Dedication

This book is dedicated in loving memory of Catherine "Kitty" Arrington. From our initial meeting, she changed my life forever. Not only did she give me the idea to write the book, as well as its title, but she also unknowingly provided me with the strength and determination to keep going over the past eight years.

Mrs. Arrington moved to Manassas in 1927 to become a teacher, where she eventually became a contemporary of local teaching legends Eugenia and Fannie Osbourn and Grace E. Metz. Mrs. Arrington was even looked upon so highly that she was asked to write the first history of Prince William County to be used in the local school system.

After her husband's death in 1998 she moved to the Caton Merchant House and a few years to Annaburg Manor. With great sadness, I found out that she passed away on April 14, 2002, two months shy of the book's long-awaited release. By dedicating this book to her I can only begin to show my appreciation for what she has done for me and to memorialize and honor such a wonderful and influential person, for without her this book would not have become a reality. Kitty, you will be greatly missed by everyone who's life you have touched, no matter for how long or how briefly.

The Shortest Dynasty
1837–1947

THE STORY OF ROBERT PORTNER;
A HISTORY OF HIS BREWING EMPIRE;
AND THE STORY OF HIS BELOVED ANNABURG

By
Michael Gaines

Second Edition

HERITAGE BOOKS
2007

HERITAGE BOOKS
AN IMPRINT OF HERITAGE BOOKS, INC.

Books, CDs, and more—Worldwide

For our listing of thousands of titles see our website
at
www.HeritageBooks.com

Published 2007 by
HERITAGE BOOKS, INC.
Publishing Division
65 East Main Street
Westminster, Maryland 21157-5026

Copyright © 2003 Michael Gaines

Other books by the author:
The Shortest Dynasty: 1837-1947

All rights reserved. No part of this book may be reproduced or transmitted in any form or by any means, electronic or mechanical, including photocopying, recording or by any information storage and retrieval system without written permission from the author, except for the inclusion of brief quotations in a review.

International Standard Book Number: 978-0-7884-2450-2

Preface

Merriam-Webster's Collegiate Dictionary defines a biography as:

> Main Entry: **bi·og·ra·phy**
> Pronunciation: bI-'ä-gr&-fE *also* bE-
> Function: *noun*
> **1** : a usually written history of a person's life
> **2** : biographical writings as a whole
> **3** : an account of the life of something (as an animal, a coin, or a building)

By no means can anyone call the task of writing a biography easy, especially when the person who is being written about lived in an era where records and other documentation have rarely survived the past century completely intact. Once information has been collected on a person's life the writer has to then decide what can be considered important or significant enough to merit an entry into a written record.

In 1994, during my senior year of high school, I had the pleasure of meeting Kitty Arrington while working at the Caton Merchant House. Upon our initial meeting, Mrs. Arrington found out about my budding interest in the history of the Annaburg Manor nursing home. Having lived only a few blocks from the facility, she knew much of its past. She told me that while Annaburg had been briefly mentioned in a number of books on local history, its history was so rich and interesting that it ought to have a book of its own. Knowing of my fascination with the place, she felt that I should be the one to write it. After considering her suggestion, I decided to go ahead with it. My initial interest had already gathered me a few pages of notes from files at the Manassas Museum, but I now had a stronger reason to collect information on and research the subject.

As I went about researching Annaburg's past, I gradually began learning about the Portner family, who lived there. Piece by piece, I started to paint a portrait in my mind of what this man and his family were like; the patriarch, Robert Portner, a German immigrant fulfilling the American dream of rags-to-riches by creating one of the largest beer breweries in the south; the matriarch, Anna von Valaer Portner, an immigrant from Switzerland who raised a large family and presided over it with proper Victorian sternness, but more than enough love and devotion to suffice every member of her family; and thirteen children, eleven of whom reached adulthood and led their own interesting lives, however short- or long-lived they may have been.

Before long, I had as much information on the Portner family, if not more, than I did on Annaburg. I soon began to realize that to fully appreciate and understand the history of a place such as Annaburg, I in turn had to appreciate and understand, but most importantly respect, the man who had created a veritable turn-of-the-century utopia in a sleepy little post Civil War town like Manassas.

Only then did I find out just how difficult writing a biography can be. When one sets out to write a biography or a history, the writer wants to create the best and most accurate account they possibly can. One of the most frustrating things I quickly learned was that no matter how hard I tried, I could never get all of the information I wanted.

In all of my research and writing, I have tried to come up with a way to describe Robert Portner and his life, in a summary, to give the reader an idea as to what kind of man he was. The best description I found was in a letter I received from Barbara Portner Whitbeck, the last Portner grandchild still living at the time of publication (two others passed away during my eight years of research). She said of her grandfather, "Just an observation – but I do think it is very interesting to put together the story of a young man from Germany – arriving in this country to seek his fortune, true he had brothers already here, but teaching himself English – seeking opportunities – working hard and building a rather unique life. I think he started out with a good education and high values – he enjoyed life – he traveled, he wanted a good life for his children and a good education. He was popular and well thought of and even an inventor – I am sure he was like many new arrivals in this land in the middle and end of the

1800's. He felt there was a "right" time to build and a "right" time to marry and a "right" woman to marry. I do not think he suffered fools and I wonder sometimes if he was not a little disappointed in some of his children and perhaps more so because he cared for them all so much."

    I do not claim that everything written in these pages is one hundred percent accurate, but rather I have made the best effort that I possibly could to portray the life of Robert Portner and the history of Annaburg the finest way I knew how. I have seen several articles on both subjects and have found that there are many different thoughts and ideas on Annaburg and Portner. With any luck I have corrected several of these misconceptions and notions, as well as having answered several popular questions about Portner and Annaburg's pasts. My only wish is that in reading this book it brings the reader as much joy and insight as it has for me to write it. And with any luck the reader will feel as much a part of the Portner family as I have had the pleasure to be.

    Michael B. Gaines
    Author

Foreword

Below is an excerpt from another letter written by Barbara Portner Whitbeck. Because she is the last direct link to the first generation of the family I have been writing about, I asked Barbara to help write the forward. In her own words, she had to say this:

"I've always felt a great pride in being a member of the Portner family, Annaburg was a lovely estate. My grandfather accomplished much and was apparently well liked and respected but most of all, I'm most impressed and touched by his love of his family and his hopes and desires for their happiness and well being. He wanted the best for his children in education, as he was an educated man himself. He wanted their happiness and saw to it that they had every advantage. Annaburg was to be a safe haven, meeting place and home for all and he very much wanted his children to be close and stick together.

"After my grandparents died, discontent and family squabbles certainly dashed any hopes of his dreams of family unity, perhaps even some "input" of some in-laws and maybe jealousy and greed surfaced, too many had too much. Perhaps had my grandfather lived longer he would have ruled his children with a firm hand until they were older and more established in their own lives. My father [Alvin] and my

Uncle Oscar would have made him proud; Paul and Herman played hard and died young but did nothing much to establish a good reputation.

"My Aunt Nana established herself as the head of the family, Elsa was the wealthy one (after she married Augustine Humes) and raised a great family. Alma, my father's favorite sister, died just before my father; Etta was the outcast and Aunt Hilda was so shy and naïve she was dominated by all (perhaps because of her hearing loss). I was closest to Aunt Hilda, she was so pretty and sweet, very tiny and soft spoken. To this day her face is just as clear in my memory as if I had seen her just yesterday.

"I think I may have mentioned before, but my grandfather's diary was a great insight into his life and thoughts and accomplishments. It was a real treasure for me. The pictures in the Manassas Museum along with the diary bring my family to life for me. My grandparents were very much into pictures for special occasions and very much into family gatherings. They all were a rather good-looking bunch, not an ugly one in the bunch! I'm sorry I have no idea what happened to Aunt Felixine Wilkening and her family as they were usually included in family events."

Author's Note

Due to the scarcity of sources available to me pertaining to Robert Portner's early life and details of his brewing industry, a majority of information contained in the first three chapters has been obtained from his personal diary. Unless otherwise noted any quotes within these chapters are directly from this source with the page number in parentheses.

In all of my research, I have come across many different spellings for the maiden name of Robert Portner's wife, Anna von Valaer. These spellings have included, but are not limited to, Valer, Valaer, Valär, and even Vollor. How it is spelled in German, more specifically with or without an umlaut adds even more variations to the spelling. When spelling Mrs. Portner's maiden name throughout the book, I have used the spelling Valaer, since that is the one that I have seen most often. Also, I have come across two different spellings for Robert Portner's hometown, Rhaden and Rahden. In the first edition of the book, I used the more prominent one, Rhaden. I have since found out, however, that Rahden is the correct spelling of the town and have made the appropriate changes throughout the text.

Contents

Dedication	iii
Preface	v
Forward	ix
Author's Note	xi
1. The Beginning of A Dynasty	1
2. Foundations	27
3. The Middle Years	53
4. The Last Days	89
5. Contributions to a Financial Empire	135
6. The Next Generation	181
7. A Palace in the Countryside	247
8. A Dynasty Ends, A New Era Begins	293
Postscript	325
Bibliography	327
Index	355

1

The Beginning of a Dynasty

> "Some have asked, 'Why write about Robert Portner?" In reply: Prior to 1900, a millionaire was a rare specimen and especially in a town of a few hundred people, so we of Manassas of this remote date remember with significance Robert Portner and [his] family."

This is how Ethel Maddox Byrd started a narrative she wrote about the Portner family in a book on Manassas in the late 1960's. Several residents of Manassas can remember the Portner estate when it was still in private hands or undeveloped while a very small number of people can still remember members of the Portner family themselves. But how did a man such as Robert Portner come to reside in Manassas and leave such an imposing legacy?

One of the most prosperous and influential men in the brewing industry during his time, the life of Robert Portner began over one hundred fifty years ago in a small town in the former European country of Prussia. Throughout his lifetime there were plenty of men who became millionaires in their fields of endeavor. Some, such as Andrew Carnegie, lived the American dream of rags-to-riches while others, such as J. Pierpont Morgan, were born with a silver spoon in their mouth. Portner's story, however, is unique in itself as it combines aspects of both lifestyles to weave a story filled with failures and successes, tragedies and triumphs.

ooo

Robert Portner was born on March 20, 1837 in Rahden, Prussia. His father, Heinrich, was a county clerk, judge and local attorney there while his mother was a housewife. Heinrich had been fortunate enough to receive the position of judge in recognition of his participation as a Brigadier General in the War of 1813-1815 and at the battle of Belle Alliance. The Portner family totaled seven children: two daughters, Augusta and Felixine, and five sons, Louis, Hermann, Carl, Robert, and Otto.

After Easter of 1848, at the tender age of eleven, Robert began his education at the military academy Castle Annaburg, located in the Province of Saxony. Like most young men of his time, Robert planned on entering a career in the military. At Castle Annaburg, often considered the 'West Point' of Prussia and Germany, Robert and his brothers received a good education, all of which was paid for by the King of Prussia, Frederick Wilhelm IV, in recognition of their father's service to the country. Robert completed his education and graduated on April 4, 1852 at the age of 16.

At the same time Robert began studying at Castle Annaburg, Louis and Hermann moved to the United States. Like many of their fellow countrymen, the brothers immigrated to the United States for a chance at better economic opportunity. A few months after Robert graduated, his brothers wrote to him, asking him and Carl to join them in New York. In an effort to persuade them even more, Louis and Hermann even sent them tickets. Finally convinced, Carl and Robert departed from Bremen Harbor aboard the schooner *Amaranth* on May 21, 1853. Loaded with merchandise and two hundred and two other passengers the ship arrived thirty-seven days later on June 27 at the Port of New York in New York City.

Though fresh out of military school, the brothers declared their occupations as bakers on the ship's manifest. As soon as they arrived in the United States, Carl and Robert went to work for Louis in his pie bakery. After a few weeks of being up to his elbows in pie dough, Robert left the bakery and found a job in a grocery store. Eight months later, in February of 1854, Robert left the store to become a bookkeeper for a factory on Long Island, which produced items such as combs and buttons from animal bone. He stayed with the factory for just over a year but had to leave because he was constantly suffering from fevers and chills. By this time Robert was 19 years old and had been in the country for nearly two years. In the time since his arrival he had been able to pick-up the English language very well. More impressive was the fact that he never took a single English lesson but instead learned his vocabulary through newspapers and general conversation.

In April 1855, after having just left the bone factory, Robert decided to leave New York and head to Williamsburg, Virginia, where Louis had relocated. Louis operated a tobacco factory there and Robert was hoping to become a salesman for his brother. Initially things went well but six months after Robert's arrival Louis had to close his business because he was spending more money than he made. Once again, Robert was out of work. He enjoyed Williamsburg and did not want to return to New York City just yet so he decided to start his own business.

Pawning a gold watch he had inherited after Herman's death earlier that year, Robert used the fifteen dollars he received for it to buy some cut tobacco. Wrapping it in tin foil, he sold the tobacco to grocery stores and restaurants the following day, repeating this procedure every day. Before long Robert had established a reputable name for himself within the area. Content, he was hoping to expand his business, but unfortunately he did not have the money for it.

Louis had borrowed a large sum of money from him and had yet to repay any of it.

At the time Robert owned a wagon and a harness but was without a horse. His luck soon changed when a German man came along and offered to become Robert's partner. The man had his own horse and Robert felt he would make a good business partner. Once a partnership had been established, Portner did all of the preparation and packing of the tobacco while his partner rode throughout the countryside to sell their product. At 20 years old Robert now had his own business.

Unfortunately, after less than a month, he realized that the pairing would not work. Unbeknownst to him at first, Robert soon realized that his partner drank to excess quite often and as a result sold very little. Discouraged with the man, Robert walked away from the partnership and returned to New York, penniless. The day after he returned, he was able to get a job with the same grocery he had previously worked for when he came to America. The store had since changed ownership and was doing quite well. Though the store did good business, Robert found himself discontented with his salary of fifteen dollars a month.

As luck would have it, a saloon across the street from the grocery was for sale for one hundred fifty dollars. Upon the advice of some friends and customers, Robert bought the business with money they lent to him. It did well, but four months later he sold it for six hundred fifty dollars because Carl needed to borrow money to open a pie bakery. Since Carl already had a partner, he brought Robert on as their bookkeeper. It was only a matter of time before Robert realized that he was not needed in this capacity. Relinquishing his position, he became a traveling salesman for his brother. Unfortunately, the partnership dissolved a few weeks later. Rather than go with his Carl, Robert decided to stay with the former partner and continued to work with him for nearly a year and a half before leaving.[1]

Throughout his early endeavors and various jobs, Robert had always had the desire to be independent. Having tried his hand at his own business in Williamsburg and New York, he felt that both could have been successful had it not been for other people. Since returning to New York, Robert was always looking for a better place to establish a business. He finally found a house he liked, 148 Chambers Street, and signed a five-year lease on it, paying sixty dollars a month for the place.

After making some repairs and improvements to the house, Portner and an acquaintance of his, Nicolas Hoffman, opened a saloon in the house in the spring of 1858. The pair ran a successful business together up to the end of 1859, at which time they parted ways. Hoffman had become engaged to a widow who had her own business that he would manage so when he told Portner he wanted to leave, Robert paid Hoffman what he asked, enough to finance the marriage. "In the winter of 1859-60, I sold the café, that is, the lease, for $1650 cash, and when I had the money (all in gold) in my pocket, I thought I was the richest man in the world." (3) After paying back six hundred dollars in debts, he rented a new store at 272 Greenwich Street and opened a new saloon there. Unfortunately, this one did not fare as well as the previous.

1860 would prove to be an exciting year for both Portner and the nation. After having become a legal citizen of the United States on October 20, 1859, Robert was now presented with his first opportunity to vote in an election. Like many recent immigrants, Robert easily identified with the anti-slavery, pro-industry feelings of the North and of the Republican Party. With the presidential election of 1860 quickly approaching he set about establishing a meeting place in his saloon for the local chapter of the party. He became the chapter's secretary and their party's candidate, Abraham Lincoln, won.

Being so far north, Robert remained largely unaffected by the troubles brewing in the south, but it was only a matter of time before these troubles began affecting the entire country. Within months after Lincoln's election, the Civil War erupted. Business had been going slow for Portner up to this point, but when it became clear that the War would be more than just a simple skirmish in the countryside of Virginia, business came to an abrupt halt. "I did not feel like becoming a soldier, and yet, I did want to see the battlefields just the same." (3) A friend of Robert's by the name of Frederick Recker had the same desire, so in September 1861 the pair traveled to Washington, D.C.

ooo

During the time of the Civil War, Washington was a city of approximately fifty thousand residents. When Congress was in session, the city became quite crowded and busy, but with soldiers now in the area because of the war, the city was utterly miserable, barely tolerable at best. In spite of this unpleasantness, along with an overabundance of swamps and dirt roads, Portner and Recker found themselves captivated with the Federal City and decided that they wanted to stay and start a business together. A business acquaintance of Robert's, Mr. Flaake, offered to provide them with the money and goods needed to open a store there, all they needed to do is find a location. Much to their dismay, this proved harder than they had expected.

After scouring the area for five or six days they had yet to find anything overly promising. Being visitors to the city, neither Portner nor Recker had a pass allowing them to cross the bridge into Virginia. The bridge led into Alexandria, a

Union-occupied city within a Confederate state, thus explaining the need for a special pass. To get around this, Robert was able to hide in a sutler's wagon and cross the bridge, hoping to find something better across the river. Once he was safely in Alexandria Robert went to see a cousin of his who was stationed nearby. The two visited with each other and caught up on what had happened since they last saw each other. Robert stayed the night with him and the following morning ventured into the city.

When it became clear to the residents of Alexandria that the Civil War was something that would not end anytime soon, most of them fled, leaving the city barren and practically deserted. Upon seeing that most of the stores were closed, Portner found himself disappointed at the emptiness of the place. Even though the city was lacking in residents, he quickly realized that the citizenry the city lacked was counter-balanced by the large number of soldiers stationed at the numerous forts surrounding the city. Plus, being so close to Washington and could prove profitable for business.

Portner spent the rest of the afternoon looking around town before obtaining a pass back into Washington. Once back in Washington, he went directly to the hotel Recker had been staying in and told him of his plan. The following morning, Portner and Recker went to Alexandria and bought a grocery store that had been abandoned for several months.

They paid one thousand dollars for the building and everything it contained, which was located at 146 King Street on the southeast corner of King and St. Asaph Streets. Due to the location of the store near the border between the North and South, the store was able to sell to both Union and Confederate troops. But since the store was located in a Confederate state, regardless that it was in a Federally-occupied city, Mr. Flaake refused to loan them any money or deliver any goods to them, a move he would later regret. Because of this stubbornness and Flaake's loyalty to the Union, Portner had to travel to New York immediately to borrow some money since they had to pay five hundred dollars up front.

Once he arrived in New York, Robert went directly to his saloon, which Otto had been caring for since he left. While there, Portner ran into an old friend, Louis Müller. After hearing about Portner's predicament, Müller loaned him the five hundred dollars he needed. He even saw to it that Portner and Recker could buy goods on credit.

> Four months later we had paid him back everything, but I shall be eternally grateful to this man. As a matter of fact, later on when he came to visit us, I gave him a beautiful horse, a

deed which was greatly appreciated by him."
(4)

On September 21, 1861, the day after Portner returned from New York, he and Recker opened their store, which they had aptly named 'Portner and Recker.' Since the store had barely anything to offer on its opening day, Portner and Recker displayed the few items they did have as best as they could to make the shelves appear as full as possible. On the first day, a few people walked past but their only business came in the form of two dollars from some soldiers. Once they were able to get butter and cheese to sell, business began to increase.

Before long the store was sold out of just about everything in stock. Portner and Recker began to receive larger shipments of merchandise, but obtaining these shipments by rail became quite difficult as the war carried on. On several occasions Portner had to go to Washington early in the morning to pick up a fresh shipment of lemons and oranges, which he would turn around and sell out of that very same morning. Before long the pair was operating the largest grocery business in Alexandria. "My partner, Recker, was a good businessman. Although a little to meticulous, he was otherwise a fairly nice man, and we always got along very well and never quarreled." (4-5) Since the store was doing so well, Portner decided that it was of no practical use to carry on with his saloon in New York, so he signed the lease over to Louis and Otto. Carl, however, left New York and came to work for Robert in the store.

"These were hectic days; sometimes there were only a few soldiers in our district, while at other times there were many. Fort Lyons, Fort Ellsworth, and all the other forts on the surrounding hills were occupied." (5) The store sold many items to the soldiers, including beer which was shipped directly from New York. For a long period of time their store was the only one allowed to import and sell the beverage within the city, which made it quite difficult to acquire the product, much less keep it in stock, despite the presence of two breweries in Alexandria.

Unfortunately, soldiers tended to abuse their privilege to drink alcohol. Many times they would be arrested while leaving a bar in a drunken stupor and held overnight to sober up, or even carted in wheelbarrows over rutted streets. The more tragic incidents happened when proprietors of saloons would rob drunken soldiers and dumping them some ways away. After several deaths, Brigadier General John P. Slough, the new military governor of Alexandria, banned the sale of all alcoholic beverages, but only after a certain hour. Not long after Slough's "Special Order No. 3" went into effect, Colonel H. L. Taylor, the Provost Marshall of Alexandria, signed a

General Order[2] stating that stated, "...the distribution of Spirituous Liquors by sale or gift either to Officers, Soldiers, or Citizens, is hereby prohibited. Any person violating this Order will be arrested and their liquors confiscated."

In November 1862, Slough completely banned the sale of any and all alcoholic beverages in the city, but this only applied to liquor since few considered beer to be harmful or intoxicating. But with the Orders in place, Portner and Recker concentrated their sales on the soldiers and their sutlers stationed outside of the city, a place that was beyond reach of Taylor's Order.

By the winter of 1862 obtaining beer had become more difficult than ever. One of the store's regular customers, Edward Abner, went to Portner and Recker with an idea. A sutler who bought a considerable amount of beer himself, Abner suggested that they begin brewing their own beer. After giving the idea some thought, Portner and Recker saw just how practical this would be. By doing so they could eliminate the worries of trying to import beer from New York and keeping it in stock.

The pair approached Abner and asked him if he wanted to become a partner in their brewing venture, since it was his idea, after all. Upon agreeing to a partnership, Abner received Portner and Recker's approval to bring in a fourth partner by the name of Kaercher[3]. Kaercher was a friend of Abner's who had been trained as a beer brewer. Portner and Recker owned one-third of the venture, Abner the second, and Kaercher the final third. Since Abner and Kaercher had little money, Portner and Recker had to provide all of the funding for the new business. Kaercher's contribution was his brewing-know-how while Abner's was the ability to sell the product through his sutler business.

When the partnership was established the four men were then faced with the task of deciding upon a name for the business. Eventually the name 'Portner and Company' was chosen. Now that they had the partners and name, Portner and Recker had to find a location, but somewhere close to their business. They found a warehouse on the northeast corner of King and Fayette Streets and began renting it immediately from Philip H. Hooff. At the time, beer brought about twenty-five cents a glass from soldiers in the field. The beer, however, was much stronger than today's product. While today's product is less than ten-percent proof by volume, beer sold to soldiers during the Civil War was considerably higher.

By February 1863 Portner realized that he was sick with what he presumed to be malaria. He was so weak that he could hardly tend to business, so he left on May 23 for a trip back to his homeland. Robert boarded the *City of New York* and arrived in Liverpool, England on June 1. From there he went to Bremen and on to Minden where he met his sister

Felixine. From Minden the two traveled home to Rahden. "Never in my life have I experienced such emotion and joy as when I saw the tower of Rahden[4] and when I was able to embrace my mother shortly afterwards." (5) After visiting with his mother for a while, she, Robert and Felixine went to visit Augusta and her family where they stayed for a few weeks.

While visiting with Augusta, Robert received word that he was to be arrested on charges of not having registered as a soldier at the age of twenty-one (he was now twenty-six years old). Being a legal citizen of the United States, Robert wrote to the Ambassador in Berlin for help. The Ambassador replied saying that it might take a few months to get him free, should he be arrested. Fearing an arrest and still not feeling well, Robert left to visit the mineral baths and spas at Oeynhausen for additional treatment. Upon his arrival, doctors examined him and found that he had been suffering from liver trouble, not malaria.

After finishing his initial treatment, he stayed a little while longer at Oeynhausen before leaving to visit an uncle near Rahden. He stayed with his uncle for a few weeks, visiting his mother and other relatives daily. Fortunately Robert was never arrested. It turned out that the reason behind his possible arrest was due to the lack of an effective agreement between Germany and America. A few years later, a treaty would be signed between the two countries allowing people like Portner to stay in Germany and Prussia as an American citizen without being accosted. After staying with relatives a few days longer, Robert left for Paris. Accompanied by his friend Samuel Barth, the two visited Paris and took in sites along the Rhine River. After returning from his trip, he went back to the spas at Oeynhausen for a few more weeks to improve his health before returning to America.

When Robert returned to America in the fall, he brought Barth, Felixine and his niece Paula Strangmann back with him. Feeling much better and stronger, he left the girls with Louis and traveled from New York to Alexandria, returning to the brewery and grocery immediately. Finding everything in order, Robert set about finding a house to rent. He soon found one that would accommodate him, Felixine, Recker and Otto.

One evening in the winter of 1863-4 Robert left his home to go to the store. As he was walking down the street he happened past a gunsmith working on his front porch. Without warning a shot rang out and Robert felt the piercing sting of a gunshot wound. He looked down to find that, sure enough, he had been shot in the arm. The round bullet had entered his arm, flattened by the bone, and exited as a flat piece. When he removed his shirt to examine the wound, the bullet rolled out of the shirt. The gunsmith came rushing over, apologizing profusely and explaining how he had been examining a pistol someone had brought him for repair. Not knowing the gun was loaded the gunsmith had pulled the trigger with the unpleasant result. Robert went immediately to a doctor to be treated and within three or four weeks was completely back to normal.

"All in all, I lived to see many good things during these war times. I was on good terms with most of the commanders, so that we enjoyed many privileges and, at the same time, could help others." (6) Using his good standing Portner was usually able to help get people regain their freedom from prison after they had been in captivity for six months. Before long, he was quite busy with applications for help as people around town learned of his ability. Through his intervention, cases were examined on an individual basis and the men were then released.

One commander in particular, Wyman, who had since replaced Col. Taylor as Provost Marshall of Alexandria, had quite a bit of confidence in Portner. Unfortunately a new commander, Gwynne, replaced Wyman in the winter of 1863-1864. Gwynne had been appointed by General Slough, a selfish individual disliked by many people (Slough would die four years later after a gunfight with a lawmaker in New Mexico). Up to this point Portner and Recker enjoyed their privileges and did not complain as they often proved that they were faithful Unionists.

Many people, among them loyal and successful citizens, were very unhappy with this order and held a meeting in the spring of 1864 and signed a petition for the removal of General Slough. The petition was then delivered to Edwin M. Stanton, Lincoln's Secretary of War. "My partner (Recker) had attended this meeting and, without my knowledge and against my will, had signed the petition to the Secretary. This was very stupid, indeed." (7) Having connections within the Federal government, Slough received a copy of the petition. Once he found that Portner and Recker's names were on it, his loyalty to them stopped immediately and all of their privileges were revoked. This now meant that they were no longer allowed to sell their beer in Alexandria.

One afternoon a local innkeeper was arrested and charged with selling beer to soldiers. Upon inquiry the man said he had bought his beer from Portner and Company. The next day, Robert received word that he was to report to Captain Gwynne's office immediately. When he arrived, Gwynne took Portner into a private room. There, he asked Robert how much he would be willing to pay Gwynne for special permission to continue brewing his beer as he had always done. Knowing that he had been allowed to brew his beer, Portner told Gwynne that he would not pay him a single cent, especially since he felt that Gwynne could not do anything to stop him. Angered, Gwynne told him that he would imprison Robert for sixty days and close the brewery. He told Portner that he had until that afternoon to make a decision. "If I had been as sensible then as I am now, I would have gladly paid him five hundred dollars or more, but I believed myself to be in the right." (7)

After leaving Gwynne's office, Portner went directly to Circuit Court Judge Andrew Wylie. Wylie had once told him that should something like this happen to come and speak with him directly. After telling the Judge what had happened, Wylie told him that he would take care of the matter and to let him know if anything new developed. Robert left Wylie's office and headed back to see Gwynne and tell him that he would not do as he had been asked. Gwynne had Portner arrested immediately and sent to prison. Robert soon found himself in a cell with eleven other men, most of them being political prisoners as well. As the night passed, each man told Portner how he came to be in prison. After hearing all the stories, he made a promise that once he was released, he would help each of them. He kept his promise to these men, which later provided him with many business and social connections in Alexandria and Washington.

In the morning the prison commandant summoned Portner to his office. Not being too fond of Gwynne himself, the commandant offered to make Portner's stay as pleasant as possible. Robert and another gentleman were able to stay in the commandant's quarters for the remainder of the day, and within a few days were allowed to sleep there and even have their food sent in from outside the prison. The pair was also allowed to receive visitors and leave the prison at nights, but Robert decided not to risk the latter of the two.

As the days passed, several people tried to intervene on Robert's behalf, but nothing seemed to work. At times when he was alone in his new room, he took the time to write to Judge Wylie and explain everything that had happened since they last spoke. Upon receiving Portner's letter, Wylie went directly to Secretary of State Stanton, who promised to look into the matter. Unsatisfied, Wylie went above Stanton directly to President Lincoln. Unfortunately, Lincoln was so busy with the war that he could not do anything to help him.

Frustrated, Wylie appealed to a Senator and asked him to help. The Senator introduced legislation to the Senate demanding an investigation into General Slough and his administration, which proved quite successful. At 9:00 that same evening, after having spent a total of nine days in prison, Robert received word from the General that his sentence had been commuted to a fine. Once he was out of prison, Robert returned to work at the grocery and the brewery, but from that point on, they sold beer on order only. After being thoroughly investigated, Slough was dismissed a new General appointed. Much to the delight of many, the new General allowed breweries and inns to sell to everyone once again, including soldiers.

Not long after Robert's release, one of the larger local regiments was transferred to Fredericksburg. Rather than loose the business, the grocery rented a ship and sent goods to Fredericksburg. Portner stayed behind to watch the store while Recker went with the shipment. In two weeks time everything had been sold. A second shipment was sent, but this time only half of it sold since the regiment moved once again. While packing up their remaining goods, Recker was arrested. Over the course of the next week, he was relocated several times before finally being returned to Alexandria under heavy police guard. During his entire ordeal Recker had no idea why he had been arrested. Once back in Alexandria he had his hearing, which Carl attended. Recker was put under a two thousand-dollar bail, which Carl vouched for. When Robert asked him how he could guarantee the money, Carl replied, "I would sell my little finger for the sum."

Upon investigation Recker's innocence was quickly proven. He had been arrested on charges of crossing enemy lines and selling his wares to the Confederates. In all actuality he had never left Fredericksburg. One of their employees, given permission by Portner to transport a wagon of goods to a regiment they supplied, had sold the items to the Confederates instead while posing as Recker. Two days later the same man returned to Alexandria and told Portner that he had lost his way because of bad roads. This is why, he said, he returned to Alexandria after having sold the goods as best as he could within the surrounding area. He gave Robert the money he claimed to have made from sales, but Portner learned he had made much more than he claimed. As a result, the man was fired immediately.

When the regiment moved on to White House Landing, Virginia, the store shipped a cargo there and opened a tent. Just as quickly as they had set up the regiment received word they had to leave the area. Carl was in charge of this particular shipment and decided to load the best merchandise into two wagons and send them to Abner's regiment. The next morning the wagons reached the site of Abner's regiment only to find they had already moved on. No sooner had they arrived that a rebel Calvary marched in and seized everything. All of the men were taken prisoner and transported to Richmond and the Cavalry took everything they could carry and anything left behind was destroyed. These proved to be great losses to the store but Recker, Carl and all of the other employees managed to return home safely. Because of the heavy losses and the instability of a regiment's movements, that proved to be the last cargo the Portner and Recker grocery would ever ship. Regardless, both businesses did well and every so often a large army would stay in Alexandria for a while.

By this time, Portner was getting tired of renting and was ready to own his own home. He bought a house on the corner of Duke and St. Asaph Streets, where the Marquis de Lafayette once stayed during a visit to America. A Federal era house three-stories in height, Portner bought the house from the Federal government, who had seized it at the onset of the Civil War. Recker married and everyone, including Felixine, moved into the new house.

> "We enjoyed a very pleasant life, had many parties and much fun. We also founded a club, the Concordia Glee Club, of which I became President. Later on we merged with the other German club and adopted the name "Eintracht." This one split again later into "Harmonie" and "Eintracht." Each club owned a stage, and I believe these were the most pleasant times we had in Alexandria."[5] (9)

Though he was still a partner in the brewery Abner was never in Alexandria because of his military service. That same year his partners bought him out for $1,800. A number of years later Abner co-founded the Abner-Drury brewery in Washington, which lasted until it declared bankruptcy in the 1930's (the site as then bought by the Christian Heurich Brewing Company).

In 1865 the Civil War finally ended. On April 14 a large parade was held in Alexandria to celebrate the peace. The joy and celebration did not last long, though. The following day gloom settled over the city as word spread that President Lincoln had been fatally shot the night before. Being a member of the City Council, Portner was present at the funeral ceremonies in the Capitol.

When the war ended, so did the tranquility of Portner's business affairs. Recker seemed to hardly care for anything anymore and left everything in the store for Portner to take care of. The remaining partner in the brewery, Kaercher, had also started taking business rather lightly. He was constantly withdrawing more and more money from the business until he was finally able to open an inn next to the brewery. Since he was so preoccupied with his new venture, Kaercher neglected his duties at the brewery.

Frustrated by everyone's carefree attitudes, Portner decided to dissolve all of the partnerships himself. At first Recker and Kaercher were not willing to end the partnership but Portner stood firm. In his first step to dissolve the brewery partnership, Portner had all of the accounts temporarily closed.

Next he and Recker offered Kaercher the option of taking over the brewery himself. To do this he would have to pay Portner and Recker a certain amount of money within thirty days. But since he had just opened his inn, Kaercher did not have the money to do this. As a result Portner and Recker bought out his share in the brewery, which left both businesses to themselves. Once he was bought out, Kaercher stayed in Alexandria to run his inn and later became a partner in another brewery.

In his final step to end all of the partnerships Portner offered Recker his choice of one of the businesses. At first Recker took the brewery, but a week later, after Portner had just finished settling into the grocery business on his own, Recker came to him and asked if they could switch. Apparently Recker underestimated the difficulty in running a brewery and now wanted the easier of the two. Before the partnership ended Portner and Recker had earned roughly $32,000 together. This amounted to the value of both businesses and the house. Portner paid Recker $16,000 for the brewery and Recker paid Portner $11,500 for the store. After the men parted ways Recker continued to run the grocery until his death in 1872. Portner, however, was now left to run the brewery all by himself.

Endnotes

[1] It is not known what kind of business Robert and Carl's partner worked in, though one might assume it was the pie bakery. The circumstances of Robert's departure are not known either.

[2] General Order No. 4, dated August 29th, 1862.

[3] "Portner does not provide Kaercher's first name. In fact, there were three men in Alexandria in the 1860's with similar last names, John Kaercher (or Kircher), Andrew Kaercher (or Kaircher), and Gottlieb Kircher (or Kircherer or Kitcher). John Kaercher had a beer garden in Washington during the war and may not have come to Alexandria until 1865 or 1866, when he briefly owned a tavern. Alexandria Water Company records showed that he occupied a building one or two doors away from the King Street brewery in mid-1867, and Porter states that Kaercher was becoming preoccupied with running an inn next to the brewery at the end of the war. On the other hand, Andrew Kaercher was likely the brew master, because his capitation assessment is listed next to Otto Portner's in the Alexandria tax records for 1864. John Kaercher was likely a relative of Andrew. Gottlieb Kircher as a farmer and butcher in the village of West End but also had a home in town." (Dennee 25)

[4] Some theories suggest that the tower Portner built at Annaburg (known as 'Portner Tower') was designed to model the tower of Rahden.

[5] The exact location of these clubs is not known, but newspapers of the time carried notices of functions that took place at Harmonie Hall, which is assumed to be the same place.

2

Foundations

When Portner and Recker's partnership ended, it was the summer of 1865. The war that had torn a nation in half had ended two months earlier and the country was beginning its healing process. In addition to mending broken hearts, families and friendships, the country had to rebuild itself both financially and structurally. Robert Portner, like so many other businessmen, found himself in a similar situation.

Portner found himself running the entire brewery by himself, and with that control came the ability to run his business any way he saw fit. To be successful on his own Portner was faced with the task of establishing a name for himself, separate from that of 'Portner and Recker' and 'Portner & Company.' He also had to prove himself as a successful businessman and brewer. His first step was to reopen all of Portner & Company's former accounts to reestablish a loyal customer base.

Having a product to sell was not a problem for Portner. Before dissolving Portner & Company, he and Recker had purchased some beer cellars on Washington Street, between Pendleton and Wythe Streets. In addition to renting a warehouse on King and Henry Streets, Portner expanded his operations that summer by renting the old Shuter's Hill brewery site[6] from Francis Denmead, a Baltimore maltster. When the spring of 1866 arrived Portner had plenty of beer to sell but all of the soldiers (the majority of his customer-base) had left. With inn after inn closing and beer sales plummeting Portner was not able to sell enough beer before it started to spoil. To make matters worse, he had accumulated an outstanding debt of $20,000 from money borrowed to purchase malt, hops, and barrels. Before he knew it, he was not even able to raise enough money to pay his bills, muchless his debts.

Facing mounting financial pressures and a continued decline in sales, Portner had to weigh his options, deciding whether or not to continue with the business. Like so many others had done after the war, Portner was on the verge of financial collapse. Needling advice, he visited S. Furgeson Beach. Beach was a personal friend of Portner's and happened to be a lawyer and President of the First National Bank of Alexandria. He suggested that Portner send a compromise to his creditors, explaining his situation and asking for more time to settle his matters to pay them what he owed. As a consolation he offered everything he owned as collateral. Portner did as he was advised and all but one told him to continue with his work and to pay them back as soon as he was able. Denmead, who also happened to be one of Portner's creditors, offered to assist him further if Portner would give him a deed of trust on everything that he owned. He took a security deposit for $12,000, and since Portner already owed him $5,000 this left Portner with $7,000 worth of credit to work with.

> After thinking over carefully whether I should give up the business and start something else, I decided to stay in the business where I had lost my money. But I had to learn the trade and become a brewer, in order not to depend on other people and to be able to supervise a brewery. I was a good businessman, but I knew very little about breweries. At that time, brewing was regarded as a secret or an art [as opposed to a business]. (10)

Starting over with new energy and determination, Portner traveled to New York in the fall of 1866. With the state's colder temperatures, it was an ideal location for a brewery. Though breweries were a fairly common occurrence, New York was home to the most breweries in operation in the entire country. This was also where Portner hoped to find his new brew master. He finally found what he was looking for in a man named Carl Wolters. Though he was inexperienced as an actual brewer, he had been educated in the trade quite well. "Although Wolters' knowledge was merely theoretical rather than practical, I preferred him to other applicants because he was an educated man." (10) After securing his release from his current employer, Portner brought Wolters to Alexandria and they quickly set about getting business in order. Their first task was to neutralize all of the old beer that was still sitting in the Washington Street cellars. They counterbalanced the flat beer as best as they could with a bicarbonate of soda. To their advantage this secret was unknown to the older, more established brewers, thus allowing them to sell some of their "new" beer. Unfortunately this trick only lasted for a short time and it soon became difficult to compete against the other breweries fresh beer.

Since they could no longer sell their product, Portner and Wolters began production of their own fresh beer. Portner assisted Wolters while he taught Portner everything he knew about brewing. The pair applied several different methods to their brewing as they slowly began perfecting their product. In a heavily populated German community, lager was the preferred type of beer, but when being produced it required fermentation in cold temperatures for up to two weeks and then stored for upwards of three months in near-freezing temperatures. In the humid south, this proved quite difficult so they started brewing ale first. Unlike lager, ales ferment quicker and at higher temperatures, which allowed them to be produced and delivered more quickly.

By November of 1866 their first beer was ready, but Portner and Wolters were hesitant to release it. In their opinion, they had not perfected their craft enough yet and the end product did not taste just right. Though it did not taste right to them, they were able to sell three or four kegs of ale a day, which at least gave them some money. As time went on the taste of their product improved, as did sales. Keg sales soon reached five to six, and even sometimes ten, per day. Once the beer had been crafted to their satisfaction Portner was ready to expand his customer base and soon began traveling throughout the state to advertise the brewery.

After months of preparation Portner and Wolters' lager beer was finally ready to be taken from the cellars and sold on May 1, 1867. The old beer had been pumped out to make way for their new lager. So it was not a complete loss, Portner and Wolters had converted some of the old sour beer into vinegar, but the vast majority was simply dumped. Their new beer was good, but sales were unexpectedly small. Eight hundred barrels had been prepared in anticipation of big sales, but only three hundred were sold to the local inns. Though Portner had a customer base, the brewery showed a loss of $2,000 that year.

Shortly after the lager beer was brought out for sale, Wolters left Portner to open his own brewery in Philadelphia. Portner was now able to supervise his entire brewing operation himself, but he still wanted a brew master to oversee the production of his product. He hired Jacob Biehle, who had been assistant brewer with the Yuengling brewery in Pennsylvania. Each day, Portner went to the cellars to continue studying and learning more about the beer and its fermentation processes. He continued his hard work, which showed as his sales continued to rise and his customer base had since expanded into Washington. At the age of 30, Portner now had his own successful brewery.

By the beginning of 1868, Portner's balance sheets showed no more losses, but the costs of shipping his beer from his two facilities to the Washington Street cellars and back again were too high. The easiest and cheapest solution for him was to build a brewery on the site of the cellars. Denmead raised Portner's credit to $16,000, and later to $20,000, and in the summer of 1868 construction began on his new facility. Portner drew all of the plans himself and moved all of his equipment, both old and new, into the new building as it was gradually completed. Six months later Portner had the finest breweries in Alexandria. To add to his convenience,

Portner fixed up two small wooden cottages, located on the same block as the brewery, for him and his family to live in.

In early 1869, Portner received two visitors, Christian Mathis of Manassas and Peter von Valaer, a friend of Mathis' visiting from Switzerland. During the course of their visit Valaer often spoke of his brother Jacob who lived in Philadelphia and ran a brewery and tavern there. Jacob had been looking for a partner in his brewery and, hearing of Portner's success, sent his brother and Mathis to look into his brewing style and product. Though he had finished his new brewery only a few months prior, Portner was always looking for ways to expand his business interests. He had avoided financial collapse after the war by establishing a customer-base in Alexandria and Washington, but if he could expand it even further, Portner knew that it could only strengthen one of the foundations upon which his brewery was built, a loyal following of customers.

Before he would commit to a partnership Portner wanted to see the brewery first. Upon seeing the facility, not only was he impressed with the brewery, but he was also quite enamored over Peter and Jacob's sister Anna, who had come from Switzerland to help Jacob with his tavern in High Bridge Mansion. It has even been said that Portner fell in love with her at first sight. Once he agreed to become Jacob's partner, Portner was more than willing to travel to Philadelphia to check on his new business, as well as to see Anna. As time went on, Portner visited the Valaer's more frequently, as well as joining them on visits to see Mathis in Manassas.

ooo

By now Portner was ready to expand the clientele of his Alexandria brewery even further. A number of his competitors had opened summer gardens within the past few years, each of which was met with great success. Two years prior, Robert had leased a portion of his Washington Street property to his brother Otto and Henry Herbner, where they opened Potomac Gardens, a "most attractive resort in the city for respectable people." Aside from Portner's own beer, the garden also offered an ice cream and soda water bar. Evening dances, concerts, and special events such as sparring exhibitions were not uncommon there, as well as private picnics, festivals, and balls. After the first season, Otto withdrew from the venture, but Herbner continued for another year.

With the completion of his new brewery in 1869, Robert was ready to serve the public himself. He cut out the "middle man" by discontinuing Herbner's lease and in April, he re-opened the grounds as "Portner's Garden."

> At this time, I opened a beer garden which, although it caused a lot of trouble, made the

beer known. On Sundays, many Washingtonians came to Alexandria, and the beer, taken fresh from the cellars, tasted very good and helped me to get some customers in Washington. I tried everything and worked, making about two to three thousand dollars. That gave me new courage, and I kept on enlarging and beautifying. (11)

Despite the change of name, loyal patrons kept coming to the beer garden. He knew, though, that loyalty alone would not draw more customers, so he had to think of something that would lure in more people. About this same time, the *Alexandria Gazette* reported a new innovation that was causing quite a stir in New York and New Haven. Taking advantage of the public's curiosity of this new 'contraption,' Portner invited "Professor" Alfred J. Schultz from Baltimore to come to Alexandria and demonstrate how a velocipede worked. He even allowed Schultz to open a riding and training school, complete with a rink, at the garden. The school opened on April 26 and was an instant success. And so with the opening of the school at Portner's Garden, Robert Portner had successfully introduced the bicycle to Alexandria society.

The pavilion there has since been daily crowded from early in the evening until a late hour at night, and some even practice in the morning. Among the numerous young gentlemen who take lessons several have proved themselves apt scholars, and one has so far progressed in his studies that he astonished the citizens yesterday by appearing on the streets mounted upon one of the new vehicles.[7]

At the close of the first season of Portner's Garden, Robert had made between $2,000 and $3,000. After seeing his success, he began thinking of new improvements for the 1870 season. Shortly after the close of the 1869 season, the *Alexandria Gazette* published an article saying how the city was lacking a public billiard table, keno, faro, roulette, or ten-pin alley. Essentially, the article was saying that the city was lacking, and desperately wanted, a gambling house.

When Portner's Garden opened for the 1870 season, its patrons were delighted to find that bowling alleys had been installed. This, however, did not mean that Alexandria society was becoming corrupt; Portner only admitted "respectable" people and refused to serve any hard liquor. He continued to operate his summer garden through the end of the 1875 season.

ooo

In addition to his customers in Washington and Alexandria, having an interest in Valaer's brewery helped Portner expand his own business into the Pittsburgh area as well. Eventually, though, he would limit his business to the south.

Every year Portner made trips to see the progress in other breweries and to see how he fared against his fellow brewers. One trip in particular left a lasting impression on him. Shortly after his return to Alexandria, Portner decided to make another addition to his brewery. In 1870 construction began on an icehouse, the first of its kind in this part of the country. Even though it was only partially finished by the spring of the following year, it had greatly helped beer sales. Even with such a jump in sales, Portner was still not able to sell everything he brewed before it went bad. He continued to make more and more money, which allowed him to pay off some old debts and enlarge his icehouse. The building, as it was constructed, was a large insulated building Portner used for the storage of natural ice and the cooling of beer. He was not satisfied, however, with the use of natural ice.

During the same time Portner's icehouse was being built, he hired Peter Wolters, Carl's brother, who had left earlier that year. "He [Wolters] was a good brewer and a hard worker but had a bad character." (12) In April of 1871,

Wolters was fired and replaced by a young man named Edward Fielmayer, who had been a barkeeper in Washington and the son of a Philadelphia brewer. He stayed with Portner through the summer before returning home to his parents in the fall.

Portner and his workers knew the brewing process so well by now that replacing Fielmayer was not a necessity. In addition to his brew master, the brewery employed a wide variety of additional workers.

> My main helpers in the brewery were some very good and able negroes [...] Even if I had to change master brewers now, it was not so critical, since the workmen knew their duties well and I myself could supervise everything. (12)

After Fielmayer left, Portner hired Paul Muhlhauser, who had come to him under the recommendation of Mr. Schwartz, owner of a brewing school in New York. After hiring Muhlhauser, Portner traveled to Philadelphia to check on the brewery there. Unfortunately, he came down with a fever shortly after his arrival and could not spend much time with Anna. After recovering, the two spent as much time together as possible over the few remaining days before

Portner had to return to Alexandria. During those last days, Portner did a lot of thinking, but since he could not find the right time to talk to Anna alone, he had to write down his feelings on the trip home. "Among all the girls I knew, there was only one whose charming character pleased me so well that I wished her to be my wife." (12) Upon receiving his letter, Anna immediately said yes to Robert's proposal of marriage and a date was set for a spring wedding the next year.

After much anticipation, April 4, 1872 finally arrived. Robert and Anna's wedding ceremony was held in a hotel parlor in Philadelphia where Pastor Mann of the same city wed them. The ceremony was followed by a dinner, after which Portner and his new bride headed to New York for their honeymoon. Mr. and Mrs. Portner spent a few days in New York before they had to head back to Alexandria. They stopped in Philadelphia to pick up Anna's personal belongings and then headed to Alexandria, where they were greeted by a warm reception. The new couple soon moved into a house with Paul Muhlhauser, his wife, and Felixine.

Initially, Robert and Anna did not mind sharing a home with three other people, but they soon began thinking about having a family. In the fall of 1872 Portner bought a large lot on Washington Street. The entire block had been filled with rowhouses, but a fire had destroyed them all, thus making it a prime spot for Robert to build a house upon. Before the house could be completed, Robert and Anna were blessed with their first child when Edwin was born on February 13, 1873. Shortly after Edwin was born, the family moved into their new home. "We enjoyed very much owning such a beautiful home, and we felt very happy. I arranged the garden myself, planted all the trees and shrubs, and considered it a great accomplishment." (12) This newfound happiness was short-lived. In the early morning of July 28, Edwin died of cholera at only five-and-a-half months old. At three o'clock the next afternoon, funeral services were held at the Portner home and Edwin was buried in Alexandria afterwards.

Though he was always busy with his business interests, Portner still longed for a family. Despite the devastating loss of their first child, Robert and Anna were adamant on having a family. On April 4, 1874, Anna gave birth to a healthy newborn son, Robert Francis. Robert and Anna were overjoyed that they had a family once again and wanted to continue expanding it. A year and a half later, on November 14, their second child, Edward George, was born.

As time went on the brewery progressed and grew. In an effort to keep his mind off of the loss of his first-born son, Portner spent more time at the brewery supervising, calculating, and writing many letters. He continued to make improvements within the brewery as well as continuing to build and expand it. Little did Portner realize, however, that big changes were right around the corner.

Since the brewing industry began, brewers had always been limited to a regional marked for their product. In some cases, this did not pose a problem but most brewers were always looking for new ways to expand their marked and build a bigger clientele base. To accomplish this, brewers had to be able to ship their beer over longer distances. But before this could be done, two things had to be accomplished. First and foremost, a way had to be created to prevent the fast spoilage of beer, but brewers also needed to come up with a form of fast and cheap transportation.

In 1874 these needs became a reality. That year, Anheuser-Busch became the first brewery to introduce pasteurization to the brewing process. The following year a new and different type of seal was invented and patented. The Lightning stopper was revolutionary in the fact that it enabled a bottle to be sealed and resealed, making them both air and water tight.[8] A few years later the Hutchinson stopper was invented. The only different between these two devises were their design as they had the same practical purpose. These seals also enabled beer to be stored and transported for lengthened periods of time without spoiling or going flat. Both of these new bottling styles were incorporated into Portner's brewery.

Once the problem of preventing the spoilage of beer was solved, attention was turned to the task of developing quick and cheap transportation. Once this was established, brewers would be able to create the regional and national markets for their beer that they had been craving for so long. During this time, the railroad was fast becoming the dominant mode of long-distance travel and cargo shipping. Because of the rail's fast speed and ability to transport large quantities of goods over long distances, it became the most cost-effective way to transport fresh beer, as well as transporting the ingredients needed for brewing.

Brewers across the country tapped into these resources as quickly as they could, but they then realized that there was still one more obstacle to overcome – advertising. Portner had done a fairly good job of it already with his beer garden, but if the wanted regional or even national recognition, as opposed to just local, he would have to advertise more. Giving away items were one way of getting your product known, but to really catch the attention of consumers, one needs to have a catchy name or slogan. Though it was his namesake, the Robert Portner brewery was just a bit too plain, so he had to think of something catchier. In 1877, he chose the name "Tivoli" for his product. While this name had traditional roots tied back to both Germany and Italy, it was rather clever in regards to marketing because if it is spelled backwards, it reads "I lov(e) it."

Now that he had the name of his product, as well as his brewery, he could begin advertising. Soon, trays, stoneware mugs, etched drinking glasses, cigar boxes, posters, and no doubt a plethora of other items were created and given to restaurants and saloons all over, each of which was met with great success. Sometimes advertisement propaganda was not enough to gain business. Often times brewers would offer deals to saloonkeepers to insure that the saloon carried their beer only. Sometimes brewers would to one or two steps further by helping a businessman purchase the needed to fixtures to open a saloon, even paying the licensing fees.

But then again, there were brewers who went that final step to ensure that their beer, and only their beer, was sold at a saloon. Many times the brewery would purchase the land and open the saloon, though someone else would run it. By 1877 Portner had an operation like this up and running. He owned a plot of land on the northwest corner of Washington and Wythe Streets, but according to the business directories of 1876-77 and 1877-78, it was George Biehl who ran the saloon, not Portner.

Aside from this saloon, it is known that Portner operated at least one other establishment of similar nature. In

June of 1877 he leased a building on Cameron Street. An article in the *Alexandria Gazette*, dated June 18, reads:

> Improvement – The old El Dorado House, on Cameron Street, near Royal, has been leased by Mr. Robert Portner, and is being fitted up in magnificent style as a first-class restaurant and bar room. The front has been modernized, the ceilings and walls frescoed, handsome bars are being built, and electric bells and all the modern appliances put in. Mr. Morgan Davis is in charge of the work, Higgins & Kell are doing the painting, and Blomquist & Henkel the frescoing. The whole work is done in the best style, and reflects great credit on the workmen.

One week later, as renovations neared completion, another article appeared in the *Alexandria Gazette*. Providing more details and paying more compliments to its designers, the article, dated June 30, says,

> New Restaurant – The building, No. 71 Cameron Street, long known as the El Dorado House, which has heretofore been under

various proprietorships, has been leased for five years from its owner by Robert Portner, esq., and has been refitted in the most splendid style of modern restaurant. The lease has spared neither pain nor expense in the adornments or conveniences of the building. The walls and ceilings have been elegantly and tastefully frescoed, and the rooms wainscoted in dark walnut, and the upper rooms have been put in the finest order for the use of clubs and select parties. The work does credit to Alexandria mechanics and artisans by whom most of it was done. The restaurant is designed to be conducted on the first-class German plan by Messrs. Otto Portner and Louis Faber, and will be open to the public on Monday next.

It is safe to assume that only Portner's beer was offered in the restaurant and bar.

With the operation of the saloon and restaurant, and possibly others, and the success of his brewery, Portner had little interest and time to tend to his partnership in the Philadelphia brewery, so he left it.

Once Robert had given up his interest in the Philadelphia brewery, this gave him more time to spend with and concentrate on his family. On June 12, 1877, Robert and Anna celebrated the birth of their fourth son, Alvin Otto. The family's first daughter, Alma Meta, was born on July 10, 1879 and their second daughter, Henriette Marie, followed on November 5, 1880.

Unfortunately, Robert spent so much time working at his brewery that by the spring of 1881 he was sick again. To help him recover, he embarked on a trip to Europe with his family that spring. Shortly before leaving, Portner settled all of his business affairs as best as he could so that when he returned, there would be less to worry about. He also instructed that during his absence his friend B. Edward J. Eils was to look after the brewery and other business duties. Though Eils was not a brewer by trade, Carl Strangmann, Robert's nephew, was there to help Eils.

When Robert and his family left for Europe, he only weighed 131 pounds, but by the time the ship arrived in Prussia two weeks later, he had already begun to feel better and had gained fifteen pounds on the voyage alone.[9] The entire family traveled throughout Prussia for eight weeks before heading to Anna's homeland of Switzerland. After six weeks in Jenaz[10], they returned to Rahden. Robert and Anna left the children with a family friend and traveled back through Prussia and Switzerland for an additional four weeks.

Towards the end of their trip, Robert and Anna stopped in Minden, Prussia.

> At Minden we received the bad news from Rahden that dear Robbie had been taken sick with pneumonia. We got very excited and went to Rahden as quickly as possible. Thank God, Robbie improved very quickly, and, on November 22, 1881, we were able to return to America on board the steamer *Necker*.
>
> It was a terrible crossing. One of our companions was Jefferson Davis, with his wife and his daughter, a nice young girl of 18, who had been in Germany for six years. We became good friends with the family, mainly on account of the terrible storm we encountered.
>
> After we had been away from Southampton for twenty-four hours, a storm broke loose. Earlier, the captain, Willi Gerde, had shown me a telegram from New York which said that we would meet two gales. For seven days, the storm was stronger than any that captain had

ever before encountered. While we were sitting at a table, a huge wave tore away the bridge, several lifeboats, and the navigation house. One man had both legs fractured. Another was thrown overboard, and when he had somehow got hold of a rope, he was thrown back by the next wave. Another one was lost and never seen again. The nose of the first officer was fractured when he was thrown off the bridge.

Another wave swept across the ship, and brought so much water into the smoking lounge that all of us, including Jefferson Davis, had to climb onto tables. Eddie, who was with me at the time, became so afraid that he kneeled down on a bench and prayed, "Dear God, please let the waves go down so that the ship won't go down with Mamma and Papa." He prayed so fervently that everybody present, including Jefferson Davis, was really touched. Davis said if God would not listen to such a fervent prayer, praying could not help at all.

Later on, there came another wave which tore away the pilothouse and practically all the boats, and brought so much water into the lounge that everybody had to get up on tables and beds. It looked terrible when the water, which was two feet deep, was moving back and forth. The passengers in steerage were also several feet deep in water. Now we all set to work trying to bail out the water... All the exits to the decks were nailed down. The ship rolled back and forth, and wave after wave went over the deck. We made only a little progress; one day we merely covered sixty miles. After a week, when we approached Newfoundland, it became better.

After seventeen days, we reached New York. Here I was welcomed by a delegation of the brewers of New York and I was invited, very generously, to the Hotel Rush. Jefferson Davis joined us there in a glass of champagne.

Mamma became seasick once more, and we had to wait another day before we could leave for Washington, where I was welcomed by a

> delegation from Alexandria, and, in a special coach, we went home. There, another reception was given. There were wreaths everywhere, and thousands of people had gathered. Our house was fixed nicely, the table was set – Felixine had taken care of everything. Mamma dear and I were very happy and glad to be home. (15-16)

Unfortunately, all of the excitements, stress from the voyage, and trying to return to his businesses proved to be too much for Portner at once, and he became nervous again. He took the whole family, as well as a governess and some friends, to Atlantic City, New Jersey, where he rented a cottage for the winter.

Rested and relaxed, Portner returned with his family to Alexandria in the spring of 1882. Shortly after their return, the family moved into a new house at 724 12th Street in northwest Washington. This home, however, would only be a temporary one. That summer, Robert bought a lot at 1104 Vermont Avenue, NW, with the hopes of building a newer and bigger home for his family; Robert and Anna had to make room for more children. On January 22, 1883, the family welcomed the arrival of their seventh child, Paul Valer. A few months later, construction began on his new house.

In addition to this he expanded his real estate holdings. While the new house was being built, he traveled to Manassas and bought the Mathis estate from Christian Mathis' widow, Anna.[11] After having spent much time there, the house and surrounding lands had made quite an impression on Mrs. Portner. With a commanding view of the nearby mountains, the area reminded her of her homeland. Plus, the house and area would provide Portner and his family with a relaxing getaway in the summers. "In the spring of 1883 I bought Annaburg, because Mama liked it so much. I started to build there, too, and had everything repaired, and we were able to move there [that very same season]. We all liked it there very much." (16) What Portner did not realize was the incredible timing for his newfound place of relaxation. Big changes were just around the corner for him, his family, and the brewery and he would need all of the rest he could get.

Endnotes

[6] Shuter's Hill had been the site of Klein's brewery, one of Portner & Company's competitors during the Civil War.

[7] *Alexandria Gazette*, April 29, 1869.

[8] Before this invention, bottles had been sealed using a cork wire bail, similar to that of a champagne bottle. But since cork is porous, the beer would often spoil and go flat quickly.

[9] Not knowing Portner's height, it is hard to know how a weight loss down to 131 pounds or a weight gain of 15 pounds affected him. However, it has been said that he was small in stature and he was never a large man.

[10] Anna's hometown.

[11] Prince William County Deed Book 33, pp. 557-559.

3

The Middle Years

Once Robert's new summer home was settled and taken care of he could start making yet another big chance in the brewery.

> In May 1883, I had the brewery incorporated, and, from now on, everything became a little easier for me. But in spite of that, I could not work very much. I had sold some shares to my best employees to have five shareholders and a board of directors. I gave one share each to Paul Muhlhauser, Carl Strangmann, C[harles] G. Herbort and B. E. J. Eils. From now on, everything improved. Throughout my absence and my disease, the business had not received the necessary attention, but without much effort I rearranged everything. (16)

In 1884, Portner's new home in Washington, located at 1104 Vermont Avenue, NW, was finally finished and ready for the family to move in. They enjoyed the house very much and it also allowed Robert to be able to tend to business better from there. Though he now resided in Washington, he was still quite committed to the welfare of the German community in Alexandria. This became especially evident one particular afternoon while walking down the street. Robert passed the new German Lutheran church being built. He asked the foreman if he could view the plans and was surprised that there was no steeple planned for the building. He asked why it had been left out and was told that the congregation was too small and poor to afford one. He argued that "without a steeple it will be no church. Draw a plan for one, bell included, and I will pay the costs."[12]

Over the next six years Portner's health declined to the point that he could only attend to the most necessary of business affairs. This also prevented him from contributing to the community to ways he would have liked. In an effort to help improve his health, Robert often spent the summers at Annaburg with his family.

> When I was there, I usually was well and could do some reading and writing. But as soon as I started work in the brewery, I became nervous again. The business was going along as usual, I attending only to the most necessary affairs, and taking great

pleasure in driving, horseback riding and taking small trips. (17)

Through all of these good and bad times, he was still able to concentrate on his family. On November 11, 1884, the family's eighth child, Oscar Charles, was born, and on October 4, 1886, their ninth and last son, Herman Henry, was born.

For Christmas of 1886, Robert took his sons Robbie and Eddie, along with their governess, to the Bermuda Islands. The following spring the family traveled to German for the summer. By the time they returned in the fall, they had seen a considerable amount of the countryside, much to the delight of Robert. That winter, Robert took Anna, his friend Henry Bartholomay, and young Paul to the Bahamas, spending three weeks there. They had a remarkable time on the islands, seeing many wonderful sites for the first time. Plans had included going to Cuba as well, but when they learned of an outbreak of smallpox there, they canceled their plans.

During their winter absence, Robbie, Eddie, Alvin, Alma and Etta all stayed in Manassas with the Weems family, where they went to school. Much to the delight of the children, the Weems family lived next to Annaburg, so they were not too far from home. Oscar and Herman, being so young, stayed with Felixine in Alexandria. Robert, Anna, and

Paul soon returned home to their family, relaxed and rested from their vacation. Unfortunately, each time Robert tried to return to Washington and the brewery he would become sick and nervous again.

In 1888 the family decided to go to Annaburg a bit early. The family would usually head to the country sometime in June, but with Anna pregnant, Robert wanted her to be in the comfort of Annaburg when she gave birth. Plus, he knew he could use the relaxation there.

> When we arrived, Robbie, Eddie and Alvin had already prepared the dinner, while Cora [a servant] had baked fresh bread and ground fresh coffee in the coffee grinder. In was very amusing. All the children stayed at Weems' until June, only Robbie returned earlier, because he was sick. He saw everything double, as a consequence of a blow to the head he had received while playing. At first I was worried a great deal, but it gradually became better, and after six months it was completely gone. (17-18)

On May 23, twin daughters Anna Florence and Clara Louise were born at Annaburg. Ten days later, they were baptized at Annaburg, along with Felixine's children (she had since married Henry Wilkening). The family had asked Pastor Louis Schneider, a Lutheran minister from Washington, to perform the ceremony. He had planned on retiring but waited one more day so that he could do the baptism. In previous years, he had baptized six of the other Portner children, so he was certainly no stranger to the family.

When the fall of 1888 arrived, Portner's health had deteriorated to the point that he was forced to retire temporarily from the brewery. In hopes of improving his health and to provide his children with the quality of schooling that he had received, Robert decided to move his family to Germany for two years. On September 15, the family left from Hoboken, New Jersey aboard the ship *Aller* of the North German Lloyd Line. Along with the family came two friends, Lisbeth Steinkäuler and Bell Lucas.

> Two days later, Oscar became very ill. He was already suffering from a cold when we arrived, and when the doctor said he had scarlet fever, he was taken to the hospital immediately. We found a house for us to stay in, located at 42 Schiffgraben. In a week's time, everything was ready and we could move in. We were very satisfied with the house and the city, and

we believed that we could hardly have found a more beautiful and more quiet place. We brought the pleasant memories back to America. (18)

Robbie and Eddie were sent off to Osnabrück to the school there while Alvin, Alma and Etta were sent to Hildegarde Hertzog's school in Pyrmont. Alvin, though, only stayed six months.

We brought him back home because Frau Hertzog could not handle him; he was too full of life and difficult to manage. He then went to the gymnasium in Hanover for six months, but we too had much trouble with him because of his lively disposition. (18)

The family lived a very enjoyable life and Robert's health and strength improved as time went on. At Christmas the entire family was together and Robert's dear friend Louise Rose was with the family when they received their presents.

At about that same time, I had my favorite horse and buggy shipped from America, and from then on went horseback riding very often, this being my most pleasant pastime. In the company of one Herr Brunkhorst and one Baron von Gornberg, with both of whom I became good friends, I took many rides in the Eilenriede and its surroundings. (18)

In March 1889, Robert and Anna left on a trip for Italy, leaving Lisbeth, Bell, the cook, and the butler at home with the children. Paul, however, was sent join his siblings at Frau Hertzog's. A train took Robert and Anna via Frankfurt and Bagel, through the Gotthard Tunnel, to Milan. After spending a few days there they went to St. Remo for a week, followed by Monte Carlo. By way of Nizza, they next went to Genoa, then to Naples, passing Pisa and Rome along the way. With so much to see, they stayed in Naples for a week. There, they celebrated Robert's fifty-second birthday.

By the end of the week their schedule only allowed for one day at the Blue Grotto, which Robert did not care too much for, and one for Pompeii and Herculaneum before they had to return to Rome. Spending a week there, they visited many sites, including the Vatican, St. Peter's Basilica, St. John and St. Peter's churches, as well as the King, Queen, and Prince's suites. From Rome, Robert and Anna traveled to Florence to spend four days there. While in Rome, the couple bought several pieces of artwork, including a painting and pair of marble statues to decorate their home with. "From there we wanted to visit Venice, but when we came to the station, your dear mother became homesick. So we went directly to Milan, and from there to Hanover, where we found everything and everyone alright." (19)

A few weeks after returning to Hanover Robert became sick again. Under the advice of his doctor, Robert and Anna took a trip to Göttingen to see Professor Ebstein. After evaluating him, Ebstein kept Robert there for four days for a more thorough check-up and observation. Ebstein told Robert that he was not sick, but rather extremely weak from an overload of work. He suggested that Robert try to regain his strength through a proper way of living, including a strict diet of one-quarter pound of butter daily, little bread, and otherwise meat, fresh vegetables, and fruit. Before long, Portner had regained his strength and was able to resume his business activities.

During the summer Robert did quite a bit of resting and relaxing in the spas at Bad Kissingen. On one particular trip home, he met with Anna, Robbie and Eddie in Cassel, France. The group toured Thuringia, visiting the Wartburg Castle, and returned home shortly thereafter. Not long after returning home Robert and Anna left on another trip, this time to visit Hamburg to see the World's Fair. After touring the fair, they left for Neumünster and planned to visit the Holstein

Schweiz, Kiel, and Copenhagen. Unfortunately, while in Neumünster, Anna became homesick again so they left without seeing the other cities they had planned to visit.

During our stay in Italy we had met a Dr. Schwartzbach who was the head of a large school in Ostrau, near Filehne. Your dear Mamma liked the charming old gentleman so much that it was her greatest desire to send Alvin to his school, and if possible, Robbie and Eddie, who she did not wish to stay in Osnabrück. Since I got only favorable information about the school everywhere, we took Robbie, Eddie and Alvin there. Upon Alvin's urgent request, we allowed Robbie and Eddie to stay there too. The school was hardly as good as we had anticipated. Nevertheless, Alvin learned very much, as did Robbie and Eddie, who certainly learned more there than in Osnabrück.

Little Hilda [Hildegarde Rose] was born on December 19, [1889 at 3:45 a.m.] in Hanover. That was the reason why we could celebrate Christmas only on New Year's Day, when the whole family, including Mamma and Hilda, were gathered around the Christmas tree. It was a wonderful celebration.

In the winter of [1889-] 1890 I made a little trip with my friends Rose and Bartholomay and his wife to Italy and the south of France. We went to Nice, Cannes, Florence and on to Venice. From there I went to Vienna in the company of the Prince of Liechtenstein [Prince Johannes II].[13] The Prince had stayed in the same hotel in Venice as I, and he had say opposite me at the table d'hôte, so that I suspected him to be an officer in civilian clothes or some high official. He was very tall and had such a beautiful waistline that the American lady next to me asked me if he was not laced.[14]

At the station I learned that the sleeper car had not arrived on account of the snow, and that we had to sit in a compartment until we reached the border. I took a private compartment. Afterwards I saw the gentleman and his valet looking for one too. As he could not find one that suited him, I offered him a seat in mine that he accepted gratefully. I did not know that he was a prince. He said at once, "You are an American. At the table I often heard you talk with the ladies about America." He told me that his brother had been there once and that he was very enthusiastic about this country. He knew very much about American conditions, and we had a nice conversation and became very friendly with each other.

As it became very cold, he offered to share his fur coat with me, which I gratefully accepted. We talked about our families and other personal problems, but he did not tell me his name. I intended to hand him my card as soon as we reached the border. But when we arrived there, the conductor said, "Your Highness, the sleeper is ready." They bowed so much that I thought to myself that the people in Austria must be very friendly because they even addressed me as "Highness." My companion answered the conductor, "Alright but I also want a compartment in the sleeper for this gentleman." My trunk passed through the customs officials unopened, and I was told that everything was alright, "Highness."

We had dinner together and then went into the sleeper which we and the valet had all to ourselves. I realized from all the compliments which were paid him by the officials that he was some high person. When I asked the conductor, he told me that he was the richest man in Vienna, the Prince of Liechtenstein. The Prince and I kept on conversing for a long time and then went to bed. But I did not hand him my card since I did not feel like addressing him as "your Highness." The next morning I awoke so late that the train had already entered Vienna. He came into my room when I was not yet quite dressed and bid me good-bye. I hurried as much as I could, but I only saw him leave in a beautiful coach from which he nodded to me. He was a very pleasant and educated man, a little younger than I.[15] He told me that his whole family was tall as he and had the same physique." (19-21)

Because of bad weather, Robert only stayed a few days in Vienna to see the best points of interest before returning to his family in Hanover. Once he returned home, he found everyone doing quite well.

> In Hanover, the spring of 1890 was very pleasant; the lovely parks and the Eilenriede made walks very enjoyable, and nobody need be bored there during this season or in the summer. Only the mosquitoes became very disagreeable when the warm weather started. (21)

During the spring, Robert and Anna took a trip to Paris, which Robert had not seen since attending the World's Fair in 1878. They returned to Hanover after a week and shortly thereafter, the family returned to America. Robbie and Eddie, however, stayed behind to finish their schooling.

On August 14, 1890, the family left aboard the steamer *München* for America, arriving twelve days later in Baltimore. After leaving the ship the family headed directly to Manassas to spend the summer there. Shortly after the family returned to America, Robbie and Eddie came home as well. In the fall they began attending high school in Washington while Alvin was sent to a private school until he reached the seventh grade, at which time he started attending public schools. Alma attended a private tutor named Mrs. Summers and Etta, Paul, and Oscar all attended the Franklin School in Washington.

No sooner had he returned from Europe did Robert find out that he had an emergency at the brewery. The morning following his return to Manassas, he received word that Paul Muhlhauser had died suddenly a week prior to Robert's return. Feeling much stronger, he headed directly to the brewery where, as he expected, there was much for him to do. The first order of business was to find a replacement for Muhlhauser, in which he took on Joseph Schneider. Aside from the sudden death of Muhlhauser, Portner received a second shock once he arrived at the brewery. While he had been away, the patents for his beer cooling and air purifying machines had been stolen. He filed numerous suits to get the rights back, but in the end Portner ended up selling the rights to the patents for $50,000, undoubtedly one of his biggest disappointments of his life.

Perhaps Robert was working too quickly to fill the void left by Mulhauser's sudden death, but Schneider proved to be very less-than-satisfactory replacement for his predecessor. Initially he was a good man and brewer, but over the course of the next two months, the appeal wore off and by October Robert was ready to find a replacement. Having put the brewery back in order, Robert could now concentrate on finding someone who was a young and efficient brewer, but also had business experience. He finally found what he was looking for in John M. Leicht, who had previously owned a brewery in Newburg, New York. In addition to this, Leicht had worked for or been part owner of breweries in Chicago, Milwaukee, Cincinnati, Cleveland, St. Louis, Boston, and New York, all of which had a high concentration of breweries. As soon as he was hired, Leicht bought 250 shares of stock and became the new Vice-President of the Robert Portner Brewing Company, complete with a salary of $3,000 a year.

Around this same time, low prices and competition caused sales in the south to drop. In an effort to bring the brewery's earnings back up, Robert decided to combine his beer business with the sale of mineral water, which he sold under the name 'Hygeia.' He soon set about establishing branches for his new venture with plans that included the opening of ten branches over the following year. These branches included Norfolk, Lynchburg, Petersburg, and Richmond, where the brewery had recently bought a large depot from the Continental Brewery. "Everything is running smoothly now; my assets keep on increasing without much effort on my part, because I am careful and do not start anything which might involve losses." (22)

On March 20, 1891, Robert celebrated his fifty-fourth birthday. "To my greatest surprise, dear Mamma had invited a large party, forty people. A play entitled "Papa's Birthday" was presented, in which Carl Strangmann, Henry Wilkening, Anna, Robbie, Eddie and all the other children took part." (22) While at Annaburg, he began working on plans for a new home there. He and his family loved the house they had but it had become too small for the still-growing Portner family. Working with Washington based architect Oscar Vogt, the pair created a home which combined the styles of Robert's favorite European mansions.

The family spent the summer at Annaburg that year quite happily. At 10:00 p.m. on May 12, Anna gave birth to her and Robert's thirteenth, and last, child, Elsa Eugenia. By this time Alvin wanted to go to military school, so Robert took him and Robbie to the Virginia Military Institute in Lexington. Unfortunately, at only fourteen years old, Alvin was too young to attend. Robbie, however, was of age and liked it there so much that he was sent in September 1891 to begin studies. Still wanting to be in military school, Alvin was sent to the Danville Military Academy.

With the exception of Robbie, all of the children were home for Christmas that year, and much to the delight of Robert and Anna, everyone brought home good report cards. Even Alvin, who had grown to dislike the Danville Military

Academy, brought home a good report card. By now Robert was nearly finished with the plans for his new home at Annaburg and set construction to begin in the spring. Not wanting to destroy the current house, Robert arranged for it to be moved to where some stables had been located, safely out of harm's way during construction.

"Today, March 28, I made a new will, and with it, I believe I did the best I could do." (23) In his will, he named the National Savings and Trust Company of Washington, D.C. as the new executor for his will and that they would receive one percent of all the money that they distributed.

> Dear Mamma is going to receive our house in Washington and the farm, our beloved Annaburg, to retain it as a home until all the girls are married or as long as they wish to keep it. Each child is going to receive an equal share of the stocks and other tangible assets at the age of twenty-five. The National Savings and Trust Company is going to administer the real estate, the income of which will go to dear Mamma or to the children respectively. The whole estate will be equally divided among the grandchildren when the youngest turns twenty-one years old. In this way, each of you will be

protected against any emergency, even if you should lose the money that you will have already received. I am very happy that I settled this affair to my own satisfaction. I am 55 years old now, but I feel better and healthier than I have in years. (23)

On April 27 1892, Robert bought the 400-acre Weems farm, Windemere, for $8,000 from Robert and Bessie McPherson.[16] Within the next day or two, the cornerstone was laid for the new home at Annaburg. Anna's birthday was celebrated shortly after that and, much to her surprise, Robert gave her photographs of the entire family.

Over the course of the next year, everything proceeded to run quite smoothly. On March 5, 1893, Robert and Anna had little Elsa baptized by Pastor J. Kunding of Reading, Pennsylvania. Recently, Alma and Etta had been in Reading for a few weeks to visit a family friend, and when Robert and Anna went to get them, they had asked the pastor to perform the baptism. Kunding told Robert that he and his family would be in Washington for the inauguration of President Grover Cleveland and that he would be happy to perform the ceremony while there. "All the children were present, as Robbie and Eddie had come home from school for this occasion. All twelve stood in a row, and it was a charming picture." (23)

ooo

As time progressed, Robert would build secondary buildings for his brewery and make adjustments whenever they were needed. The brewery had continued to expand during the 1880's, even to across the street onto a second block. In 1886, Robert made a substantial change to his brewery. Up until this time, all of the power in the brewery had been supplied by coal-burning steam engines. By March of that year, Consolidated Electric of New York (forerunner to Consolidated Edison, or ConEd) had installed a new electric dynamo in the brewery. With the dynamo installed, Robby proceeded to install electrical lighting fixtures throughout the entire plant. Initially the dynamo was used to power 100 incandescent lights throughout the building, the first use of electric lights in Alexandria. Before long, though, the dynamos were being used for brewing tasks as well.

In addition to this new marvel, the brewery soon featured another scientific wonder within the complex. In 1881, a Southern Bell telephone exchange had been established in Alexandria, but only the wealthy and large businesses could afford this costly new invention at first. By 1892, the Robert Portner Brewing Company was able to receive orders over the phone instantly and keep up with its far-reaching distribution network by simply picking up a receiver.

Throughout all of the brewery's expansion, though, there was one thing that the complex still needed. In December of 1893, construction of a new five-story brew house began at the south end of the plant. Not only would this new addition increase production totals, but it would also allow for modernization of the facility.

In 1894, the *Alexandria Gazette* wrote a glowing review of the new Tivoli Brewery.

> [In 1892] the management of the Robert Portner Brewing Company had under consideration the feasibility of remodeling their old brew house, but after mature deliberation of the several projects and in view of the impossibility of attaining satisfactory results to the space, it was thought best to defer the proposed alterations until the increase in demand should justify a more extensive and complete improvement. About the closing of last year [1893] it was decided by the management that the time was ripe to go ahead.

The object was to increase the present capacity of the brewery and also simplify and facilitate the different operations by means of constructing a plant which should combine all the best features developed during the last ten years. The architect was directed to use only the best quality of materials and workmanship throughout but to leave off all unnecessary and expensive embellishments.

The brew house proper, of 40 feet 4 inches by 44 feet 8 inches, has three main stories with a height of 54 feet from the street level to the top of main cornice, and a total height of 80 feet. The structures are entirely built of brick, stone, steel and iron, lumber only being used for windows, doors, the purloins and top layers of roofs. The thicknesses of walls above ground are 21 ½, 20 and 16 inches respectively.

The entire interior framing for floors, platforms, galleries and other supports, also main roof, is of steel, the floors being fitted between beams of concrete arches. There is an unobstructed view from one point to another at all levels, and also light in the remotest nook and corner through the large windows. The roofs are covered with slate, and all guttering is done with copper. Broad flights of iron stairs lead from floor to floor and a power elevator of two tons' capacity furnishes access to all main levels.

All the tanks, tubs and hoppers throughout are built entirely of steel, with the exception of the hot water tank and the brew kettle, which are constructed of copper. On the [ground floor] is the new Corliss steam engine of 65-horse power, fitted with a pulley weighing four tons, and an eighteen-inch wide belt. The whole driving system is arranged so as to transmit the power in the most direct way and at the same time not interfere with the overhead or passage room anywhere.

The [brew] kettle is designed to carry the great load of 55 tons when full, its own weight being over 5 tons. It is entirely of copper with a double bottom, and is fifteen feet in diameter with a total height of 14 feet. The mashtub is

15 feet 6 inches in diameter by 8 feet high and is provided with a machine with a grain-removing device of the latest pattern. The rice conversion tub is entirely built of steel to withstand the high pressure exerted, and weighs about 6 tons. All the service, feed and discharge pipes from one vessel to the other are of copper.

The old brew house will be remodeled into a malt storage of 40,000 bushels capacity, and when completed will enable the handling of the malt in bulk, discharging it from the cars to the bins. Through these extensive improvements, when entirely completed, the capacity of the plant will be at the maximum 250,000 barrels per annum. The cost of the new brew house, mill room and plant will be about $75,000 and with the malt storage included, $100,000. The engineer and architect under whose direction the work was executed is Mr. C. F. Terney of New York and the result fully justified the company's confidence in his taste and ability.

With the additions described above, the brewery is now one of the most imposing and capacious in the country. It is also an ornamental structure, and adds greatly to the beauty of the northern section of Alexandria.[17]

When the new brewery was finally finished in November of 1894, it must have come as no surprise to anyone that the Robert Portner Brewing Company was now the largest brewery in the South. To accommodate the new production capacity, Portner equipped the new brew house with new coal-burning power plant, which devoured 2,500 tuns of coal yearly.

During the same year the new brew house was finished, the Virginia Glass Company opened in the West End of Alexandria. The opening of this company could not have been more perfectly timed. With the brewery expanding at such a fast pace, it needed a steady supply of bottles to meet he demands of its customers. Within a year the brewery had signed $20,000 worth of contracts with the factory.

This helped to alleviate the worries that came from ordering bottles from companies located farther away. Previously, the Robert Portner Brewing Company had ordered their bottles from Karl Hutter of New York, E. H. E. of Ohio, and Dean & Foster of Boston. With a bottle company so close, the brewery no longer had to worry about bottles getting broken while being shipped so far, as well as the shipping costs themselves. Alexandria soon became the local hub for bottle production when three more factories opened shortly thereafter, each one working around the clock to produce tens of thousands of bottles daily. The Robert Portner Brewing Company continued to purchase a majority of its bottles from the Virginia Glass Company until a series of fires forced the plant to close in 1914.

One of the benefits to having had built his brewery over his beer cellars on Washington Street was Portner's access to the railroad. Extending down the middle of St. Asaph Street, stopping between Pendleton and Oronoco Streets, was a rail spur. The spur had been part of an old railroad that once had its depot on the corner of King and St. Asaph Streets shortly after the Civil War. With immediate access to this line, the brewery's fleet of fifty refrigerated rail cars, all painted a vibrant blue, could steam up to the brewery, be loaded with its precious cargo, and head back out to any number of the brewery's depots throughout the south. The spur ran past the ice plant, where the cars would receive their refrigeration before being loaded with beer. There was also a shop beside the icehouse for the maintenance and repair of the cars.

Once the fleet of cars left the brewery, they would stop at various depots throughout the southern states. Stops in Virginia included Norfolk, Lynchburg, Danville, Richmond, Chesapeake, Newport News, Fredericksburg, Petersburg, Roanoke, and Charlottesville, while stops in North Carolina included Charlotte, Wilmington, Goldsboro, Greensboro, Raleigh, and Salisbury. In South Carolina, the fleets would make stops in Columbia, Charleston, Greenville, and Florence. The only known stop in Georgia was in Atlanta. Though Robert limited his sales to the south, the company had continued to sell within Washington, D.C. until 1890.

In 1893, the United States was hit with the greatest depression that it had ever faced up to that point, the Panic of 1893. Grover Cleveland was in his second term as President and not only had he upset many people with his political tactics, but his term happened to coincide with one of the most devastating business panics in history. The Panic of 1893 started with the collapse of the Philadelphia and Reading Railway Corporation on February 20. Within the next five months, two other high-profile companies would collapse as well; the National Cordage Company on May 5 and the Eerie Railroad on July 25.

Despite all of these closings, as well as many others, constant reckless spending of the Democratic Party caused the underlying weakness of the Panic. For many years, they had been intentionally inflating the national money supply through the overvaluing of silver as compared to gold. Such a disastrous combination resulted in millions being out of work, over four hundred different banks to collapse, and for the first time in its history, the United States Treasury was in the position of being bankrupt.

The Panic caused strikes across the country, including the infamous Pullman Strike in 1894. Citing grounds that the movement of U.S. mail was being prevented, President Cleveland sent in troops to break up the strike. Unfortunately, with the collapse of some major railroad companies and the strikes of others, every business was hurt in more ways than just financially. The resulting depression was not lifted until 1897 when three New York banks combined themselves and offered to redeem people's bank notes, which regular banks would not touch.

Because of its reliability on the railroad to ship its product throughout the south, Portner's brewery was affected considerably throughout the depression. In 1890, Robert had become the Vice-President of a new brewery in Washington. Fortunately, this brewery sold its product exclusively to Washington and the surrounding areas so they were not hurt nearly as bad.

ooo

In December of 1894, Portner went on a trip to Boston. Unfortunately, he suffered an attack of rheumatism and had to return home where he was confined to bed for about ten days. Once he was feeling better, he returned to the brewery where he found things running in a less-than-desirable fashion. As a result, Robert once again resumed active management of the plant. He asked Carl Strangmann, his nephew who had been with the company since 1875, to resign from his positions of Secretary and Treasurer, and replaced him with Percy McKnight Baldwin. After leaving the brewery, Strangmann left for Germany. Upon his return, he sold his and his sister's shares of stock in the brewery, 200 in all, back to Robert at $175 per share. Now, Robert owned all but one hundred twelve shares, which were owned by Leicht.

By 1895 the Alexandria branch had spanned to three city blocks and was able to offer the public seven distinct brands of beer: "Vienna Cabinet," "Tivoli Lager," "Tivoli Select," Tivoli Extra Pale," and "Tivoli-Hofbräu," the latter of which was the premium of Portner's beers. Prior to adopting the 'Tivoli' name in 1877, Portner only brewed two brands, "Vienna Cabinet" and "Vienna Lager."

The plant yielded 100,000 barrels for 1895, employed over 110 workers within the Alexandria brewery itself, and had an annual payroll of $68,835. Besides being one of the largest assets to the economy of Alexandria, Portner financed his other branches as well. With all of the branches combined, Portner employed 168 workers for a payroll of $71,000 yearly. With the brewery and branches combines, the company totaled over 278 employees with a payroll exceeding $140,000 per year. In October, Robert extended his brewing family when he brought Eddie in to begin working at the brewery.

On January 29, 1896, Robert and Eddie left New York aboard the steamer *Fürst Bismarck* for a cruise to the Orient. Six days later, they arrived in the Azores. The two stayed through the evening before heading off to the Madeira Islands. Over the course of three days, the two took in many sites they had never seen before. On February 8, they arrived in Gibraltar, which they followed with Algeria on February 10 and Genoa on February 13. Throughout the remainder of their trip, Robert took Eddie to many southern European and African cities, including Monte Carlo, Malta, Alexandria, and Cairo, where they visited the Pyramids of Gizah, the Nile River, and the tomb of King Ramses II.

After leaving Egypt, they headed to Jerusalem and Bethlehem, seeing everything that they possibly could while in the Holy City, before heading off to Greece. On March 4, they arrived in Smyrna, but only stayed one day before heading to Athens. Here, they visited many sites, including the Parthenon, the Acropolis, and the Royal Castle. Next,

Robert and Eddie went to Eleusis. They toured the area for a little while, but returned to their ship at three o'clock because the King and royal family of Greece were expected then. "They were congenial people, and they all speak German well. The royal family had some champagne and, afterwards, dinner on board ship. Then they returned to their boats and landed accompanied by three cheers." (27)

After Eleusis, Robert and Eddie headed to Constantinople, where they arrived on March 10. They saw the sights there, but soon left for Messina, where they spent one day before heading to Palermo. "I believe this is the most beautiful and interesting, and at the same time, the cleanest Italian city." (27) On March 18, they arrived in Naples, just in time to celebrate Robert's fifty-ninth birthday. After a celebration on the ship, Eddie left for Genoa via Rome. Robert stayed behind a few days with friends, finally meeting Eddie in Genoa on March 24. Two days later, they left for America. When they finally arrived in Hoboken, New Jersey, they found Anna and the rest of the family waiting for them. On April 6, they finally arrived back home.

Robert did not stay home for very long, though. On April 9, he left for Germany. Leicht was resigning from the brewery effective June 1, so Robert wanted to visit his family for a while to rest before having to take on extra responsibilities at the brewery. While in Germany, Robert took some time to visit his friends he had not seen in some time. First he went to see Louise Rose in Hamelin, followed by Henry Bartholomay in Frankfurt. Six weeks later, Robert returned to Alexandria.[18] Upon his arrival, he immediately hired a new brew master named Peter von der Westlaken, the brewery's only non-German brew master. He also bought back Leicht's shares in the company, gave Eddie ten shares, and made he and Baldwin members of the Board of Directors. As it now stood, Robert was President and Chairman, Eddie the Vice-President, and Baldwin as Secretary and Treasurer.

The course of the following year was another uneventful time. "In January [1897] I went to Hot Springs, Virginia for my rheumatism. There, for the first time, I read through the description of my life. I found it to be a little confused, but I cannot copy it, although I would like it to be different." (28) On March 4, 1897, William McKinley was inaugurated as the 25th President of the United States and Robert had served as a member of the reception and civic committees for the occasion. Later that evening, Robert and Anna, along with their friends Rose Meredith and Mrs. Wright, attended the inaugural ball. The following day, the family hosted a large reception at their home in Washington.

> On March 5, we had a formal dinner at which were present the German ambassador, Dr. von

Holleben; the minister from Switzerland, Mr. Peoda; Count Götzon; Baron Herman from the German Embassy; Congressman Barthold[19]; Robbie; H. Xander; and E. H. Droops. (29)

By this time, Robbie and Eddie were going to the brewery each day with their father. Since he was the oldest son, it can be assumed that Robbie was following his father, being trained to assume the Presidency of the business someday. Eddie, on the other had, was in charge of the bottling houses. About this time, the brewery began to produce malt extract.

For his home on Vermont Avenue, Robert had a new wing added. "On Christmas we had a house warming party for the new dining room. As all the children were home, we had a photograph taken of the whole group by the photographer Prince." (29)

Six months later, toward the end of June 1898, Robert embarked on another trip. He and Etta left New York aboard the *Fürst Bismarck*, arriving in Cherbourg, France a few days later. They traveled to Hanover where they met with Alma, who had been staying with the Voight family. From there, the three spent the next few months traveling throughout France, Germany, and Switzerland, visiting many cities and friends along the way. At the end of August Robert and his daughters returned to Cherbourg. They boarded the steamer *Augusta Victoria* and headed back to New York, arriving on September 4. By the next morning the family was back at Annaburg. With the new school session, Robert sent a young fifteen-year-old Paul to the Virginia Military Institute.

By all intents and purposes, the Robert Portner Brewing Company had been a smooth running operation, with no major catastrophes or strikes to mar its reputation of product line. But even the brewery could not escape the vagrants and vandals of society. In 1899, the *American Brewer's Review*[20] reported, "The safe at the agency at Newport News, Va., of the Robert Portner Brewing Co., was cracked and $50 in cash and some checks stolen and the building damaged by the explosion." Fortunately, no one was hurt during the robbery and the brewery and depot were soon able to return to business as normal.

ooo

In early-1899, the Portner family suffered their first family tragedy since Edwin's death twenty-six years earlier.

> On Sunday evening January 15, 1899, our dear Clara died [of remittent fever] in Atlantic City, where we had taken her on the advice of Dr. Gardner and Dr. McDonald after she had suffered from an intermittent fever for about

seven weeks. Mamma and Etta were with her. I had left for Washington two days earlier because we were not aware of the danger, and the doctor had assured us that there was none. Her illness started with a cold and stiff neck, then she ran a temperature for a few days. On January 18 she was temporarily interred in Rock Creek Cemetery [in Washington]. All the children were present, and the oldest brothers were pallbearers. (30)

Endnotes

[12] *The German Element in Virginia*, 184-187.

[13] Members of the royal family of Liechtenstein bear the title Prince[ss] von und zu Liechtenstein (Serene Highness), or HSH Prince[ss] for short. At the time Robert met him, Prince Johannes II had been the ruling Prince for thirty-one years.

[14] Wearing a corset.

[15] Robert was now 52 years old, the Prince 48.

[16] Prince William County Deed Book 41, pp. 338-339.

[17] *Alexandria Gazette*, April 18, 1894, p. 3.

[18] After leaving the Alexandria brewery, Leicht joined former Portner employee Carl Strangmann at the brewery he had purchased in New York, the German American Brewing Company.

[19] Congressman Richard Barthold of Louisiana.

[20] The American Brewer's Review was a publication put out once a year at the annual meeting of the United States Brewer's Association.

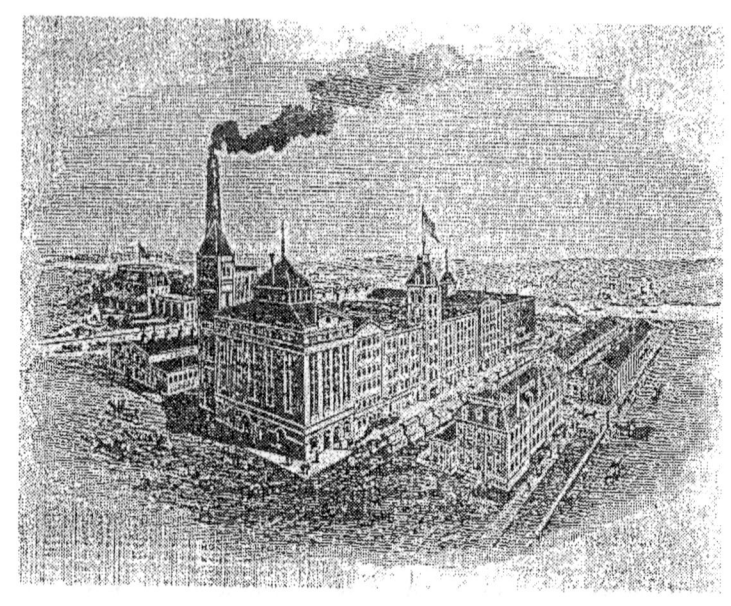

Lithograph of the Robert Portner Brewing Company in the 1880's

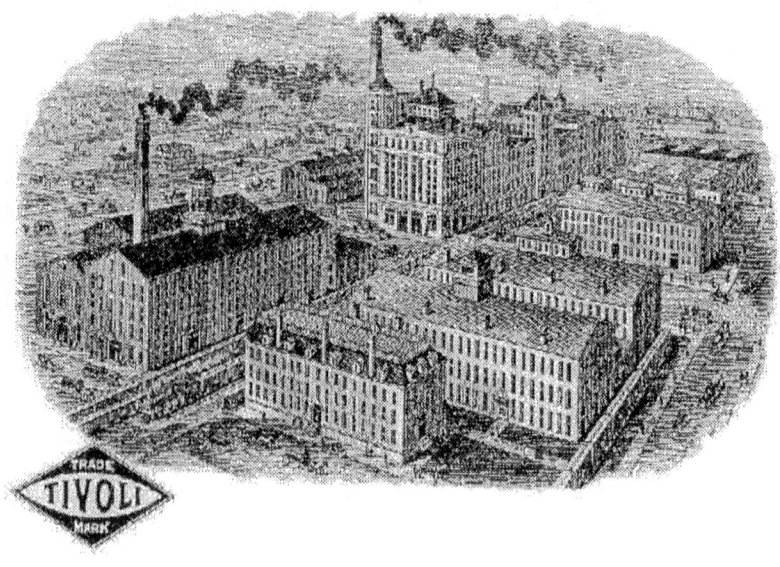

Lithograph of the expanded Robert Portner Brewing Company in the 1890's

Copy of letterhead from the Robert Portner
Brewing Company, dated 1898

Copy of letterhead from the Robert Portner Brewing
Company, dated 1900.

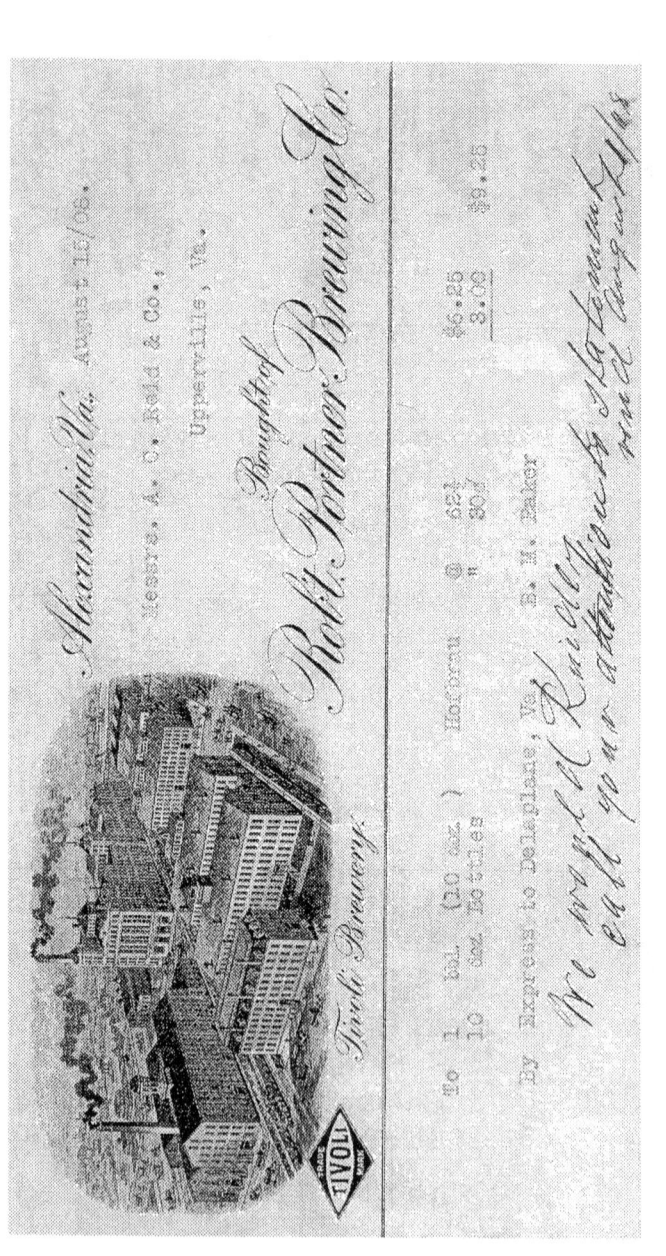

Receipt from the Robert Portner Brewing Company dated August 1908
Courtesy of Anna Schoellkopf Lacher

Slide # 1
Picture Here

Slide #2
Picture Here

Poster advertisements for the Robert Portner
Brewing Company
Courtesy of The Smithsonian Institute

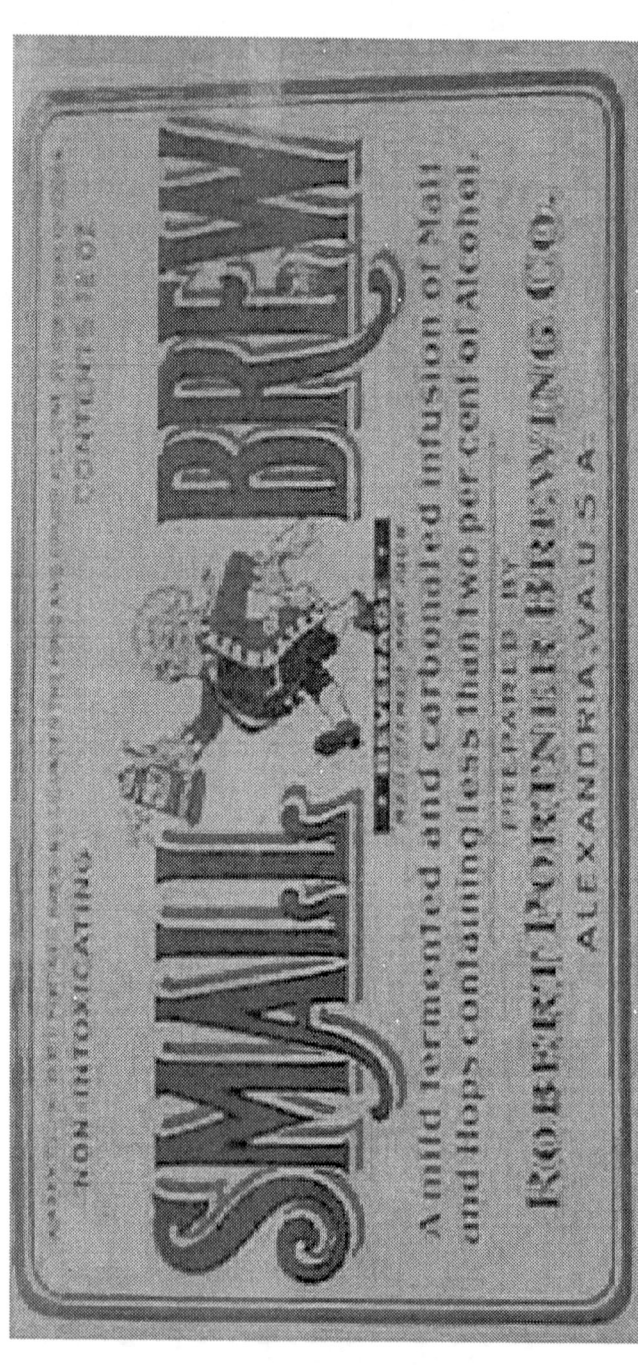

Label from one of the brewery's many different varieties of beer. The label says that it was registered in 1908. The product, as best as one can tell, is similar to a "near beer."
Courtesy of Peggy E. M. Portner

Bottle caps from sodas made by the Portner Brewing Company

Label from one of the varieties of beer.

4

The Last Days

According to Victorian custom, women in mourning would wear black for one year after the loss of a child or husband. No sooner had Anna hung up her black crepe dress in mourning for Clara did she have to take it down as tragedy struck the Portner family once again.

> Robert died of exhaustion [typhoid fever] on January 23, 1900 at eight o'clock in the morning as a result of hemorrhages after an illness of seven weeks. He was a good and noble boy, and I do miss him <u>very</u> much. (30)

Robert "Robby" Francis Portner had died at the age of 25 at his father's home in Washington. Two days later, his body was buried in Rock Creek Cemetery, presumably along side of Clara's. Only a few years earlier, Robby had graduated from the Massachusetts Institute of Technology with a degree in electrical engineering, and later with a degree in the same field from Columbian University.

If Robert had a favorite child, it was Robby. The boy shared the same mental inventiveness as his father. While attending the Virginia Military Institute, Robby wrote a letter to Eddie, explaining a new kind of microphone he had invented. With utmost confidence in him, Robert had been training Robby to follow in his footsteps and to take his place when Robert chose to retire from the brewery. By 1898, Robby had begun to work at both the brewery and his father's construction company. Robby had clearly been his father's pride and joy. But, as any parent must, Robert had to move on.

In May of 1900, Robert took Alma on a trip to Europe to get Etta, who had been at school in Morgan. They met her in Frankfurt, where the three then traveled to Wiesbaden and stayed for ten days. The trip then went on to Cologne to visit friends, then to Pyrmont where they met with Mrs. Marwede and her daughter, Mrs. von Schenck.

> On June 28 we received a cable that Paul, who had been sick for some weeks, had become works, and so we, i.e. Etta and I, left right away. Alma followed by the end of October; we left her under the protection of Mrs. Marwede. Etta and I took the steamer *Columbia* and arrived in New York on July 6, and in Washington on July 7. From that day on

Paul improved, and by now he is almost completely well, but he was very ill. (30)

In 1900, Robert bought a large plot in the newly formed town cemetery in Manassas.[21] With three children buried in two different cities, he preferred that they were all together, as well as having room for others in the future. Plus, in spending more time in Manassas each year, it would make it easier for the family to visit the graves of their loved ones as compared to if they remained in Washington and Alexandria. On January 12, 1901, Clara and Robby were removed from Rock Creek Cemetery and interred in Manassas. Around this same time, Edwin was moved from Alexandria to Manassas as well.

Two weeks later, Robert, Alma, Etta, and Paul embarked on a cruise to the Caribbean for thirty-five days aboard the new yacht *Princess Victoria Louise*. They visited such islands and countries as Haiti, Santo Domingo, Puerto Rico, St. Thomas, Venezuela, Jamaica, and Cuba. From Nassau, they returned to New York on March 2 and were home in time for McKinley's second inauguration on March 4.

By the time the summer arrived, Robert was not going to the brewery much since he wanted Eddie to have the opportunity to conduct the business alone. They also built and opened their third, and largest, icehouse that same summer, which produced up to twenty-five to thirty tons of ice daily. Once the new icehouse was in operation, Robert was able to leave on June 31, along with Alma and Etta, aboard the steamer *Deutschland* for another trip to Germany. Though they spent much time visiting cities throughout Germany, they also visited Holland, Belgium, Catende and London, where they stayed for ten days. On August 30, they left Europe aboard the *Princess Victoria Louise* and headed back to America. "After our return, we stayed in Manassas until the middle of October. Then we went to Washington, where Alma and Etta gave their first tea; they came out [were presented to society] in December." (31)

On December 10, 1901, Robert made the last rewrite of his will. He left the houses in Washington and Manassas to Anna to be used and enjoyed throughout the rest of her life. He also named the American Security and Trust Company as the new executor of his will. Robert instructed them to pay thirty-five dollars per month to his only surviving brother, Otto, for the rest of his life; five thousand dollars to Felixine, in addition to one hundred dollars per month for the rest of her life; and fifty dollars per month for the rest of her life to his other sister, Augusta Strangmann, who was at present a widow and living in Prussia. Should Anna not survive Robert, he arranged for five thousand dollars to be paid to Anna's brother, Hans Valaer, who was living in Jenaz, Switzerland,

and for the items within the Washington and Manassas homes, as well as the homes themselves, to be equally divided among his children.

Being a man of good conscience, he could not go without leaving an annuity for some of the organizations in the towns he resided in. He set aside his fifty shares of stock in the National Bank of Manassas, or an equal amount of five thousand dollars, to be used in a trust fund for the poor of Manassas. He also left five thousand dollars to the Manasseh lodge of Masons A. F. & A. M. in Manassas for a new temple to be built, and five thousand dollars to the Mayor and Town Council of Manassas for general street repairs. Lastly, Robert had his executor invest and reinvest his shares of capital stock in the Robert Portner Brewing Company in ways to best benefit his children, and he had other incomes of money set aside for his wife and children as well.

On March 1, 1902, Robert left for a trip to Palm Beach with Alma and Etta. They returned eleven days later after having an enjoyable time. Upon their return, the family celebrated Robert's sixty-fifth birthday. Later that month, all of the children were home again in Washington. Alma and Etta had returned from spending a few days in New York and Oscar and Paul were home from school. Once the family was together, they traveled out to Manassas and spent the Easter holiday there. In August, Anna went abroad with the children, and Robert, Alvin, and Etta followed on October 23. Later in the year, after the family returned from Europe, Alma became the first child to become engaged. Robert and Anna proudly announced her engagement to Washington society, saying that Alma and Julius H. Koehler, a native of St. Louis, Missouri, were to be married in the fall of the following year.

ooo

In 1902, the brewery was only at satisfactory production levels, but by the beginning of the next year, business had once again improved. After opening his newest icehouse the previous year, it was met with more success than Portner had anticipated. In fact, it produced more ice than the brewery could effectively use. Being the money-conscious businessman that he was, Robert saw an opportunity to make a profit from waste.[22] He made an agreement with the Mutual Ice Company of Alexandria to sell them his surplus. In the agreement, signed January 11, 1902, the brewery would sell all of this extra ice from April through September at $2.50 per ton during April, May and September, and $3.00 per ton between June and August. It was also agreed that the surplus would not exceed 800 tons (1.6 million pounds) each month.

Later that year, the brewery purchased the Mount Vernon Cotton Company building, located on the other side of Pendleton Street from the brewery. In early 1903, work began on refurbishing the building into a new bottling plant. To do this, the four wooden floors were removed and replaced with iron beams and concrete floors, which were more suited to support the weight of the bottling machines.

ooo

In January 1903, Robert embarked on a trip to Nice with his entire family. Alvin and Etta returned with him while Anna, Paul, little Anna, Hilda, and Elsa stayed behind. By March, Robert could feel his age. "My state of health is not very good. I feel that I am getting old and shall not hold out much longer." (32) Anna Paul, and little Anna returned the next month while Hilda and Elsa stayed behind a bit longer to finish their courses at a finishing school in Oldenburg. Not long after Anna's return with the two children, Alvin, Etta, and Paul left to visit Florence, Venice, and Rome. On one of the last overseas trips he would take, Robert met the children in Naples and headed off to Cairo with them. After a few weeks there the group returned to Washington.

By this time, Robert was sixty-six years old, and he knew that he would not live too much longer. With his advancing age and failing health, Robert decided to practically retire from his businesses and let his sons run them on their own. He would visit them from time to time, though, to check on their progress. Since it had always brought him so much relaxation and pleasure, Robert wanted to move to Annaburg to spend his remaining years. "Today [May 21, 1903] we will move up to Manassas. Mamma left with Hilda, Elsa, the cook, and the governess at 11:15 a.m. I will follow them this afternoon because I want to go to the brewery first." (32) Unfortunately, this would be Robert's last entry into his diary.

Once at Annaburg, Robert lived there for three more years before he passed away. In late May of 1906, Robert briefly went to stay at his home in Washington for a few days[23]. While in Washington, he developed bronchial trouble so on Sunday, May 20, he headed back to Annaburg to recuperate. By Tuesday his condition had grown worse and he continued to grow weaker and more ill as each day passed. At 4:45 in the afternoon of Monday, May 28, 1906, Robert Portner finally passed away. Anna and their ten surviving children were at his bedside throughout his final hours.

A private funeral was held at Annabug for Robert while his casket was placed on display in the east parlor, surrounded by bouquets of flowers. The casket, purchased from Gawler & Sons of Washington, was made of solid bronze and was to be hermetically sealed. The chaplain of the Manasseh lodge of Masons A. F. & A. M. conducted the service. Edward, Alvin, Paul, Herman, Oscar, and Julius Koehler served as pallbearers. On Wednesday, May 30, 1906, Robert was laid to rest with Masonic ceremonies in the family plot in the Manassas cemetery.

ooo

After her husband's death, Anna continued to spend time both at Annaburg and her home in Washington. In November 1908, Anna proudly announced to Washington society that a second of her daughters was engaged. Etta was now engaged to William Payne Meredith, a native of Manassas who was a lawyer in Washington. As the children were growing up, the couple's parents had been close friends. William and Etta were married the following fall.

On March 10, 1910, Anna made the last rewrite of her own will. To her four nieces and three nephews in Switzerland, she left two thousand dollars each; to Elisha Meredith, Etta's father-in-law, Anna left one thousand dollars; to Anna Merchant, a close friend, two hundred dollars; and to the American Security and Trust Company, five thousand dollars in trust to be given to her brother Peter during his lifetime, then to his wife after his death, and their children after hers.

The large family portrait that hung in Annaburg was to go to Edward, but should he die without issue, then the portrait would go to the oldest surviving child, but the portrait was to remain in Annaburg so long as it was used as a home (it ended up hanging in Annaburg long after it stopped being used as a home). A particular portrait of Robert was willed to Etta, but all other paintings were divided up amongst the children. With the exception of her shares of stock in the Robert Portner

Brewing Company, all of Anna's other belongings were to either be sold or divided between the children. Anna specifically requested that all one hundred and thirty shares of stock that she owned be sold for the best price obtainable. Should Edward want the stocks, however, he could buy them for the appraised value, paying in five payments, the first being when they were sold to him. Should he have no interest in the, the same offer would go to the other children, from the eldest down to the youngest.

As time progressed, Anna continued to spend more and more time at Annaburg. Like her late-husband, she found comfort and relaxation there, and felt it was very helpful in her attempts to recover when she began having minor strokes in January of 1912. On Tuesday, July 2, 1912, Anna suffered a massive stroke. For the next ten days she lingered, trying to make a recovery, but she finally passed away at the age of sixty-four on Friday, July 12, 1912.

Anna's funeral took place at Annaburg on Sunday, July 14 at 6:00 in the evening. Reverend U. G. B. Pierce of All Souls Unitarian Church, Washington, officiated. The internment, however, had to wait until the following day. As her casket was being taken from Annaburg to the family plot, a terrible storm broke out. The downpour of rain, bright lightening, and loud thunder scared the horses, forcing the procession to return to the house, where her casket lay overnight.

> Several persons including John R. Tillett, Ira Reid and The Democrat's representative took shelter from the terrific storm, Sunday evening, in the pavilion at the Manassas cemetery to await the arrival of the Portner funeral cortege. The storm was the most severe that has passed over this section within the memory of the oldest inhabitant. The lightning cast its vivid glare, with slight intermissions, and the terrific peals of thunder came in quick succession.
>
> It was noticed that Mr. Tillett and Mr. Reid repeatedly picked up and swallowed the hailstones which were pelting the concrete floor of the pavilion. It developed that it has been said that if one swallows hailstones in a storm there is immunity from lightning stroke, and from the number of hailstones swallowed by the parties named it is a great wonder they did not freeze to death.[24]

The following day, internment took place in the family plot where she was buried alongside of her husband. Pallbearers consisted of her sons Edward, Alvin, Paul, Herman and Oscar, her nephew Peter Valaer, and two of her sons-in-law, William P. Meredith and Lorimer C. Graham.

In his memoirs, Peter Valaer recalled his aunt fondly by saying:

> Aunt Anna was very proud of her family history in that Paul Valaer, one of our ancient relatives, as General of the Swiss Army, saved Switzerland from the warlike Austrians. I will be ever grateful to the Portner family for their kindness and helping [my brother] Paul and me to get a college education. I will always remember Aunt Anna's kind words, "Peter, hold your head up and be ever proud of your family because it has a noble background."

Anna von Valaer Portner was born in Jenaz, Switzerland on April 16, 1842, and as a young woman, she came to America to help her brothers Peter and Jacob with their business in Philadelphia. Once she married Robert, she became actively involved in various charitable organizations throughout Washington, including being a member of the board of governors of the George Washington University Hospital, the German Orphan Asylum, and the Washington Home for Foundlings.

Mrs. Portner was also very prominent in the social life of Washington. For many years, Anna was one of the city's most lavish and hospitable entertainers. The home on Vermont Avenue, up until two years before her death, was the center of many of Washington's more attractive social events. In 1910, she leased the house to the Chilean minister and it was still being used as the legation at the time of her death. After the house had been leased, she used Annaburg as her summer residence and the home at 1523 New Hampshire Avenue as her winter home.

ooo

After Robert's death, his family and employees now had to adjust to life without the leadership and guidance from the man who had built the environments they had come to know and cherish. When the Board of Directors met in 1907, Edward was officially elected as President and Alvin as the Vice-President. In 1910, however, Edward stepped down and Alvin assumed the role of President with Paul as Vice-President.

But at first the boys were like princes regent; still young, they undoubtedly leaned heavily on the more seasoned executives hired by their father. At the Alexandria brewery, Secretary-Treasurer P. McKnight Baldwin and assistant Secretary George Beuchert "held down the fort," handling much of the business end of the firm until Prohibition, while the "boys" remained at their Washington homes and commuted as necessary.[25]

At the time Edward assumed control of the brewery, *Wedderburn's Souvenir Virginia Tercentennial 1607-1907* said of the complex,

> The present fine plant of the Robert Portner Brewing Company covers the greater portion of four city blocks, about 250,000 square feet, and all the latest scientific improvements in brewing, refrigeration and bottling machinery are applied in its construction. Their brewing department has a capacity of one hundred thousand barrels and the bottling department twenty million bottles. Their refrigerating, power and light equipment consists of a 300-ton refrigeration and ice-making plant, 1,200 horse-power boiler capacity, and electric

engines and dynamos of 100 kilowatt power. They manufacture 50 tons of ice daily.

In all actuality, from the time of Robert's death in 1906 until Prohibition took effect in 1916, very few changes were made to the brewery. Capacities, sizes, and even locations remained the same for the brewery's machinery, and the few physical changes made outside of the plant were the erection of some sheds and the demolition of a water tower.

The most significant physical change at the brewery, and the last one to occur, was the erection of a new bottling house in 1912. With depots having closed in all other states, the brewery now concentrated its bottling operations in Alexandria, thus the demand for a new bottling house. In 1912, it bought the last piece of privately owned parcel of land on the 600 block of North St. Asaph Street. With this purchase, they now owned the entire block, which cleared the way for construction. Designed by E. R. Weller, the brick, steel, and concrete building was constructed by the Boyle-Robertson Construction Company of Washington and was considered to be the most modern structure in the entire complex. Studies in industrial design, as well as using modern materials, led to the erection of this impressive 93 foot by 180 foot building building, complete with reinforced concrete floors, steel beams, and natural light coming through the ceiling. With all of the bottling now under one roof, the brewery saved money not only in general costs, but it is believed they had pipes installed in a tunnel underneath St. Asaph Street to pump the beer directly to the bottling house, which reduced shipping costs and time as well. The state-of-the-art building was completed in 1913.

ooo

Unfortunately, Robert's death was a blow that the brewery and his other business would not recover from. Even though he had taught his sons how to run his company with the skill and determination that he had, none would ever reach or exceed the production totals that Robert once had them at.

This, however, was not because his sons were less 'competent' or business savvy than he, but rather it was the increasing pressure from the temperance movement that caused production levels to drop. In 1907, Georgia voted to go dry, as did North Carolina in 1908. By the end of the year, the Robert Portner Brewing Company had pulled out of Georgia, South Carolina, and North Carolina completely. Wanting broader coverage for the brewery, depots were opened in Maryland and Washington to help alleviate the drop in sales.

As all good things do not last, so did the harmony of Portner's brewing family. By the time of incorporation, the numbers of employees had grown so much that it was next to impossible to keep track of everything, as well as to be as closely involved as he had been in the past. Having depots and agents in various cities as far south as Atlanta, Georgia made this task all that much more difficult.

> Having been completely absorbed in operations until the early 1880's, Robert Portner decided both to take more vacation time and to move his family away from their home on the brewery block. The legal and physical separation of Portner from his business was more than symbolic. It meant that he would spend less time observing operations, and that the workers would be dealing with a board of directors instead of one man.[26]

It should come as no surprise, then, that the brewery workers were hardly impressed with the new management, even though they were Portner's own sons. By 1910, rumors had already been circulating of an impending strike at the brewery. In May, employees went on strike for higher wages and shorter workdays. Initially, the board of directors agreed to raise wages in the brewery to between seventeen and nineteen dollars per week and between twelve and fifteen dollars per week in the bottling house. Citing competition as the cause, management did not concede to shorter hours. This, of course, did not sit well with the workers.

> The rumors of a strike...crystallized into a movement this morning by which Alexandria was made the scene of a May-day strike, the employees in the various departments of the brewery walking out. They will await orders from the central body in Washington [the Brewery Workers' Union]... The brewery officials are employing other men to take the place of the strikers, and they say their business will suffer no material interruption from the walkout. It is said that the employees at the brewery have no issue with the officials, who have granted an increase in pay, and if left to themselves, would not have quit work. They are, however, obeying mandate of the leaders of the union in Washington.[27]

One day after the strike began, it was over as the board of directors gave in to the demands of their employees. Not only had the workers won an increase in wages, but also their workday was shortened to eight hours, year-round. In an effort to keep the brewery running longer, the management created two work shifts, even though it often claimed that it could not afford to pay its employees the same as what their contemporaries were making in Washington breweries.

In an effort to hire more employees for this new second shift, the brewery started hiring a number of non-union men who would work for lower wages. Plus, some records indicate that the management may have even singled out union members when it came time for layoffs. All of this came to a head in 1915 when, on January 11, bottlers, brewers, and drivers all walked out once again. In addition to these men, others walked out just to show their support for their fellow worker. All in all, seventy-eight of the two hundred employees failed to show for work the next day.

The workers remained on strike in defiance of the company's practices, but the brewery had to keep their factory running, so they brought in outside help from New York, as well as local areas. Ultimately, the workers gave up their strike after seeing the brewery running without them, and using cheaper, non-union labor.

The Rise of the Downfall

Anyone who has ever taken an American history course knows of Prohibition and its effects on the country during the thirteen years it was "enforced." Most people, however, do not realize how the movement came about and evolved over the many decades before Prohibition was made into law. In 1996, a student at George Mason University wrote a paper entitles *End Game: Anti-Prohibition in Alexandria*. This paper does an excellent job of explaining the movement, from beginning to end. The following are excerpts from this dissertation, which will help the reader to understand how a brewing empire such as Portner's came to meet its demise.

> By 1909, the Anti-Saloon League concentrated its efforts on tighter dry laws and the gubernatorial race. It threw its support to William Hodges Mann and made temperance a major political issue. The Methodist Church, through the Virginia Annual Conference and Baptist State Association, also backed Mann.
>
> The gubernatorial primary election of 1909 pitted Mann against Henry St. George Tucker.

Mann, who was personally dry, was backed by the political machine of Senators Thomas S. Martin and Hal Flood[28], who served as architects of the campaign. That organization had traditionally relied upon funds from the liquor industry to maintain its political power. They were able to craft a coalition of liquor interests and the temperance movement to maintain party unity and gain both wet city votes and dry support even though Mann's dry position offended the traditional, wet supporters. Senator Martin urged Mann to take a conservative position and offer local option as a reasonable approach to statewide temperance.

Tucker, a wet candidate, favored local option as a means of satisfying dry preferences yet allowing for alcohol consumption for those who so desired. Both sides, therefore, supported local option but with opposite intentions; Mann saw local option as a means of drying the state while Tucker saw it as a means of keeping it wet. Both sides shared another similarity – support for a statewide referendum on prohibition. In his Richmond kick-off speech on February 2, Tucker declared support for a statewide referendum. Mann followed suit. But quietly, Martin assured supporters that Mann would not support prohibition. The wets were therefore able to safely vote for Mann.

Primaries were held on August 5, 1909. Mann won the election by 5,000 votes – 39,281 to 34,203 – assuring him of election as the next governor of Virginia. Mann's support included not only traditionally dry areas but also wet cities including Alexandria, Portsmouth, Richmond, and Norfolk. It was a closing act in the local option era for Virginia. By 1910, the Anti-Saloon League, at the head of prohibition forces, shifted the fight from local option to statewide prohibition and to use a statewide referendum as the vehicle. The ASL was prepared to take on the Machine.

Over the next four years, the ASL continues to push statewide prohibition, slowly gaining support every step of the way. Seeing where things were headed, beer, wine and liquor retailers within the state came together to fight the ASL's petition drives circulating throughout Virginia.

On May 14, 1914, 2,000 businesses and professional men formed the Virginia Association for Local Self Government (VALSG). Not nearly as powerful or effective as the Anti-Saloon League, they worked against statewide prohibition. Their primary argument, as expressed by various self-proclaimed prominent individuals, was that statewide prohibition would not prohibit.

Little did anyone realize just how accurate this statement would become. In September of 1914, the issue finally came to a vote.

Within a day, the results were known and statewide prohibition had passed by 35,000 to 40,000 votes. Dry forces had carried four cities and sixteen counties. Of the eleven jurisdictions in the Eighth Congressional District [the northern Virginia area], only Alexandria City, and King George, Prince William, and Stafford counties had voted wet.

The latter three counties voted against by 56, 57, and 64 percent respectively. The District-wide total was 6,181 wet to 6,070 dry, the balance tipped by Alexandria's 1,121 to 358 voted for local option.

The Association for Local Self-Government accepted defeat when the results were announced and promised to support the ban. A brief suggestion also appeared for retrocession – to return Alexandria to Washington, D.C. where alcohol was still, and for some time, would remain legal and available. The idea quickly and quietly passed.

The statewide ban closed the state's remaining retailers, distillers, and manufacturers. Over 566 retailers or retailers and shippers and another 54 wholesale or manufacturing operations were closed by the ban. Alexandria closed 34 retail establishments, 5 retail and shippers, a wholesale dealer, and one malt manufacturer, Robert Portner's brewer.

Portner's Brewery, an important business fixture of the city since 1861, was Alexandria's malt manufacturer casualty of the statewide ban. The brewery was the largest industry in Alexandria and its largest employer. Contracts, contract and factory workers, machinists, and other laborers also profited from his business. He supplied almost every saloon in the city. All of this ended in November 1916 when the ban became effective.

By 1916, a statewide ban on the sale, transport, or manufacture of alcohol superseded any controlled distribution or local option – Virginia became dry. Federal prohibition, passed in 1918, strengthened by wartime prohibition measures, and incorporated into the Federal constitution in 1920, made Virginia, and the rest of the United States dry. Until 1933, prohibition was the law of the land.

For years, the state of Virginia had been able to put off petitions and attempts to enforce prohibition throughout the state. In some cities, including Alexandria, prohibition meant an end to one of their largest sources of economy.

Unfortunately, it was something that they were only able to postpone, not prevent.

When the "law of the land" went into effect in Virginia in 1916, the Robert Portner Brewing Company had no choice but to obey the law. Rumors began circulating in May that the brewery was closing, at which time the plant reduced its level of production. The brewery remained open until October, at which time Alexandria's largest employer and manufacturer was forced to close its doors, shut off its steam, and stop its massive convoy of rail cars forever. "It was difficult to understand how a nourishing, healthful beverage would be classified as intoxicating liquor."[29] Portner's sons were not going to step down so easily, though.

> In mid September 1916, the brewery management announced that the company would enter new fields. Alvin and Paul Portner and [assistant] secretary George H. Beuchert rechartered the company as simply "The Robert Portner Corporation," with Alvin remaining as president, to engage in real estate, farming, and the manufacture of feeds and other products.[30]

Citizens of Alexandria will be glad to learn that the Robert Portner Brewing Company will engage in the manufacture of stock, dairy and poultry feeds, and that the present buildings owned by the company will be utilized for that purpose. The company is already investigating and arranging for the purchase of the necessary machinery, and it is expected that they will begin operations around the first of the year. The plant will have a capacity of 20 tons per hour of the various kinds of feeds they will handle. The industry will supply a long felt need [of] this locality which may be readily understood when it is known that the State of Virginia alone consumes about 200,000 tons of these feeds per year, nearly all of which comes from the western States. All will join the Gazette in wishing the new enterprise abundant success and prosperity.[31]

Under the name the Virginia Feed and Milling Corporation and with Oscar as president and Paul as vice-president, the company invested into the refurbishing of the buildings for this newest business. Unfortunately, the business was not large enough to fill the entire brewing complex, so they primarily used the icehouse as a "manufactory" and the brew house for storage. The 1903 bottling house, which had been empty since 1913, was rented to the United States government for storage. Hoping for an eventual reopening of the brewery, the buildings on the east side of St. Asaph Street were rented out to the United States government as well. This way they would at least be used and not fall into complete disrepair. The Virginia Feed & Milling Corporation could hardly be considered a success as compared to the brewery. This, combined with Paul's death in 1919, all contributed to the demise of the business.

Alexandria historian Ray Gallagher once wrote about the Robert Portner Brewing Company:

> With the closing of Portner's, naturally came the closing of every saloon served by Portner's, since the brewery was their chief supplier. The closing of the brewery robbed the neighborhoods of their feeling of community...since the saloons were the gathering places for the neighborhood locals...it was quite a blow to the economy when the 18th Amendment went into effect and the brewery was closed down. Seemingly, all the saloons prospered, and it was quite a blow

to the local economy with The Law (prohibition) went into effect, and the brewery closed down.

Unfortunately, all of Portner's sons died before Prohibition was repealed, which made a reopening of the brewery virtually impossible. In the same article by Gallagher, he also said:

> Living in the 400 block of N. St. Asaph Street in the late 1920's, I early became aware of the past history of Portner's, and the saloons it spawned and supplied. Even then, 1927, Portner's dominated the skyline on the 600 block, but by then it was a hulking red-brick ruin, with all of its windows out, and its vats and tubs exposed.

In 1937, the Robert Portner Brewing Company was officially dissolved. Though Prohibition had been repealed four years earlier, none of the Portner sons were still alive and no one else in the family wanted to attempt a reopening. Plus, the brewing complex had fallen into such disrepair that it could hardly be considered worthwhile to attempt to repair and reopen the plant. Within four years of the dissolving of the company, the main brew house which had dominated the Alexandria skyline for nearly fifty years had been reduced to nothing more than a pile of rubble.

What Remains Today

When people hear of the story of Robert Portner and his brewery, they often wonder and ask if there is anything left of the old complex. The answer is yes. Though Alexandria has changed considerably since the days of horse-drawn buggies and dirt roads, some of the buildings from the Robert Portner Brewing Company do remain, though they have been adapted to more 'modern' uses.

Unfortunately, nothing remains of the brewery buildings located on the block between St. Asaph, Washington, Pendleton, and Wythe Streets. By 1941, the entire block had been demolished and a few years later a Woodward and Lothrop department store built on the site. Commonly called "Woodies," the business remained until 1968, when the W. J. Sloane Company purchased the building. In the early 1980's Mastercraft Interiors purchased the site and used the building to display their home décor wares. Today, a brand new office and shopping complex, completed in 2001, sits on the site. As for the block behind it, the only building remaining is the 1912 bottling house.

By 1921 the United States Government had gained control of the entire block, using the buildings as storage for the Department of Agriculture's Bureau of Exhibits. For easier mobility of the exhibits, the government even had a new rail spur put into the block. By 1931, most of the buildings on the lot were vacant, with the exception of the bottling house, which was still being used as a warehouse. Shortly thereafter, the government sold the block and the bottling house was remodeled into an arena, affectionately known as "Portner's Arena," and served as a venue for various forms of Depression-era entertainment, including boxing matches. Around 1936, it was remodeled once again, this time for use as a used car showroom for the Parkway Motor Company. Two years later, it was used as a soundstage and production facility for the American Film Corporation. In 1940, it was transformed yet again, this time into a skating rink. Like its predecessors, the business only lasted a short while and the building was sold once again.

The 1941 Sanborn maps show that, after the closing of the skating rink, the block had been sold to the Red Cross. When the Red Cross unveiled its plans to convert the site into their new Eastern Headquarters, plans called for the demolition of all of the buildings on the site, including the

1892 bottling house. Fortunately, the Red Cross saved the 1912 bottling house and incorporated it into their plans as office space. A new building was built adjacent to and connected with the old bottling house. The Red Cross used the site as their Eastern Headquarters until 1997, when the building began its biggest transformation to-date.

Two years earlier, the Red Cross phased out its Eastern Headquarters, merging it with the National Headquarters in Washington and no longer needed the site. The Red Cross sold the entire block to developer Madison Homes, Inc., whose planners envisioned a development within the block consisting of apartments, townhouses, and condominiums. Fortunately, the history of the building and the area was not lost on them. Naming the development 'Portner's Landing,' Madison Homes hired Torti Gallas CHK to design the project for them.

The challenge was to design homes consistent with the architectural heritage of Alexandria, but at the same time, planning for enough units to make the project feasible. The end design was a pleasing combination of new construction with an update of the existing building. To accommodate the townhomes, the bottling plant was gutted and redesigned for condominiums, including an additional story on top. Where the Red Cross addition had been built, a new four-story apartment building was built and named the 'Portner House.'

In addition to all of this, a new road was added through the middle of the complex, appropriately named Tivoli Way.

Aside from this building, two others survive. The 1903 bottling house, formerly the Mount Vernon Cotton Company, still stands at 515 North Washington Street. In 1918, the building was sold and became the Express Spark Plug Factory, which was in operation until 1928. The building sat empty until 1935, at which time it was remodeled and converted into the Belle Haven Apartment Building. The apartments were eventually closed and in 1981, a group of patent attorneys converted the building into offices. In July 1992, the International Association of Chiefs of Police bought the building and continues to use it as their headquarters today.

The building, however, does have a bit of a colorful past, tracing back to before Portner even came to Alexandria. In 1854, a 21-year-old night watchman at the Mount Vernon Cotton Company was killed in an attempted robbery. In an effort to lure the killer back to the scene of the crime, local police placed a six-foot tall look-alike mannequin in the cupola on the roof, dressed in the night watchman's clothes. Unfortunately their ruse did not work, but the Silent Watchman still survives and remains in the cupola, keeping an ever-watchful eye over his building almost one hundred fifty years later.

During the Civil War, the building had a number of uses, including a hospital, logistics center, jail, and barracks for convalescents and Union stragglers in 1865. One can only wonder if this is the jail Portner stayed in while under arrest by General Slough during the war.

The last building associated with the Robert Portner Brewing Company that is still standing is his 1901 icehouse, located on the northeast corner of St. Asaph and Wythe Streets. Since the closing of the brewery, it has served as the home to number of different businesses, including a laundry from 1937 to 1950 and, more recently, a bank. In the late-1990's, the building and lot were purchased by a developer who wanted to build an office building on the site. Using the existing building (the original icehouse, through additions and alterations, had nearly doubled in size since it was first built) as a starting point, plans for the "Riverport" office project called for the building to be partially demolished and encased within the new structure, which would double the original building both in width and height. The interior was remodeled extensively and only the piers visible on the exterior give a hint as to its original usage.

A Man and His Brewery – A Commentary

What was it that made the Robert Portner Brewing Company so successful? When Portner entered the industry, beer brewing came so few and far between that it was not considered by most to be an industry, but when the process of artificial refrigeration was introduced, the country saw an explosion of breweries popping up everywhere. By 1910, the brewing industry was ranked sixth of the nation's largest moneymaking industries.

Before artificial refrigeration was introduced, most breweries within the United States were located in the northern states. The cold weather played a major role in beer production. In the beginning, the beer brewing process was very long and complicated, and temperature played a large part in this. However, once artificial refrigeration was introduced, breweries could be established anywhere. Besides this development, advancing technology played a part in the increase of breweries. Large steel and copper cisterns and tanks for fermenting were developed to help lift some of the pressure off of the demand for beer.

Another reason that Portner was so successful was the introduction of lager beer, which had become easier and cheaper to make compared to the previous ports and ales. Plus, lager beer had a more appealing taste. As more and more people began drinking it, the market expanded drastically. A book written on brewing in 1933 stated:

> The people now had within easy reach and at moderate price a refreshing beverage of sparkling appearance, possessing the lively quality of a carbonated drink, of much greater stability, lighter in both body and in alcohol content than the old-style beers.

Since lager beer had lower alcohol content, people were still able to go out and drink beer, but they would not get as intoxicated as they would have drinking the same amount of the old-style beer.

One of the biggest attributes to the success of Portner's industry was the demand for beer itself. In 1810, there were merely 150 breweries in the United States. By 1850, the number had nearly tripled to 431 breweries. As the next ten years went by, the largest jump occurred when the number hit 1,269. The peak of breweries occurred in 1873 when the count showed an impressive 4,131 breweries in the United States. From here on, the numbers only dropped as breweries grew larger and bought-out or forced the closure of its rivals. By 1930, a count showed that there were only 186 still in operation. This shows just how powerful of an effect prohibition had on the industry. As the number of breweries decreased, however, the demand for beer increased.

When Portner entered the market in 1862, the average person consumed around 2.75 gallons of beer yearly. By 1914, the average consumption had increased by thirty-four percent to 20.6 gallons a year. There were three main reasons as to why demand increased as breweries closed: mass production of beer, extensive shipping networks for outlying markets, and the prohibition movement. Doing the same thing as Portner did, other breweries developed their own forms of mass production and founded large networks in order to ship their beers to markets outside of the city the brewery was based in. As the prohibition movement shut down breweries, the number of "wet" counties, or counties where breweries were located, decreased, which resulted in mass production for the ones that did remain open. Of the few breweries that did remain open, many turned into massive industrial breweries, Anheuser-Busch and Miller being prime examples.

Even though industrial technology, timing, and social acceptance all played key roles in Portner's success, the most credit ought to go to Portner himself. With his strong drive and determination to keep going, rarely did he encounter a barrier that he could not pass. But Portner was also a man of great character, social tolerance and acceptance. He did not judge a man on his social or economic class, or even the color of his skin. Instead, Robert Portner was a man who subscribed to the beliefs that the only limits placed on a person were those placed by himself, and that one only got out of life what he or she put into it.

Robert also understood the practice of treating your employees with the kind of respect you would give your own family. In the beginning, Robert ran his brewery as if it were a family, all of his employees being a second set of children to him. The employees respected a boss who shared in the labor and showed a knowledge and respect for the trade. And many times, the workers were related as trades often passed from father to son. But not only were his employees related, but also Portner had his own family working in the brewery. Carl Strangmann and Christian Valaer worked for their uncle in one capacity or another, as did Robert's brothers Otto and Carl and his sons Robby, Eddie, Alvin and Paul. Even Robert's niece, Louise Strangmann, married brew master Paul Muhlhauser.

His commitment to his employees, though, was quite evident. Robert was known to have some of his best employees sit on multiple boards of directors within his companies. Those who were not as high ranking, but were higher than the "common laborer" and trusted by Portner were known to have been placed in directorship positions. But

Robert's devotion to his employees was not limited to the affluent within the company.

In the early years, he, Otto, and Felixine were known to have served meals to employees, and in Christmas of 1874, Robert even presented each of his workers with a turkey and a new jacket. But even when employees left to seek work elsewhere, Robert did as best he could to find them work in other communities that were heavy in German population.

In nine years of research on Robert Portner, two poignant testaments to Portner as a man have come to light. The first is found in the memoirs of his nephew, Peter Valaer, when Peter writes about his first visit to Annaburg in 1902.

> Uncle Robert Portner was in Manassas at that time but he was very sick nearly all the time. I had a number of nice talks with him. He was a very inspiring and truly great man and he was loved and admired by everyone, particularly in Alexandria, Virginia, where he was rated as one of their finest citizens, during years of building up the Robert Portner Brewing Company and his other projects.
>
> It was said that when as a very young man coming from his home in Germany to America,

young Robert Portner threw his few remaining coins overboard; he said he would begin his career in the United States without one cent, but by hard, hard work and fine character he built up the Robert Portner Brewing Company in Alexandria on St. Asaph Street. In his early beer garden near the brewery he waited on the garden customers himself. His beer was famous and he could hardly make it fast enough.

The second testament to Portner can be seen in a letter written in 1977, just a few years after Valaer's memoirs and seventy-one years after Portner's death, by E. R. "Ren" Conner, III. Though Conner never knew Portner personally, and most likely did not know any of the Portner children, the moving words he wrote would make one thing that the two men had been neighbors, or even close friends.

[Portner's] wealth made him a special man in Manassas, but like the working man he perfectly reflected the hopes, beliefs, and above all, the tastes of his age. Strangely enough, the mid- to late-nineteenth century seems more remote to us today than the Civil War era, or even Colonial times, these more dramatic periods in American development. Mark Twain called the late nineteenth century the Gilded Age, and it was during this time, from Grant's administration through the second term of Grover Cleveland, that Robert Portner amassed his fortune. The rich, unburdened by government restriction and taxation, were very rich. Portner's Annaburg estate at Manassas was the most lavish display of wealth that the little village had ever seen. Here in its midst was a man who had celebrated the American Centennial in 1878 by inviting President Grant's entire cabinet to the launching of his new clipper ship from his own Alexandria shipyard. Robert Portner did this, and he also, by his presence in Manassas, provided the first overlay of culture, of cosmopolitan living, to a community trying to keep pace with the new age. And like the Carnegies, the Rockefellers, the Vanderbilts who were his contemporaries, he recognized the obligations of great wealth. He was never aloof from the community. When he died in 1906 and left Annaburg for the last time on the way to the family plot in the Manassas cemetery, the whole town turned out to mourn. He was a millionaire many times over, but he respected every class of man and in his way, helped them.

Portner turned miles of brush and straggling corn patches all the way from Manassas to Bull Run into productive farmland. He paved Main Street from Portner Avenue to Center. He laid out the streets of northwest Manassas. He built the finest hotel that the town would ever see. Without him, the Masonic Lodge would not have been able to rebuild after the Great Fire of 1905. Without him, quarry stone would not have been available for the new Courthouse, the new National Bank, or for scores of other buildings and their foundations.

On the level of national importance, he invented the first home air conditioning apparatus in 1878 and installed it in Annaburg when the house was built. He organized the first German bank in the Washington area. He served as President of the American Brewers' Association and patented the earliest beer cooler in the country. He built ships and apartment buildings. In short, he was the classic entrepreneur, the man who was not afraid to take the risk so that society might benefit. And in so doing he rose from an immigrant peddler to a multi-millionaire.[32]

Brew Masters

- _____ Kaercher[33]   1862 – Spring 1865
- Carl Wolters   Fall 1866 – May 1867
- Jacob Biehle   Summer 1867 – 1870
- Peter Wolters   1870 – April 1871
- Edward Fielmayer   April 1871 – Fall 1871
- Paul Muhlhauser[34]   Fall 1871 – August 1891
- Joseph Schneider   August 1891 – Oct. 1891
- John M. Leicht[35]   Oct. 1891 – June 1, 1896
- Peter von der Westlaken   June 1896 – Nov. 1916

Brands and Dates of Incorporation

1862-1865	Over 1,700 barrels of lager beer brewed.
1866	Ale production begins and continues into the early 1870's.
1869	Portner's brewery begins production of cream ale and a porter, in addition to ale.
1873	"Vienna Cabinet" introduced.
1877	Tivoli trademark first used; "Tivoli Cabinet" begins production.
1887	Bock beer introduced.
1891	"Hygeia", a brand of mineral and carbonated waters, is introduced.
1894	"Tivoli-Hofbrau", Portner's premium "export" lager, and "Tivoli Select" introduced.
1896	Bock beer re-introduced; renamed "Bavarian Tivoli-Extra (Dark)" the following year.
1898	"Red Cross" brand of malt extract introduced.
1899	Brewery ceases production of its "Bavarian Tivoli-Extra (Dark)" bock beer.
1900	Line of flavored sodas introduced, ultimately offering six different flavors.
1908	Low-alcohol "Small Brew" introduced.
1914-1915	"Tivoli-Hofbrau" renamed "Virginia Extra Pale Export Lager" due to increasing anti-German sentiment in the U.S.

Endnotes

[21] With room for thirty people and almost half full, the Portner family plot remains the largest privately owned plot in the city cemetery to this day.

[22] This was not the first time Portner and the brewery conducted business in this fashion. In the early-1870's, Portner sold his surplus grain at 15 cents per bushel directly from the "New Brewery." His advertisements declared it to be the best feed for cows.

[23] 1410 16th Street, NW

[24] *Manassas Democrat*, December 1910.

[25] Tim Dennee, *Robert Portner and His Brewery*, 168.

[26] Tim Dennee, *Robert Portner and His Brewery*, 175.

[27] *Alexandria Gazette*, May 3, 1910.

[28] Ironically enough, Flood married one of Portner's daughters five years after supporting Mann in the gubernatorial race.

[29] Peter Valaer's memoirs.

[30] Tim Dennee, *Robert Portner and his Brewery*, 202.

[31] *Alexandria Gazette*. September 16, 1916.

[32] Letter written by Manassas Museum Curator E. R. "Ren" Conner, III to Manassas Mayor Harry J. Parrish in 1977.

[33] See Endnote 1, Chapter 1.

[34] Brew master at the time the brewery became incorporated.

[35] Also served as Vice-President.

5

Contributions to a Financial Empire

Aside from his brewery, Portner made an additional sum of money through various other businesses in Manassas, Washington, and Alexandria. This chapter covers the successes and failures of each of these ventures.

Banking

In 1869, Portner made his first business venture outside of brewing when he helped established the German Banking Company, a mutual savings association and the first of its kind in Alexandria. In addition to Portner, several prominent businessmen and builders comprised its Board of Directors. What made this particular bank so prosperous was the fact that it let the small businessman get money from them when larger banks had previously turned them down. More importantly, its customer base had very strong ties to Alexandria's thriving German community. Unfortunately, despite its success, the bank only lasted ten years.

Business had been doing well until Portner's resignation as President in 1880. The Board of Directors, however, did not accept his resignation until the following year. Upon Portner's departure, Isaac Eichberg became the President. It was around this same time that the cashier, James H. Reid, began to drink in excess and became quite reckless with his duties. He did not keep the books as he should have and embezzled some funds, all of which led to him getting fired. When the bank finally closed, all debts were paid off and stockholders, who originally bought stock for one dollar per share, were given about seventy percent of their original investment back.

Another banking venture Portner helped establish was the German Co-operative Building Association. Founded a year before the German Banking Company, the Association dedicated itself to buying land, where it erected buildings, and turned around and sold them to people within the German community. Stock-holding and dues-paying members were allowed to purchase a home from the Association and pay the debt at a low interest rate.

> In order to join, a man had to subscribe to buy stock, that is, to save a certain amount each week; if he did not, he was fined. When he had paid for all his shares, he became a member

and was able to borrow money from the cooperative. Any profits that were made were paid to members as dividends or else invested in real estate. Interest was charged on loans, but it was less than charged by local banks. When the association had so many shares, the cooperative's books would be closed and a new association would be instituted.[36]

The Board of Directors was not exclusively German, but did feature other prominent Germans from within Alexandria community such as Justus Schneider, who served as Secretary, Albert Rosenthal as Treasurer, and Isaac Eichberg. Like the German Banking Company, Portner served as President from its beginning until his resignation in 1880.

Ship Building

By 1870, a different type of ship was needed to haul high-bulk, low-value freight that did not require quick delivery. Before long, three- and four-masted schooners began to appear within the ports of Alexandria, Georgetown, and Washington. Most of these ships came from Maine shipyards, and though a rivalry began to develop between the local cities there, they formed a single market.

Many of the suppliers that contracted the shipyards had their distribution points in more than one location so that the ships were forced to unload their cargo in one location and retrieve their next cargo in another. Alexandria, however, had the advantage of being one of the only points on the Potomac that afforded direct access from the shipyards to railroad cars.

> Coal was the basis of trade. Schooners with fertilizer, building materials or other bulk commodities would deliver their cargoes to Alexandria or Washington and move to Georgetown to load Cumberland coal at the [C & O] Canal basin near the mouth of Rock Creek. A profitable trade grew up between Maine icehouses, some of which were owned by Washington distributors, and the butchers, dairies and ice cream manufacturers of Washington, though it was in fact the return trip to Maine laden with coal which made the round trip worthwhile financially.[37]

By 1874, Portner had already made quite a name for himself, both in the brewing industry and in Alexandria.

Working with the maritime trade to receive his beer brewing supplies (i.e. grains, hops, and barley), Portner recognized the importance of cargo ships and how industry relied too heavily upon them to survive. Knowing how vital Alexandria was to trade on the Potomac, he soon realized that there had not been an area within Alexandria or the immediate vicinity where a ship could go for repairs if needed since the Civil War. In 1849, a group of businessmen had established the Alexandria Marine Railway Company for this purpose, but the war forced its closure and the yard had sat empty ever since.

On March 18, 1874, Portner organized a meeting of local businessmen at Harmonie Hall to discuss the possibility of reestablishing a marine railway and shipyard within Alexandria. The group consisted of fourteen men, including Steven Shinn and John P. C. Agnew, two of the founders of the original marine and railway company. On March 27, the Alexandria Marine Railroad and Shipbuilding Company was officially incorporated.

Initially, the company looked to purchase the Hunter family shipyard, located on a stream bordering Wilkes Street. The family had been in business for over 75 years, but was on a steady decline. Rather than buy this shipyard, though, the company opted for the purchase of the original Alexandria Marine Railway Company site on Franklin Street. The new company provided plenty of new jobs for many people in

Alexandria. Once the shipyard was purchased, the owners immediately began enlarging it by purchasing lots surrounding the property. Before long, the company owned the entire wharf. The first railway to be established by the company was in the northern portion of the site. To construct this railway, the company reused materials from an existing railway on the property, as well as obtaining some additional supplies from the former military railway nearby. Soon, a second rail was added, this time on the southern end of the yard.

The main focus of the Alexandria Marine Railway and Shipbuilding Company was to provide repairs for the sizeable fleet of coal, ice, and fertilizer schooners on the Potomac River. They also repaired other ships, including steamers, tugs, and coasters. On July 5, 1876, one day after America celebrated its centennial, construction began on the company's first ship. Funded by Portner, he had a keel laid for the largest vessel ever built on the Potomac River up to that point, a three-masted, 631-ton schooner. The ship was to be 168 feet long with a 34-foot beam. Over the next four months, workmen swarmed around the yard to work on the ship. Progress accelerated so quickly that Portner, in celebration, hosted a reception on September 6. Over 500 people attended, including the Richmond and Washington Singing Societies, Alexandria's Board of Aldermen and Common Council,

Donch's Brass Band, and members of President Ulysses S. Grant's cabinet. On November 27, 1876, the schooner, which had been appropriately named the *Robert Portner*, was launched. "The launching took place with great applause from thousands of spectators." (13)

On December 5, the *Robert Portner* began preparations for her maiden voyage. Chartered by John P. C. Agnew, the ship was loaded with coal and left for Hoboken, New Jersey. After unloading her cargo, she was loaded with tobacco and set sail for Leghorn, Italy. Over the next year, the ship had little difficulties on her voyages as she toured the Atlantic and Eastern seaboard delivering her various cargoes.

After a stop in England in 1877, the ship headed southeast to Rangoon, a port city in India, where she was loaded with rice. The *Robert Portner* set sail to return to England but encountered a terrible storm along the way, which grounded the ship in the Hawaiian Islands. Though the ship had to be abandoned by its crew, everyone managed to return to Alexandria safely. Upon their return, the ship's captain, Captain Strange, presented the ship's flags to Portner since it was he who had originally presented them to the ship.

Four years after the *Robert Portner* was launched, the shipyard completed its second ship, the *James B. Ogden*. A 678-ton schooner chartered b New York owners, Portner owned one-eighth interest in the ship. Unfortunately, like the

Robert Portner, the ship cost the yard more to build than it made, "but Alexandrians, in loyal Democratic fashion, managed to place the blame on [President] Garfield's high tariff policy."[38] Undaunted, Portner continued with the yard, building, overhauling, and repairing several more large ships over the next five years.

Feeling that his brewery was of a higher priority, Portner eventually retired from active duty with the shipyard. In 1880 the yard was leased to John P. C. Agnew, who purchased the company the following year and combined it with his coal business to create the Alexandria Marine Railway, Shipbuilding and Coal Company. Agnew's company continued to operate on this site until its demise in 1930.

Associations and Organizations

In addition to sitting on the boards of banks, Robert was involved with many associations in Alexandria and Washington. Though many Germans had fled to America to escape the overbearing German government, they could not help but to feel immense pride when the Germans defeated the French in 1870. Serving as President, Robert helped to establish the German Patriotic Aid Association, which gave assistance to those injured or displaced by the conflict. After moving to Washington in the 1880's, Robert and his wife became quite supportive of the city's German Orphan's Asylum.

Portner had barely resigned from the German Banking Company and the German Co-operative Building Association when he was elected as the new President of the United States Brewers Association[39]. He had been interested in the association for many years, and was considered to be one of its oldest members. Whenever there were any arguments, it seemed Portner was always the one to settle them quickly. As early as 1878, the Association wanted him to be President. Upon Portner's request, though, he was not nominated since he and his family were about to embark on a trip to Prussia.

Two years later, while on his way to a convention in Boston, Portner found out that he was about to be elected President. Reluctant to accept the position, he stayed in New York in hopes of avoiding any intrusiveness. A few days later, after having finally arrived at Coney Island, Portner was notified by telegram that he had been unanimously elected. With this extra responsibility, his work increased again. Many times, he had no choice but to attend to business for the Association in Washington. On March 26, 1881, Portner resigned from the position and, under doctor's advice, left for Prussia once again with his family.

In January 1895, M. M. Parker, Town Commissioner of Washington, paid a visit to Portner. He informed him that he had been sent by the American Security and Trust Company to ask if Portner would be interested in becoming a member of their Board of Directors. "I accepted, bought ten shares for $137 each, and was elected in January. I realized that the board consisted of the best men from Washington and Philadelphia." (24) In May of the same year, Portner was asked by one of his neighbors to replace the late Henry Simken, another friend of Portner's, as the Director of the Riggs Fire Insurance Company. Once again, Portner accepted.

Word began to spread rapidly of Portner's involvement with so many associations and of his ability to effectively run so many of them at the same time. In January of 1896, the President of the National Bank of Washington offered Robert the position of Director to replace Mr. Carter, who had recently passed away. He accepted the position because he thought of the company as "an outstanding institution." He was sold ten shares of stock for $290 apiece.

Though Portner accepted a number of these positions, he never stayed with any one for very long. Many times his schedule would become so full that he would become overworked and become ill, forcing his resignation. By working with so many institutions, though, they provided him and his family with many personal and professional connections that would last for many years to come.

Inventions and Innovations in Beer Brewing

During the time when Portner operated his brewery, many contributions were made to both brewing and American industries. In 1876, scientist and microbiologist Louis Pasteur published a paper titles <u>Studies on Beer</u>, which explained why beer often turned sour during fermentation and would spoil so quickly. This study left its mark on brewers for all time. Soon after Pasteur's paper was published, inventors began creating machines that would filter, quickly heat, and then cool beer to kill any microbes it might contain. Known as pasteurizers, brewers across the country and abroad began installing these machines in their breweries. Robert Portner himself made two significant contributions to the pasteurization process.

Between 1876 and 1878, Portner began working on two devices, one that would pasteurize beer and another that would cool beer. Unfortunately, his designs were not practical, so he turned his efforts towards the invention of an ice or air cooling machine. He had heard of a man, Thomas Cook, in Pennsylvania who had been experimenting with one such machine. He traveled to Philadelphia and visited Cook at the Centennial Exposition of 1876 and once they became acquainted, Cook taught Portner about the construction of the machine and the principles upon which it was built. Portner even bought one of his machines for his own personal study.

Once he returned from Pennsylvania, Portner began redesigning the machine. By early 1878, he had what he felt to be a finished, and improved, machine. These changes, though, resulted in additional problems. Once these troubles had been worked out, Portner had converted Cook's machine into a beer pasteurizer, which was the first of its kind to both work well and be of practical use.

On February 15, 1878, Portner submitted an application for a patent on his new machine. In his proposal, entitled *Improvements in Beer-Coolers*, he wrote,

> The main objective of my invention is to provide a method and means for preserving beer and other fermented liquors by heating and again cooling the same with great rapidity, so that the taste thereof may be affected as little as possible.
>
> My improvement in the process consists in successively heating and cooling beer or other

fermented liquors while running a continuous stream through pipes or other closed vessels.

My apparatus for practicing my improved process consists of a continuous pipe for conducting the beer or other fermented liquor, one section or portion of which is enclosed by a pipe or pipes for the passage of steam or other preferred heating agent, while the other section or portion thereof is similarly enclosed by a pipe or pipes, for the passage of cold water or other preferred cooling agent.

Portner's machine received patent number 202,019 on April 2, 1878. With confidence in his new machine, he immediately had it installed in his brewery. In June of the same year, members of the United States Brewers Association, after concluding their convention, visited Robert's brewery to see this new miracle machine.

> The brewers "declared unanimously that although the capacity was not as great as several others, Portner's was decidedly the most complete and best arranged brewery in the United States." One of these brewers, Emil

Schandein of the Philip Best Brewing Company of Milwaukee, wrote a favorable account to his brother-in-law, Frederick Pabst: "So far the Cook system seems to be the best for it serves its purpose and keeps the cellars as dry as a room. With Portner's improvements it can't be surpassed."[40]

After receiving a patent for his modification of Cook's machine, Portner set about creating an air-cooling and purifying system. His goal was to create a machine that could be used in breweries to help in the beer brewing process. He asked B. Edward J. Eils, a friend and former clerk at the brewery who was now a patent attorney, to assist him on the project. On April 8, 1880, the two submitted their application for a patent on their invention. Little did they realize, but this machine would be the first step towards modern-day air-conditioning. As stated in their application:

> The object of this invention is to cool and purify air in buildings by blowing it over metallic refrigerating pipes or tubes and operating in such a way as to condense into water the main portion of the moisture with which the air may be laden, and thus to avoid

the injurious accumulation of snow on such refrigerating pipes or tubes, notwithstanding the fact that they are kept, partly, at least, at a temperature below the freezing point by the refrigerant circulating through them.

Portner named his method "Direct Ammonia Expansion," using ammonia as the refrigerant. In addition to air-cooling, the invention served another purpose.

> Another object of our invention is its special application to breweries in such a way as to draw the air from above the tops of the fermenting tubs in the fermenting room of such brewery in order to intercept and carry off the carbonic-acid and other gases of fermentation for immediate absorption by the water of condensation forming on the refrigerating pipes or tubes, so that the air in the fermenting room may be kept comparatively pure, which is a matter of prime importance to the attainment of a good fermentation and the production of pure fine beer.

In other words, besides being an air-conditioner of sorts, Portner and Eils had also designed an air-cleansing/filtration system. They received patent number 229,750 for their machine on July 6, 1880.

On May 19, 1885, a special edition of *Amerikanische Bierbrauer* (*The American Brewer*) was published during the convention of the United States Brewers Association in New York. In it, the editor commented on Portner's air-cooling invention by writing,

> The greatest credit for this development is due to Robert Portner of Alexandria, who was among the first to study the effective utilization of such machines and to evaluate them in practice. Others were Mr. [John C.] de la Vergne, then Mr. [David] Boyle in Chicago; then Messrs. Theo. Krausch, E. Jungenfeld and [Fred] W. Wolf.

Once his machine was put to use, Portner traveled to Germany to visit breweries connected with ice machines, but did not find anything of practical use. He returned home and started on a new machine in the fall of 1885. He built the first beer-cooling apparatus, also using ammonia, but before he could get a patent for it, de la Vergne was awarded one for the same type of machine. Portner kept working at his idea and applied for other patents, but since he did not have any justifiable support and the entire project was such a worry to him, he became very ill and had to partly retire from his business for a while.

Construction and Real Estate in Washington, D.C.

Even before moving to Washington in the 1880's, Robert had already begun purchasing real estate in the nation's capital, a venture that would ultimately become his second largest enterprise. Between 1877 and 1897, Portner would buy thirty-five parcels of land, though he would not use every one of them. In 1875 he purchased his first property in the District, half of a triangular block bordered by Virginia Avenue, 7th Street, and D Street, SW. With direct access to the Baltimore & Ohio railroad along Virginia Avenue, he erected a depot for his brewery here.

Between 1882 and 1883, Portner built his new home on Vermont Avenue, NW. The following year, he bought three lots on 13th Street, NW and a half a block along 15th Street between U and V Street, NW. On the three lots on 13th Street, he built three three-story townhouses in 1885 at a cost of $14,000, each one designed by Clement A. Didden.

Portner was so pleased with Didden's designs that he would later hire him to design a majority of his other buildings in Washington.

At the same time he bought the lots on 13th Street, Portner bought the Woodmont Flats on the corner of 13th Street and Iowa Circle. Built in 1879 by N. W. Fitzgerald, the four-storied building was made of brick and stone. In 1894, Portner had the building remodeled and added on to so as to accommodate more renters. When the name of Iowa Circle was changed in 1900 to Logan Circle, the apartment building changed its name to the Logan. Portner, his children, and later their business associates, continued to manage the building until 1937, at which time it was sold. The building burned down sometime in the late-1940's.

On the back half of the lot on 15th Street, Portner divided the land into sixteen individual lots, which were developed by Jacob Jones and Theodore Friebus into individual townhouses. Though Portner and his construction company owned the lots, he later sold one to his sister Felixine. All of the lots would be accessible from a new road that was put in, appropriately called Portner Place. The front half of the lot, though, remained vacant. Portner had plans to develop the site later.

In addition to buy the Woodmont, Portner built two others in Washington. The first, known as the Virginia or

Virginia Flats, was located on the corner of Virginia Avenue (now Potomac Avenue) and 7th Street, SW. Again, Portner hired Didden to design the building, which was built in 1894 by Francis A. Blundon at a cost of $28,000. The four-story building had stores on the ground floor with three floors of apartments above. Unfortunately, the building was demolished in the 1960's when urban renewal swept through to make room for new government buildings.

Up to now, Portner had been quite proficient in his real estate ventures in Washington and earned him a reputation for having sound and successful business practices. All of this was not without its headaches, though.

> Mr. Portner claims $2,000 for violation of the contract. The declaration filed states that Portner entered into a contract with [William E.] Clayton in December, 1885, to erect for him three houses in square 464, and the same to be completed by April 1, 1886. Mr. Clayton was to furnish all the labor and material, for which Portner was to pay $7,857.50 in installments. The time has passed in which the houses were to be completed, and they still remain unfinished, and hence the suit for damages.[41]

The three three-story rowhouses, numbers 629-633 D Street, were finished shortly thereafter. Unfortunately, this left a bad taste in Portner's mouth for general contractors, so from then on, he acted as his own. Using a brownstone quarry in Manassas he had purchased an interest in, he often supplied the stone for projects in Alexandria, Washington, Manassas, and for the brewery from this quarry.

In 1896, Portner began plans his last large real estate venture in Washington. Working with Didden once again, the pair began designing plans for a large, up-scale apartment building, which measured 320 feet in length, called the Portner Apartments. It marked a first in Washington by being the first apartment building to have both tennis courts and a swimming pool. Still reeling from the contractor disputes over the row houses, Portner decided to create his own construction company.

> At the beginning of 1897, the Capital Construction Company was chartered to buy, sell, lease and improve real estate in Virginia and the District of Columbia. Portner served as chairman, of course, and the board initially included Park Agnew, a real estate and insurance broker and chairman of the

PORTNER FLATS.

Portner Apartments

Alexandria Marine Railway and Shipbuilding Company; William H. Saunders, a Washington real estate and insurance broker; and Portner brewery employees P. McKnight Baldwin, John T. Johnson, and John M. Johnson.[42]

Portner states in his diary, "I founded [the] stock company...but own all the shares. I only did this in order not to get into conflict with the unions." (28)

On February 1, 1897, construction for the first section of the Portner Apartments began. Located on the northeast corner of 15th and U Streets, costs for this section were estimated at more than $100,000. The building was completed later that year and when it opened, was met with great success. Like the brewery, Robby installed all of the electrical lighting fixtures in the building, as well as the heating.

The Portner, commonly called Portner's Folly because of its remote location to then downtown Washington, was one of the city's most fashionable apartment buildings, featuring three-bedroom luxury apartment units. Adding to its success was its location one block from the 14th Street streetcar line, which had been expanded to Park Road only five years earlier. One of the most striking features of the building was the turret on the corner of 15th and U Streets. Five metal caryatids, sculpted with upraised arms and painted to look like stone, were at the base of the turret, supporting a shallow circular brick balcony above the entrance to a drugstore.

The overwhelming success of the first section forced Portner to move into phase two of the building in early 1898, less than six months after the first section opened. He and Didden began drawing plans for the new section, and on February 27, 1899, ground was broken for the new section. A month and a half later, on April 10, the first bricks were laid. Construction on the six-story section, located at the corner of 15th and V Streets, was completed and the unit opened later that year. The newest section was met with as much success as the first, and by the end of December, all but ten apartments had already been rented.

By the summer of 1901, all but one of the apartments had been rented between the two sections. The Portner was considered to be one of the most luxurious and prestigious apartments in Washington at the time, and with a demand for more rooms, construction began on a third section in the fall. Because of the design of the complex, the third section had to be built between the first two. This also happened to be where the tennis courts and swimming pool were located. By January of 1902, four floors had been finished and the rest of the building was completed later that year at a cost of $87,500.

Once the entire complex was finished, costs had totaled nearly $350,000.

At the time the center section was built, the beaux-arts style of architecture was taking over, and architects and designers began moving away from the more traditional Victorian style previously used. Unfortunately, this new style made the first and second sections architecturally outdated. To draw attention away from this, the design for the flat-roofed structure attempted to emphasize, with astounding success, upon the building's main entrance by building the center section one story higher than the first two. To draw even more attention to this section, an open, arched balcony was built within the top two floors and topped off with a poised spire and a pair of vases. Once The Portner was completed, the Capital Construction Company's main concern was to manage it, the Woodmont, and the Virginia.

When the first two sections were designed and built, they were created for apartment-style living. The third section was created with this same arrangement, but also featured "efficiencies" for use as hotel-style units. These rentals featured a bedroom, sitting room, and bath. With the completion of the newest section, The Portner offered a total of 123 apartments ranging from three to seven bedrooms, and thirty hotel-style suites. The building was also the largest apartment house in Washington, and would remain so until Stoneleigh Court opened in 1903.

To make up for the loss of the tennis courts and swimming pool, Portner had an enormous and elegant dining room created for the occupants, which would easily be adjusted for debutante parties, cotillions, and balls if need be. There were also four new parlors next to the dining room that could be used for private parties if residents chose to entertain somewhere other than in their own apartments.

As with the brewery, Portner brought his sons in to work at the apartment building. Robby and Alvin soon began working there almost daily. And when they became older and had families of their own, many of Robert's own children would have apartments in The Portner, including Alvin, Oscar, Anna, Hilda, and Etta.

The Portner Apartments would become one of the last Victorian buildings to be built on such a large and elegant scale in Washington. Prior to World War II, Washington was practically a "southern city." Once the war erupted, however, extreme social, economic, and political changes came to the city, including a change between the traditional boundaries of white and black residential neighborhoods.

After the war, many of the white residents within the 16th Street corridor of Washington began to leave the city for the suburbs of Virginia and Maryland. There, they could find single homes with spacious lawn and room to grow gardens.[43]

The significant integration that occurred in this neighborhood caused a shift from a traditionally "white" neighborhood to an almost exclusively "black" neighborhood, as residents continued to move to the suburbs, business continued to decline. In 1945, the board of directors of the Capital Construction Company, which oversaw the Portner, sold the building to a group of investors. After its sale, the entire building was remodeled and refurbished into a hotel. To utilize the space more effectively, and acquire the most patronage, the large, spacious apartments were converted into 488 rental units, each with a bedroom, sitting room, and bath. Within two years, after a cost of over $800,000, the building reopened as the Dunbar Hotel, named for the acclaimed literary figure Paul Lawrence Dunbar.

Almost as soon as the building opened, it was plagued with problems. Over the next four years, the Dunbar battled constant complaints and charges of prostitution, drug trafficking, and alcohol violations. By 1950, things had gotten to the point where the hotel had lost its liquor license and was about to lose its hotel license. After years of poor management, the hotel's owners finally stepped in and began making drastic changes in both the management and its policies.

Before long, the Dunbar became Washington's leading African-American hotels with several famous entertainers and sports figures counted among their patrons. For years, the U Street Corridor had been the center of African-American social and cultural entertainment within Washington. Theaters such as the Lincoln and the Howard hosted entertainers including Duke Ellington, Louis Armstrong, "Moms" Mabley, Cab Calloway, and Ella Fitzgerald. It can only be assumed that when in Washington, they stayed at the Dunbar.

Known at one time as the largest African-American hotel in the nation, the Dunbar slowly declined after 1956, a time when the city's major hotels were becoming increasingly integrated. By 1964, the Dunbar Hotel could no longer compete against its nicer, more modern rivals, and its deterioration increased dramatically. In 1970, the owners of the Dunbar came to a crossroads. Two years earlier, race riots fueled by the assassination of Martin Luther King, Jr. swept through the Shaw neighborhood, leaving many destroyed buildings and businesses in its wake. For years they had been losing money and business because of integration, and the riots certainly did not help matters. The hotel had tried in vain to integrate itself, but it could not shake its reputation as being an exclusively African-American hotel. To be able to contend with its competitors, the Dunbar would have had to have undergone an extensive renovation. Unfortunately, this kind of money was something the owners did not have.

After considering all of these factors, the owners realized that they only had one option left, to sell. During the 1960's and 70's, the American landscape within big cities changed dramatically from the urban renewal movement, where rundown and practically vacant sections of a city, which often happened to be one of a city's oldest districts, were razed and new, modern buildings erected on the sites.

In 1970, the Shaw neighborhood of Washington was at the height of its own redevelopment. The owners officially closed the hotel that year and sold the now empty and desolate structure to the city government. The government, however, did not have any immediate plans for the 73-year-old building. For four years, the structure sat empty. In 1974 the government announced that they would demolish the building to make way for a new assisted-living facility in conjunction with the Department of Housing and Urban Development's Section-8 housing initiative.

As soon as this was announced, preservationists and historians began scrambling to find alternative uses for the structure. Unfortunately, everything they tried was to no avail. That same year, the building was demolished and the site sat vacant for the next four years. In early-1978, construction began on the Campbell-Heights apartment building, which opened later that year. The new ten-story building for senior citizens featured a drab gray concrete façade, which replaced the beige brick and red sandstone structure that had been the Dunbar (Portner), trademarks, in a sense, of Robert Portner's taste in design, materials, and color.

A Second Brewery

By 1890, sales from Robert's brewery had been increasing considerably in Washington. Rather than continually haul his product from Alexandria to Washington, he soon began considering the possibility of building a new brewery in the city. He had purchased a piece of land on Maryland Avenue and 13th Street, SE, which he thought would be a good location for the brewery. About this same time, another man wanted to expand his brewing interests in Washington.

After arriving in Washington in 1887, Albert Carry bought an interest in the old George Juenneman brewery northeast of Capitol Hill. After three years, he sold the brewery to an English organization and purchased Henry Rabey's small brewery in the southeast section of town.

Albert Carry had proven himself a very practical and sensible businessman in Washington, so Portner approached him with the idea of merging their interests. Carry must have felt the same about Portner because he accepted Robert's offer and in October, the two founded the National Capital Brewing Company.

Initially, Portner purchased $40,000 worth of stock in the brewery, but later bought an additional $25,000 worth, while Carry invested $85,000 into stock. Additional stock was sold to Carl Strangmann, who bought $10,000 worth, and Frank P. Madigan, who also bought $10,000 worth. In order for the company to reach its goal of $500,000 in capital, the remaining $190,000 of the company's stock was sold to its customers. Since he was the largest shareholder, and had no other sizeable business obligations, Carry was President while Portner served as Vice-President. Also included in the Board of Directors were John Vogt, John D. Bartlett, Charles Carry (Albert's son), Strangmann, and Madigan.

They men soon set about building their new brewery. Since a brewery already existed on the land Carry owned, and it was in a more prime location, the men opted to build their new brewery here. Considering them obsolete and useless, Portner sold his depot and his land on Maryland Avenue, the latter of which was bought by the Richmond and Danville Railroad Company for $60,000.

On July 25, 1891, shortly after the National Capital Brewing Company opened for business, the *Washington Star* wrote a glowing review of the brewery. Not having found any other description of the brewery outside of Portner's personal memoirs throughout my research, it would be best for the reader to read the article in order to appreciate this incredible brewery.

> A brewery that turns out 100,000 barrels of first-class pure beer every year for local consumption solely is a big institution for any city, and yet Washington has recently had just such an addition made to its business enterprises in the National Capital Brewery. Organized by Washington men, officered by Washington men, and with every share of its stock owned here at home, it would seem to be a local enterprise first, lad and all the time. This business is the result of the combination of two of the oldest and most successful breweries in this part of the country, and that the new firm will be even more successful is a foregone conclusion. People who have had occasion recently to traverse D Street southeast have noticed a splendid new building on the

south side of the street between 13th and 14th Streets. This is the new home of the National Capital Brewing Company, and it is by long odds one of the most substantial and imposing buildings of the sort to be found anywhere. Although it has been completed hardly more than a month it has about it already that well-kept appearance and air of bustling activity that always denote prosperity following upon enterprise.

This fine new building, standing as it does in a very desirable location for such a business, with almost an entire block of ground about it, is a five-story structure of brick with handsome stone trimmings and surmounted by a graceful cupola. It covers a plat of ground 94 by 136 feet, and owing to the unusual height of the several stories the building itself is quite high as an ordinary seven or eight-story building. Attached to the main building are several roomy and substantial outbuildings, including an engine house, stable and cooperage shop, all pleasing in appearance and forming a handsome group. To make a good pure quality beer for local use so that it can be drawn from wood and not adulterated with any chemicals whatever in order to make of it a "beer that keeps well;" this is the purpose of the National Capital Brewing Company. They do not make beer for shipment, and hence their beer is not treated with any salicylic acid or deleterious substances that are sometimes used with bottled beer to keep it clear and lively. Pure beer is generally considered a healthful drink. The president of the National Capital Brewing Company told a [Washington] Star reporter that any person with a proper interest in the matter might take the keys of the entire establishment at any time, go through it thoroughly, and if he found anything at all used in the making of their beer that was not pure and wholesome the company would give him $1,000.

Beer drawn from the wood is almost certain to be a purer and better quality of beer than the bottled. The National Capital Brewing Company does not bottle. It serves its customers fresh every day with beer that has reached its prime in the immense cooling rooms of the brewery. F. H. Finley & Son, the bottlers, however, have a contract with the company for 20,000 barrels a year of their pale extra beer, and this they bottle and serve to customers in Washington. They get their beer early every morning, as needed, so that people who buy the bottled variety of the National Capital Company's beer are using beer that left the huge casks at the brewery that very day. J. F. Hermann & Son; Wm. H. Brinkley and Jas. A. Bailey also act as agents for the company. A [Washington] Star reporter, accompanied by Mr. Albert Carry, president of the brewing company, recently made a complete inspection of the buildings of the brewery, spending several hours seeing how beer is manufactured from the time it comes in the form of malt and the raw materials until it leaves the building a clear, cool, foaming beverage enclosed in stout kegs and casks. How much beer there is that leaves the building may be judged when the statement is made that the company uses 10,000 kegs and barrels of all sizes simply supplying the Washington trade. Nine huge wagons and thirty big horses are used steadily in carrying beer from the brewery to the consumers. In truth this is no small business. But what strikes the visitor, be he a casual or an interested one, first and forcibly of all is the absolute cleanliness and neatness that prevails everywhere. The walls and stairways, for the most part of stone and iron – for the building is fireproof throughout – and the floors are all of iron or concrete and immaculate. On all sides there is hot and cold running water, and indeed the wards of a hospital could scarcely be cleaner and more orderly than the various departments of this brewery. There are no secret chambers into which one may not go. Everything is open and above board, and the fact that the company has no objections to the beer consumer examining every branch of its manufacture is a pretty good sign that they know that everything is honest and fair.

As proof of this the company intends giving a public reception at the brewery next Tuesday, July 28, from 3 to 8 p.m., when everything will be in running order and everybody is invited to visit the brewery and inspect it thoroughly from cellar to roof. A handsome luncheon, consisting of all the delicacies of the season, will be spread. Everything will be free, and the National Capital Brewing Company intends to prove that they are as liberal in their hospitality as they are enterprising in their business. It is needless to say that beer will be plentiful and none need to go to bed thirsty Tuesday night.

Connecting the main building with the engine house is a handsome arched gateway leading into the big court yard, where the wagons stand while they are being loaded. The entrance to the offices is through this gateway. The offices consist of a number of connecting rooms on the main floor in the northwest corner of the building. They are handsomely finished in oak, and are fitted with the most improved office furniture for the convenience of the officers of the company and the corps of bookkeepers and clerks required to transact such an immense volume of business.

The National Capital Brewing Company is a combination of the firms of Albert Carry,

Robert Portner and the Robert Portner Brewing Company, the latter selling out the Washington branch of the business. The capital stock of the company is $500,000, all paid up. The company has been in operation since last November, but has been supplying from its new brewery only since June. The officers of the company are as follows: Albert Carry, president; [Robert Portner, vice-president;] C. A. Strangmann, secretary and treasurer. Directors: Albert Carry, Robert Portner, John L. Vogt, John D. Bartlett, Charles Carry, C. A. Strangmann, Frank P. Madigan.

Once Portner and Carry had established their Washington brewery, they split the market of the brewery with that of Portner's in Alexandria. The Washington brewery, offering "Golden Eagle," "Capuciner," "Diamond," and "Munich" as their distinct brands, sold beer exclusively to Washington and the north while the Alexandria brewery continued selling to the south. Unfortunately, the National Capital Brewing Company faced the problem of selling their brands in a city already saturated with products from a number of other breweries. They were able to do quite well, though, and even out-produced the Alexandria brewery on a number of occasions. The only serious competition the Washington brewery faced was from the Christian Heurich Brewing Company, located in Foggy Bottom, the only brewery in Washington to produce on a large scale.

Robert remained Vice-President of the National Capital Brewing Company until his death in 1906, at which time his shares of stock were sold back to the company and Carry's shares in the Robert Portner Brewing Company were sold back to that brewery as well. Carry continued to run the brewery until Prohibition, at which time he switched to the manufacturing of ice cream, and continued until his death in 1925.

Construction and Real Estate in Manassas

Aside from having lucrative business interests in Alexandria and Washington, Portner also owned or had an interest in three businesses in Manassas. His first venture came when he bought half of the interest in the 50-acre Tillett Brownstone Quarry from John Tillett on July 27, 1891. The name was soon changed to Portner & Tillett, but Robert later bought the remainder of the company from Tillett and changed the name to the Portner Brownstone Company.

Initially, he bought the company to supply sandstone for the construction of his new country estate in Manassas. The quarry, located on Quarry Road just outside of Manassas, ended up providing sandstone for the construction of several buildings in Manassas, many of which are still standing today.

Two years before his death, Portner established his second business in Manassas when he bought a piece of land near the railroad depot, located on West Street between the railroad tracks and Prince William Street. Here he built the elegant Prince William Hotel, which would become one of the community's most celebrated structures. Using plans designed by Oscar Vogt, the same man who designed Annaburg, construction began in the summer of 1904. The two-story structure featured thirty-five rooms and measured 105 feet in width. Portner hired John and Ira Cannon, prominent builders in Manassas, to construct the building. At a cost of $34,000, which included furnishings, the hotel was completed and opened by the end of the same year.

Portner's last business venture in Manassas was in 1906, a few months before his death, when he helped establish the Mining and Building Company. Co-founders of the business included J. S. B. Thompson, Thomas C. Lion, C. E. Nicol, W. W. Moffitt, and C. A. S. Hopkins, who served as general manager. Later known as the Manassas Improvement

Prince William Hotel

Corporation, the business had been created for the general maintenance of the town (i.e. streets and sidewalks).

After Robert's death, his sons assumed control of the brownstone quarry. Anna, on the other hand, took over ownership of the Prince William Hotel. It continued to operate under various managements until the hotel finally closed on May 30, 1908. In August of 1909, Eastern College, a school established in Manassas the previous year, bought the vacant building and all of its furnishings for $25,000. Happy to see her late husband's building be used once again, Anna donated $5,000 to Eastern College to be used toward the purchase price. The school, located one block away on Prince William Street, converted the building into a girl's dormitory, accommodating seventy-five students, until a new, permanent structure was completed.

Though the new dormitory would not be completed until September, by June of 1910 plans were already being considered for a future use of the building once it was no longer needed by Eastern College. Efforts to establish a hospital in Manassas were under way and the former hotel was one of five sites being considered. If used, the hospital would combine the college infirmary with a county hospital to help reduce costs.

The new dormitory, however, was completed two months early, before a hospital was ready to be chartered, so the building was leased to W. R. Lucas on July 26, 1910. No stranger to the hotel business, Lucas had been the owner of the Warren Green Hotel in Warrenton before coming to Manassas. He spent the next three months cleaning, repairing, and improving the building in an effort to renovate it back into a hotel before reopening it under its original name on October 15.

When the Prince William Hotel first opened, it was well received by the town, so when news spread that it would reopen, there was a great excitement in the air. As preparations were being made, local newspapers ran articles, which generated even more interest and excitement.

> Promptly at six o'clock next Saturday morning the Prince William Hotel will be formally opened...when the dining room doors open for breakfast, revealing glimpses of snowy napery, glistening silver, sparkling glass and banks of ferns and flowers.[44]

Unfortunately, the splendor of the hotel did not last long. In the early morning of December 15, 1910, only two months after its grand reopening, an alarm sounded in the hotel. Will Lynch and M. Lynch Jr. had discovered a fire on the roof of the hotel and quickly began waking and evacuating the guests and staff. As the guests left the building, every attempt possible was made to save the structure. Firemen set up large wooden tanks to receive water from a nearby water tower, which belonged to the Southern Railway Company, and stretched hoses across the railroad tracks so that the water could reach the building. Twice, though, the hoses had to be unhooked to let passing trains through. These delays, however, did not prevent the building from being saved. Unfortunately, the building was practically doomed from the moment the fire started, the strong flamed were aided by a heavy westwardly wind and were beyond control. Just as the last guest left the building, the center section burst into flames.

> No pen can picture the weird beauty of the scene presented by this early morning fire. Day was breaking when a tiny spire of flame pierced the night, mounting higher and spread into a pillar of fire, swaying into fantastic forms, and illuminating intensely, brilliantly. Apart on the crest of a knoll in a field of snow, dazzling white, the magnificent structure, wrapped in a sheet of seething flame, crumbled to ashes.[45]

By 8:30 a.m., two hours after the fire was first discovered, all that remained of the hotel was a pile of smoldering rubble. Though this was only one building, the residents of Manassas were just as devastated by the loss of their 'cosmopolitan' hotel as when the Great Fire of 1905 destroyed half of the downtown business district.

To date, the origin of the fire remains a mystery. One theory was that it was caused by a faulty gas jet located in a servant's room in the attic. Another theory came from an eyewitness who thought "that sparks from a burning out of the flue ignited the roof."[46] Another man also claimed to have seen a shower of sparks falling on the roof before it ignited. Fortunately, no one was seriously injured or killed by the fire. The thirteen guests and the hotel staff, all of whom had been staying in the south end of the hotel, were able to escape from the burning structure before the fire spread beyond the roof.

Robert Portner's Prince William Hotel was never rebuilt and nothing remains of it today. Where the elegant structure once stood is now a parking lot for the Manassas train depot, a water tower, and a small power substation. In 1912, Richard S. Hynson built a new Prince William Hotel on the corner of Main and Center Streets, which was later named the Stonewall Jackson Hotel. Sometime in the early-1960's, it was torn down to make way for a more modern 'downtowner.'

When compared to one another, the two hotels were quite the opposites. Portner's hotel was rectangular and two stories high while Hynson's was more squared and three stories in height. His also featured two porches across the front, one for each of the first two floors, while Portner's only had one, which ran across the ground level of the front and wrapped around each side. In addition to all of this, the first Prince William Hotel was considerably more elegant and featured more architectural detail. To this day, no other hotel in Manassas has even come close to the grandeur of Portner's Edwardian-style palace.

Portner's Influence in Modern Times

Though nearly every remnant of Robert Portner's brewery and various other business interests are gone, constant reminders still exist within Alexandria, Washington, and Manassas. If you walk through the streets of Alexandria today, Portner's presence can still be felt. The city has a street and park named for him[47], a microbrewery restaurant carries his name, and a few parts of his brewery still stand. Unfortunately, Washington is where Portner's influence is lest felt with only one or two of his buildings still remaining. Portner Place, located behind where the Portner Apartments once stood, still remains, though. Manassas, like Alexandria, has a street named for Portner as well, but his presence and his family are still strong there since his beloved Annaburg still stands.

What most people do not realize is that Portner's influence is felt all across the United States, regardless of whether or not anyone has ever heard of him or his brewery. The next time you walk into your air-conditioned home during the summer, think of what life might be like had Portner not invented his beer-cooling or air-purifying machines. Someone else would have undoubtedly invented something similar at some point, but it most certainly would not have had the same impact as Portner's did. In an interview with one of his daughters, Anna Portner Flood once remarked on how it had broken her father's heart that he could not convince people that his air-cooling process and machine would be a thing of the future.

Endnotes

[36] Penny Morrill, *Who Built Alexandria* (1979).

[37] Engineering-Science, Inc. *Maritime archaeology at Keith's Warf and Battery Cove (44AX119), Ford's Landing; Alexandria, Virginia* (1993).

[38] Brian Brown, "Monographs on Early Alexandria." *Alexandria Gazette*.

[39] The United States Brewers Association was originally formed in 1862 when 37 breweries in New York merged together; the official Association formed two years later.

[40] Tim Dennee, *Robert Portner and His Brewery*, 76.

[41] *Alexandria Gazette*. May 25, 1886.

[42] Tim Dennee, *Robert Portner and His Brewery*, 151.

[43] James M. Good, *Capital Losses* (1979), 185.

[44] *Manassas Journal*. October 13, 1910.

[45] *Manassas Democrat*. December 15, 1910.

[46] Ibid.

[47] The park is located on a plot of land the brewery owned quite some distance from the actual brewing complex. The street named for Portner leads to the park.

6

The Next Generation

By no means can anyone call Robert Portner's life dull or boring, muchless uneventful. Whether it was technological advances, imprisonment, or a war that tore a country apart, he was able to make the best of just about any given situation he found himself in. But even a man with Portner's vision and mental capabilities could not imagine what the future would hold for his children. Like any parent, Robert wanted nothing but the best for his children and their futures. His care and compassion for them can best be seen in a letter he wrote to his family in 1890, shortly after finishing his autobiography. Translated from German, it reads:

> Hanover, June 03, 1890
>
> Writing down my life history, I fulfill a long desire and I only was stopped because writing creates a nervousness (over reaction of nerves) created by mental stress. The reason for writing is that my beloved children should know the story of their parents as my only duty in life is to educate my children to become able

and good human beings as the other things I wanted to obtain from life, I have reached with full satisfaction. I only want to send my children with good knowledge and education in life so that my family tree, which has been removed to America, will bear good branches and fruits.

I write in German, not because I prefer Germany to my adoptive country as at the moment spending already two years in Hanover to give my children better schools and to become healthier (and I believe I reached this goal) German has again become more fluent.

Now my beloved children, I want to remind you that you have to hold together in life so that the family earns respect through the right attitudes as only this brings happiness in the last years of life.

It could be possible that some of you will make mistakes in life and others should help to bring them back to the right way with love and understanding if necessary, with all means. Let nobody go under and think that not everybody is the same and each person makes mistakes.

All of you came with the same prospects in life...use your knowledge and wealth in the right way but: <u>Do right and stay together.</u>

For this reason I've taken my beloved Annaburg and improved it and I will continue to do this to give you there a pleasant childhood and to have a real homeland which brings you all together and to refresh in your minds your childhood. This home I wish to reserve for you all. Those of you who feel tired or sick can return to this place and remember what a beautiful childhood to regain health and fresh spirit and those who have had a hard time in life should regain their strength for a new beginning.

You all meet once a year there and take care that the family PORTNER maintain a good name in America.

With all my heart, your papa
Robert Portner

Like their father before them, each Portner child would be faced with events that would test his or her individual character. Successes and failures, tragedies and triumphs, these are their lives; these are their stories.

Edward George Portner (1875 – 1917)

In the fall of 1893, Edward enrolled at the Massachusetts Institute of Technology to study chemical engineering, but returned home after only two years. After returning to Washington, he began working for his father at the brewery. In an effort to finish his education, Edward enrolled in night classes at Columbian University. Though he was preoccupied by his responsibilities with the brewery, this did not deter Edward from becoming involved in social activities here. In 1896, he was initiated into the Kappa Alpha Order social fraternity (Robby would be initiated into the same fraternity two years later). Edward received his Bachelor of Science degree in 1897 and his Master of Science degree the following year, all the while serving as Vice-President of the brewery.

Anticipating a life-long career with the brewery, Edward enrolled at the Siebel Institute, a brewing school in Chicago, the fall after receiving his Masters degree. Unfortunately, he was not able to complete his studies at Siebel as he was forced to return home after only a year because of an ear infection. Upon his return, he resumed work with the brewery. In 1904, Edward returned to Columbian University as a candidate for the degree of Doctor of Philosophy, studying Chemistry with minors in Physical and Mineral Chemistry. He never did receive this degree, though, as he opted to spend more time working at the brewery through his father's illnesses and eventual death.

Growing up, Edward was one of the oldest children and as a result, was counted on for a number of things. After Robby's death in 1900, Edward, or Eddie as he was often referred to, was given first responsibilities in business matters and, with the exception of one time in particular, always seemed to be in his father's favor. At one point, Edward has become involved with a woman known as Reetzie Peters, whom Robert did not care for. In fact, Robert disliked her so much that he went so far as to mention her in his will, saying that if Edward, or any of his heirs, were to legally live with or marry her, then anything left to Edward would be revoked and given to his siblings. Apparently this seemed to have worked as there is no mention of interaction between Edward and Reetzie ever again.

On June 4, 1913, at the age of 37, Edward married 22-year-old Nannie Moncure at St. John's Episcopal Church in Washington. A native of Stafford, Virginia, Nannie was the daughter of the Reverend and Mrs. George Moncure, as well as the great-niece of Confederate General Turner Ashby, and a member of one of Virginia's oldest families. Their romance began several months earlier when Edward had been a patient at the George Washington University Hospital where Nannie was his attending nurse. Reverends P. H. Murphy and E. Slater Dunlop married the couple and Herman served as Edward's best man. For the ceremony, Nannie wore a beautiful gray gown and carried a bouquet of lilies of the valley, while the sanctuary had been decorated in white flowers and ferns. After the wedding, the newlyweds left by train for a honeymoon in Atlantic City and New York. After returning from their honeymoon, Edward and Nannie made their residence in the Portner Apartments.

From 1897 until his father's death in 1906, Edward served as Vice-President of the Robert Portner Brewing Company and Manager of the Portner Apartments. After Robert passed away, Edward left his management position at the apartments and became the acting President of the brewery until he was elected into office the following year. By 1912, he had become the President of the Capital Construction Company, as well. In addition to running his father's businesses, Edward also spent time as a professor. From 1904 to 1910, while working on his doctoral degree, Edward taught chemistry at the George Washington University.[48] As with his pursuit of a doctoral degree, brewery matters forced him to resign as a professor.

In addition to family businesses, Edward was also involved with the production of a pigment in Alexandria for the Magnetic Pigment Company.[49] According to Peter Valaer, Edward's cousin,

> After I graduated from N. C. State and came to Alexandria, Virginia to do research for Eddie to conclude his PhD from M.I.T. but with his manifold duties at the brewery and the apartment [The Portner] and number of other important things he had to look over, he had very little time to outline the work he wanted me to do on his thesis, but he was also very much interested in the manufacturing of the black pigment which was made in a loft over the Keg House of the brewery. I was the chemist and hard labor man. We sold the pigment to the U.S. Bureau of Engraving as

one of the ingredients in printing paper money, and to Bausch & Lamb Optical Company in New York.[50]

On May 20, 1914, Edward wrote his last will and testament. In it he left his entire estate to his wife, the income of which would be paid in quarterly payments for as long as she lived. Should he have any children, once they reached the age of twenty-one, half of the quarterly payments would be paid to his wife and the other half to his child or children. Just over one year later, on July 8, 1915, Edward's only child, Edward Moncure Portner, was born.

Sadly, family life was short lived for Edward. In the evening hours of December 14, 1917, Edward collapsed from a stroke in his apartment and died. High blood pressure and heart disease were contributing factors to his death at the young age of 42. After funeral services were held, Edward was buried in the Aquia Episcopal Church cemetery in Aquia, Virginia.

After receiving a substantial estate from Edward's will, Nannie raised young Edward on her own over the next four years. In 1921, she married John Milton Ralls, a real estate broker in Washington. The following year, a daughter, Nancy Moncure Ralls, was born. To the dismay of his mother, when the Great Depression hit in 1929, young Edward's inheritance was completely wiped out.

On Tuesday, August 26, 1941, Nannie passed away at her home in Washington. A service was held two days later at Aquia, and though she had remarried, Nannie was buried next to Edward that afternoon. After Edward Moncure Portner passed away on November 14, 1965, his final wishes were respected when he was buried along side his parents at Aquia.

A photo taken in Washington, DC of Edward as a child, c.1880
Courtesy of Edward M. & Vivian S. Portner

Brothers Robert Francis and Edward George
Portner in an undated photo
Courtesy of Edward M. & Vivian S. Portner

Undated photos of Edward G. Portner.
Courtesy of Edward M. & Vivian S. Portner

Edward holding his newborn son, Edward M. Portner, at
Annaburg, c.1915
Courtesy of Edward M. & Vivian S. Portner

Alvin Otto Portner (1877 – 1931)

As a child growing, Alvin attended the public schools in Washington, as well as receiving additional private tutoring in Latin and French on the side. When the family moved to Europe in 1888, he was enrolled at the Royal Gymnasium in Hanover, Germany. By September 1891, Alvin had returned to the United States and was attending the Danville Military Academy in Danville, Virginia. Though he liked the school at first, he soon began to dislike it and returned home two years later. Once back in Washington, he attended Washington High School, where he graduated in the spring of 1894.

The following fall, Alvin enrolled in the Massachusetts Institute of Technology. Here he studied under the General

Studies program. The M.I.T. catalogue of 1898-99 describes the program as the following:

> The course in General Studies is designed especially for students who wish to secure an education based upon scientific study and experiment, but including a larger amount of history, economics, language and literature than is possible in technical courses. It is adapted to the needs of those who expect to engage in trade, banking, manufacturing, or journalism, or in the teaching of social or political science.

In addition to his studies, Alvin was also involved in several clubs, including the Walker Club, the Deutscher Verein (German Club), the Southern Club, and the Washington Club. Alvin graduated with a Bachelors degree in General Studies in 1898.

Upon his graduation, he enrolled at the University of Virginia. As with M.I.T., Alvin was very active in extracurricular activities here, including O.W.L., the Washington Literary Society, the Mandolin Club, and the *University of Virginia Magazine*. He graduated the following spring with a Master of Law degree.

After graduating, Alvin opened his own law firm in Washington, which he ran until 1901. The following year, he began working for the American Security and Trust Company. After six months, he left after having been elected the new President of the Portner Brownstone Company in Manassas and the Vice-President and Treasurer of the Capital Construction Company. In addition to accepting these positions, he had already been sitting on the Board of Directors as Vice-President of the Robert Portner Brewing Company and the Prince William Horseman's Association. During the same year, he assumed control of the Capital Construction Company. He even found time, in 1905, to become a town councilman in Manassas.

In 1911, Alvin worked on the Reception Committee for the Peace Jubilee in Manassas. The celebration was held to commemorate the 50th anniversary of the Battle of Bull Run, one of the first conflicts in the Civil War. Being a member of this committee, Alvin worked along side of his brother-in-law William Meredith; Ira E. Cannon, one of the builders of Annaburg; William F. Merchant and W. A. Newman, two close friends of his parents; and John R. Tillett, former owner of the Portner Brownstone Company.

Growing up Alvin was close with his siblings, but he had an especial fondness for Paul. Though they were five and a half years apart in age, the brothers did just about everything together, growing closer as they grew older. As the years passed by, the two ended up owning two boats together and sharing an apartment in the Bellevue Hotel in Washington.

Though his work schedule kept him busy, Alvin did have time for a social and personal life. In the early part of 1917, Alvin married Ethel Mae Old, a native of Norfolk, Virginia. At the time they met, Ethel had been a student at Mount Saint Joseph's College in Emmitsburg, Maryland. Shortly after their marriage, Alvin bought a house in Annapolis, Maryland. In 1925, the couple's only child, Helen Barbara, was born. Originally, her name was supposed to be Barbara von Valaer Portner, but two weeks prior to her birth, her mother's sister passed away. It was then deiced that she would be given the name of her aunt in her memory.

Of the seven sons of Robert and Anna Portner, Alvin lived the longest. Unfortunately, like Edward, family life was short lived for Alvin. After a long illness, Alvin passed away at the age of 54 on Saturday, December 19, 1931 in his apartment at the Portner Apartments. Services were held the following Monday, December 21, at Gawler & Sons at 12:00 noon. After the service, Alvin's body was taken to Manassas where he was buried in the family plot. Pallbearers included Stanton C. Peele, Charles F. R. Ogilby, William P. Meredith, and Augustine L. Humes.

In his will, Alvin left his home and real estate in Annapolis to Ethel, but should she and Barbara have died before him, he had a clause that arranged for his estate to be transferred to the University of Virginia. He instructed that it be used for the improvement and maintenance of their medical department.

A few years after Alvin's death, Ethel remarried to Joseph F. MacCurdy. On September 23, 1976, Ethel Portner MacCurdy passed away at a nursing home in Wilmington, North Carolina and was later buried in Norfolk, Virginia.

At the time of his death Alvin held a number of positions within the family businesses. He was the President of the Capital Construction Company and the Robert Portner Corporation, and Vice-President of the Portner Realty Company. Aside from his law practice, the only other time Alvin worked outside of the family businesses was when he worked for a short period of time at the Alexandria County Lighting Company.

Playing to the social crowd, Alvin was an avid yachtsman. Over the years, he held memberships with a number of yacht clubs, including the Century, University, Commercial, and Capital Yacht Clubs in Washington and the Annapolis Roads, Baltimore, and Saint Michael's Yacht Clubs in Maryland. He had owned several large sailboats as well as a yacht, the *Latona*, which according to his daughter even had its own personally engraved set of silverware. Being prominent in many social circles and having a home in Annapolis afforded Alvin the ability to entertain numerous guests during the summer months.

In addition to his fondness for watercraft, Alvin was also an avid hunter and lover of horses.[51] He held memberships in the Cameron Run Hunt and Country Club and the Bull Run Hunt Club in Prince William County, and owned a large stable in Virginia.

Throughout his lifetime, Alvin had the peculiar nickname 'Venus.' In a letter, his daughter explained how he most likely received this nickname.

> The Portner's, having such a large family, being well-to-do, also had a large staff of black servants. My grandparents must have called my father Alvin, pronouncing it 'Al-veen' (found this very spelling in a census record). So it was said one of the servants made up a little ditty, "Mr. Alveenus, the greatest man the world ever seenus," thus he was tagged with this nickname. I never heard him referred to as anything but Venus Portner in my life.

On a final note, in a strange twist of fate two particular names have come full circle through Alvin's branch of the Portner family tree. Barbara's daughter is the great-great-great-granddaughter of Heinrich Portner, Robert's father. Her husband, a German himself, is the great-great-great-grandson of General Blücher, under whose command Heinrich fought in the Napoleonic Wars. Plus, her husband was born very near to where Robert Portner himself was born.

Alvin 1880's
Photo of Alvin c.1880, taken in
Wiesbaden, Germany by Carl Borntraeger
Courtesy of Barbara Portner Whitbeck

Alvin & Ethel Portner with their daughter Barbara, taken in 1926 at their summer home in Annapolis, Maryland
Courtesy of Barbara Portner Whitbeck

Portner grandchildren--Bolling Byrd Flood and Helen Barbara Portner c. 1928 at Meridian Hill Park in Washington DC
Courtesy of Barbara Portner Whitbeck

Portner grandchildren--Bolling Byrd Flood and Barbara Portner Whitbeck in the 1980's
Courtesy of Barbara Portner Whitbeck

"My father (no hat), my mother and unknown friend on yacht *Latona* in Annapolis, Maryland in the early 1920s
Courtesy of Barbara Portner Whitbeck

Jean Allwine on "Topsy" (black pony) and Barbara Portner on "Jackie" (gray pony) at Annaburg in Manassas.
Courtesy of Barbara Portner Whitbeck

Alma Meta Portner (1879-1931)

On April 16, 1903, at the age of 24, Alma married Julius H. Koehler of St. Louis, Missouri. Unlike big social weddings of the time, Alma and Julius' wedding took place at the Portner home on Vermont Avenue. Their engagement had been announced the previous fall, but Alma had taken ill for most of the winter season. As a result, the couple could not plan for a large wedding and settled on the small ceremony. It was not without its intimacy, though.

Alma and Julius' wedding took place in the morning and was performed by the Reverend U. G. B. Pierce of All Souls Church. Because of its small location, guests were limited to only the families of the bride and groom. Afterwards, a wedding breakfast was served, and once everyone was finished, the happy couple departed for Atlantic City for their honeymoon.

Upon their return to Washington, the couple packed Alma's belongings and moved to St. Louis, where Julius was working for his father's brewery. Two years later, on August 9, 1905, their son, Robert Portner Koehler, was born. Unfortunately, the happiness of Alma's marriage did not last long. On June 13, 1913, after only ten years of marriage, Alma and Julius were divorced. She took Robert and moved to Annaburg where they lived for a few months before moving to New York in the winter. From then on, Alma made New York her permanent residence. Alma never remarried and spent the rest of her life traveling both the country and the world. Robert, who was very devoted to his mother, was at her side on nearly all of her journeys. Julius, on the other hand, stayed in St. Louis.

When Alma wrote her last will and testament, she named Edward E. I. Martin and the New York Trust Company as the Executors of her will and directed that her estate go into a trust for her son. She arranged the trust so that her son would receive two thousand dollars per year until he reached the age of twenty-one, at which time he would then receive three thousand dollars a year until he turned twenty-five. Once he had reached that age, half of the remaining estate would be transferred over to him while the other half was to remain in the possession of the trustees until he turned thirty.

On Tuesday, March 3, 1931, at the age of 51, Alma passed away at Union Memorial Hospital in Baltimore, Maryland. Four days later, a service was held at Gawler & Sons. Afterwards, her body was taken to Manassas and she was buried in the family plot along side of Oscar. Unfortunately, Robert was so distraught over his mother's death that he never had a headstone made for her, and her grave remains unmarked to this day. It is only through older members of the family that anyone knows where she is buried.

After his mother's death, Robert began a career as a successful murder-mystery writer, writing over thirty novels throughout his lifetime. Though he often had no fixed address, he lived out the last years of his life in Santa Fe, New Mexico, where he died on February 9, 1988.

Henriette Marie Portner (1880-1965)

In November of 1908, Anna Portner announced Etta's engagement to William Payne Meredith, a lawyer in Washington. Growing up as children in Manassas, the couple's parents had been close while William and Alvin were good friends as well. A month later, on December 16, William and Etta were married at All Souls Church in Washington. The ceremony, performed by the Reverend U. G. B. Pierce, began at 4:00 p.m. in a chapel bedecked with many varieties of flowers and palms. Thirteen ushers, including Edward, Alvin, Oscar, and Herman, seated guests while Paul had the honor of giving his sister away in marriage. Edward Frederick of Philadelphia served as the best man and Etta's sister Anna served as the maid-of-honor.

After the wedding, guests and the bridal party returned to Mrs. Portner's home on Vermont Avenue for the reception.

> The distance from the church to the house is so short that the reception was in full swing at half past 4. Mrs. Portner, Mrs. Meredith, and the newly married couple received guests in the front drawing room, where a profusion of American beauty roses and asparagus vine adorned each available space. An orchestra played in the living room where azalea decorations prevailed. In the conservatory balls of pink roses were suspended by pink ribbons from the ceiling. A pink color scheme was also followed in the dining room, where a bounteous collation was served.[52]

Upon the reception's conclusion, the couple embarked on their honeymoon. Once they returned, the Meredith's made their home in Washington. Over the next ten years, the family grew to include two daughters, Sylvia Contee Meredith, born on November 20, 1910, and Jacqueline Cabell Meredith, born on September 5, 1918.

As time progressed and the children grew, the Meredith family continued to live in Washington, though they did reside in Chevy Chase, Maryland for a short while. In late August 1947, William became ill. He suffered for a week before passing away on August 30 at the age of 68 in a Washington hospital. Funeral services were held at St. John's Episcopal Church in Washington, followed by burial in the Meredith family plot in the Manassas Town Cemetery, which happens to be right beside the Portner family plot.

William Payne Meredith had begun his professional career as a lawyer before moving into real estate and then on to the Mutual Life Insurance Company of New York for a short time. In 1934, upon its creation, he was appointed executive secretary of the District Alcohol Beverage Control Board. He served on the board until 1940, when he was elected to the national ABC board, and served there until his death. In addition to these positions, he had served as an examiner with the National War Labor Board during World War I.

After her husband's death, Etta continued to live in Washington until her death on Wednesday, July 7, 1965. She died at the age of 84 as a result of a long illness. Gawler & Sons handled funeral arrangements and services were held in Manassas on Saturday, July 10. After the service ended, Etta was buried next to her husband. Sylvia Meredith Garnett, who died in late-September of 1999, is buried in the same plot next to her late husband, Robert Sears Garnett. Jacqueline

Meredith Castle, who passed away in 1986, is buried beside her husband, William Donald Castle, on the island of Oahu in Hawaii.

Paul Valer Portner (1883-1919)

[Author's Note: A majority of information about Paul's adult life was obtained from transcripts regarding a lawsuit over his will. A fairly controversial issue, I have read and reviewed both sides of the case and have tried to write this section as unbiased and unobjectionable as possible.]

As a child, Paul began his schooling at Pantop's Academy, a Presbyterian preparatory school located on Pantop's Mountain just outside of Charlottesville, Virginia. The main reason for Paul to attend Pantop's was to prepare him for college, but he preferred this particular school because of its close proximity to the University of Virginia, where Alvin was attending school at the time. With Robby and Eddie busy working for their father and attending school, they had little time to devote to their younger siblings. As a result, Paul looked up to Alvin as a role model and for advice.

In the fall of 1898, Paul entered the Virginia Military Institute under the recommendation of many people, including his brother Robby. Unfortunately, Paul did not care for VMI and transferred to Hampden-Sydney College the following fall. During the spring of 1900, he contacted pneumonia and was sent home. His hopes of returning that semester were dashed when his illness became typhoid pneumonia. Paul managed to make a full recovery, though, and enrolled in the University of Virginia in the fall of 1901.

After he left the University of Virginia, Paul held a number of jobs within the family businesses. His only job outside of these was when he and Oscar ran a real estate business together from 1910 through 1912. Paul's other jobs included being both the President of the Portner Realty Company and Vice-President of the Robert Portner Brewing Company in 1915, Vice-President of the Virginia Feed & Milling Corporation from 1917 through 1919, and the Vice-President of the Capital Construction Company in 1918. In addition to these positions, he also sat on the Town Council of Manassas from 1907 to 1908.

Being a member of a well-connected family had its advantages. During World War I, Paul's brother-in-law, Representative Henry D. Flood, urged him to accept a diplomatic appointment with the State Department involving the custody of German prisoners in Russia. Paul, however, turned down the offer saying that he felt he would not be able to properly execute such a responsible position.

During the time Paul held his jobs and positions in and around Washington, he had at least five residences: his father's home on Vermont Avenue, his mother's home on New Hampshire Avenue, a house on V Street, a house on 16th Street, an apartment at the Bellevue Hotel he shared with Alvin, and one or more apartments at the Portner Apartments. It was not until 1916, though, that Paul finally had a fixed address. Like his siblings, Paul often stayed at Annaburg for long periods of time, but after Herman died in 1916, Paul moved to the farm permanently.

Though he was not as close to Herman as he was to Alvin, Herman's death affected Paul considerably, and it can be assumed that this was when he started to drink to excess. Prior to this time, Paul had occasional problems with alcohol, but his troubles seemed to increase from that point on. Visitors to and servants at Annaburg began to notice that he would not get out of bed until around mid-day, and once he was awake, began drinking until mid-afternoon, take a nap, and then resume drinking well into the night. They also began to notice that he developed the habit of taking a bottle of whiskey to bed with him. The bottle would be half to completely full, and by the time he awoke the following day, it would be empty.

Other people, however, did not notice Paul's drinking and were very pleased with his ability to conduct business. Some of these people included a number of businessmen in the Manassas community. During World War I, a local committee approached the Portner family and inquired about the possibility of leasing a portion of the expansive estate for use as a campsite for military training exercises. Heirs of the Portner estate signed a power of attorney, which gave Paul exclusive rights to the farm and authorized through him, at his discretion, the lease of the estate to the government for such a purpose. On several occasions, Paul made trips into Washington to meet with army officers representing the government.[53]

Fortunately, Paul's drinking habit did not change his affections for his siblings, even when they tried to intervene. While Alvin was Paul's favorite brother, he seems to have cared the same for each of his sisters and their children. Like all siblings, there were nicknames. Paul typically called Etta

'Mashie' and Elsa 'Skinny.' Though he did have the same amount of affection for his sisters, Paul tended to look out a little more for Hilda, being that she was one of the youngest and the only sister unmarried until shortly before his death. Since Annaburg was such a large place, he often tried to convince her to move there with him, in part for the company but also so he could keep an eye out for her.

In late May of 1917, Paul took ill after another bout of excessive drinking. Finding Paul practically in a coma, one of the servants at Annaburg called his personal physician, Dr. William Syme, and asked him to come to Manassas in order to tend to him. Dr. Syme arrived on May 29 and found Paul still in the same condition that the servant had described. It was not until the following morning that Paul was finally able to muster the strength needed to board a train to Washington.

Upon their arrival, Syme immediately took Paul to Emergency Hospital, where Paul had been a patient a number of times in the past for the same problem. Syme was surprised to learn, however, that Paul was denied a room. Uncertain of what to do, he did the only thing he could think of. Rather than take Paul to the Portner Apartments, where he risked many people seeing him in his present condition, Syme took Paul to the apartment he shared with Alvin at the Bellevue.

Dr. Syme left him there that evening in the care of Paul's personal servant, Ned, and Alvin. He returned in the morning to check on Paul only to find him in a similar state as the night before. With no other options, Syme left for a while and returned later that afternoon. Upon his arrival, he found Etta and her husband visiting with Paul.

Shortly after his arrival, Etta pulled Dr. Syme aside and informed him that he was being discharged. The reason for this, she said, was that the family felt Paul should be cared for by the family physician, not a personal friend. After Syme left, Etta called Dr. B. Lynn Claytor, a personal friend of hers and a complete stranger to Paul, to come in as his acting physician. Once Claytor stepped in, he contacted Emergency Hospital and was able to get Paul a room immediately. Though he was in no condition to conduct business of any kind, Paul made one phone call before leaving for the hospital. He called Charles F. R. Ogilby, a lawyer, and asked that papers for a will be drawn up for him.

The following day, June 2, Ogilby arrived at the hospital with the papers Paul had requested. After reading the will to Paul and making sure that he understood it and that it was prepared according to his instructions, Ogilby had Paul sign the will, had it witnessed, then left. Within a matter of days, Paul's condition improved and he returned home to Annaburg. Like his previous treatments, Paul stopped drinking for a few days, but was soon drinking heavily again. Aside from Etta and her husband, no one else in the family knew about the will.

Paul continued to drink heavily and be admitted to hospitals, with the same result each time. In early August 1919, he was taken sick with the flu and his health began to fail. Alma, who was living in New York, heard of Paul's weakened condition and left immediately for Annaburg. Upon her arrival, she gathered some of his belongings and took Paul to the Neurological Institute in New York City on August 17.

Though Paul's condition became better at times and grew worse at others, he continued to slip further and further away from recovery until he finally passed away at two o'clock in the morning on Friday, October 31, 1919. At the age of 36, his death was caused by cirrhosis of the liver and alcoholic neuritis. Two days later, after his body had been returned to Manassas, ceremonies were held at the family plot. For some reason, however, his casket was not buried immediately. Instead, it was placed in the nearby mausoleum of Judge J. B. T. Thornton, where it sat for two to three weeks before he was finally buried in the Portner family plot.

Soon after Paul's death, his siblings began sorting through his papers and personal effects, hoping to file estate papers. It was not until one of them opened his safety deposit box at a local bank that his will came to light. Once the will was read, it infuriated the entire family. Sometime between June 1913 and February 1916, Paul, Herman, and Alvin, the three remaining sons who had yet to become married, had made a verbal agreement that they would not write a will unless they married. Upon their deaths, this agreement would ensure that everything they had inherited from their father would be evenly distributed among their siblings. Not only did Paul break this agreement, but also he had left his entire estate, valued at approximately $250,000 to Etta and her daughter Sylvia, with a small annuity of $300 to his servant Ned Dickerson. To Augustine Humes, Paul's brother-in-law, things were starting to make sense.

Shortly before his death, Paul began to frantically call for Humes, who was a lawyer, to come and see him. Once Humes had arrived at the hospital, Paul began to tell him that he felt he had signed some papers a few years ago that he should not have and asked if he could look into it for him. Unfortunately, Humes did not get a chance to do this as Paul passed away a few days later.

After the family had read the will, they immediately filed suit against Etta. They claimed that she had influenced Paul to write the will while he was in the hospital and while he was incapable, mentally or physically, to conduct such business. On Friday, July 19, 1920, nearly nine months after

Paul's death, the case finally went to court. During the course of the trial, testimony was given that made it appear that Etta had actually influenced Paul to write the will. Some of the testimony even included a nurse admitting to having falsified Paul's charts for the night prior to and the morning of the signing of the will.

Another aspect that did not make sense was whom Paul chose as the beneficiaries. At the time he wrote the will, Etta only had one daughter, Sylvia. Between then and the time he died, however, Etta gave birth to her second daughter, Jacqueline. It was a commonly known fact that Paul loved and doted on each of his nieces and nephews equally. If that was the case, why did Paul not change his will to include Jacqueline with her mother and sister as beneficiaries? In addition to this, Paul had chosen William P. Meredith, Etta's husband, and Mr. Ogilby and his law associates as executors and trustees of his estate.

One final piece of contradictory evidence was his annuity to Ned Dickerson. Though he had left this small amount to him, Dickerson was fired shortly after the signing of the will for stealing and ordered to keep off of the Portner estate under penalty of personal harm via a shotgun, and yet the annuity remained.

Finally, on August 5, after only twenty minutes of deliberation, the verdict was announced. Much to the delight of most present, the jury awarded Paul's estate to Etta. The case had lasted for approximately fourteen days, one of the longest court cases in Prince William County history up to that point. The prominence of the family involved, the intense family feeling displayed, the wide array of legal talent involved, and the size of the estate caused the entire ordeal a widely publicized and followed media event. It had attracted so much attention that the courtroom was often packed each day. When the verdict was read, many people erupted into cheers, not for a lack of good feeling toward the family, but rather accepting that Paul was mentally sound when he had written the will. Even little Sylvia could be seen shaking the hands of several members of the jury.

For Etta's brothers and sisters, however, it was a different story. Outraged, they immediately filed an appeal with the Virginia State Supreme Court in Richmond. On June 15, 1922, the court entered its decision by sustaining Paul's will and awarding the estate to Etta. Though the decision was to sustain the will, the appeal was technically dismissed on the grounds that the appealing parties had failed to have certain papers given to the judge in time. As in Prince William County, the case was the largest ever filed in the Supreme Court of Virginia. By the time the final verdict was read, costs had exceeded into the tens of thousands of dollars and everyone involved was exhausted, physically and mentally.

Rather than pursue the case further, the family decided to let it go so that they could get on with the rest of their lives and allow Paul, and his memory, to finally rest in peace.

Oscar Charles Portner (1884-1924)

As a child, Oscar attended a variety of schools including the Franklin School, a school for the children of Washington, D.C.'s elite, and the Montclair Military Academy in Montclair, New Jersey. Unlike his siblings, though, Oscar received his entire secondary education at one school. He entered the George Washington University on October 31, 1905, seeking a "Special" degree. Like his brothers before him, Oscar found time to be involved in social activities, and following in Eddie and Robby's footsteps, was initiated into the Kappa Alpha Order social fraternity in 1905.

Sometime between late May and early June of 1912, Oscar married Mary "Molly" Amanda Dougherty (Dock-er-tee), a native of Philadelphia, Pennsylvania. After the wedding, the couple let for their honeymoon on Coney Island,

New Jersey. Upon their return, Oscar and Molly moved into Windemere, the former Weems family home at Annaburg. Taking after his father, Oscar began creating the perfect home for his family. Not only did he set about landscaping the property, but he also supplied the home with only the finest furnishings available at the time. The *Manassas Democrat* of June 13, 1912 gives a perfect example of this.

> Oscar Portner, who has recently taken unto himself a wife and has remodeled the "Weems house" on Annaburg farm, where he now resides, has purchased one of those beautiful 500 candle-power Gloria Portable lamps for his library. Mr. Portner has made many improvements to his property referred to, in the way of neatly laid out walks, shrubbery, etc., which makes it one of the most cozy and beautiful suburban residences in the section.

Other elegant furnishings included wicker furniture and hand-woven grass mats for the front porch, paintings from Europe, and beautifully carved wood furniture for the interior of the home.

Within a year, on March 14, 1913, their first child, Robert Joseph Portner (also known as Robert Portner III) was born. Three years later, on July 29, 1916, the couple's second son, John Alexander Dougherty Portner, was born. Over the years, the family divided the majority of their time between an apartment at the Portner Apartments and Annaburg, as well as time in Philadelphia. In April 1920, however, Oscar bought a home in Washington at 2409 California Street, NW. By May he and his family had moved and were settled into their new home. Not only did this put Oscar closer to the family businesses, but also a break out of Spanish influenza in Manassas contributed to the family's move.

> Oscar and Herman were the two boys I knew best. I was about Oscar's age, perhaps a year or so younger. It was Oscar who I knew best and we often discussed plans about what we were going to do. Once he worked at the brewery off and on while I was working in the ink factory. He was the nicest and kindest person I ever knew (like a brother). His sisters always said he was the sweetest of all their brothers and always so kind to them. I remember his wife "Molly" and their two fine sons, John and Robert Portner, III.[54]

On Friday, October 31, 1924, at the age of 39, Oscar died at his home in Washington from a sudden heart attack. His death came as quite a shock to everyone since he had been in the best of health prior to this unfortunate turn of events. Services were held at his home the following Monday, November 3 at 2:00 p.m., the Reverend Mackin of St. Paul's Episcopal Church officiating. Later that day, he was buried in Rock Creek Cemetery in Washington.

At the time of his death, Oscar was Vice-President of the Capital Construction Company and the Portner Corporation, as well as President of the Portner Realty Company and the then defunct Virginia Feed and Milling Company. Aside from his several business obligations, Oscar was quite well known as a social clubman. He held memberships with the Racquet Club in Philadelphia and the Congressional and Washington Gold Country Clubs in Washington. Oscar was also an avid sportsman, having interests in both golf and horses.

In his original will, Oscar asked that his body be buried in a hermetically sealed coffin and buried in the Portner family plot. He arranged for Molly to receive their home in Washington while his sons were to receive both specified and non-specified items. He also left some money to Molly's brother George, who lived in Philadelphia at the time. Shortly before his death, however, Oscar made two changes to his will. The first, he instructed that his coffin be made of solid bronze, similar to his father's, and bought specifically from Gawler & Sons of Washington. Secondly, he asked that rather than be buried in the family plot specifically he be buried wherever his wife saw fit. On April 16, 1925, four months after being buried in Washington, Molly had Oscar's remains reburied in the family plot in Manassas.

After Oscar's death, Molly and her sons moved to Aix-les-Baines, France to live with her older brother and sister, George and Lida Dougherty. They lived there for the next four years before returning to Washington in 1928, at which time they boys began attending Sidwell Friends. The following summer, Molly and her sons returned to France to visit her brother and sister. One evening, Molly went for a walk, and upon her return, found that she had caught a chill. Within days, her chill had developed into pneumonia.

Sadly, on July 6, 1929, Molly Portner died from pneumonia, leaving behind two sons who were only sixteen- and thirteen-years-old. Her body was sent back to Washington, and after services were held, she was buried along side of her husband in Manassas. Given the young ages of Molly's sons, her brother and sister assumed guardianship over the boys and raised them for the remainder of their teenage years. When each son graduated from high school, they came back to the United States to further their education in college.

As an adult, Robert married and had two children, including a son he named Robert Portner IV. In his later years, he became a resident of the nursing home in Manassas that his grandfather's house had become a part of. He entered the facility in the early-1970's and resided there until he passed away from colon cancer on July 22, 1983. Rather than be buried in the family plot, Robert requested that his body be donated to science at Georgetown University. John, on the other hand, lived all of his adult life in Washington with his wife and five children before passing away on October 26, 1990 of congestive heart failure. After services were conducted, his body was taken to Manassas and buried in the family plot along side of his mother and father. With his burial, John became the last Portner to be buried in the family plot to date.

Undated photo of Oscar Portner taken in Switzerland

Undated photo of Oscar C. Portner
Both courtesy of Peggy E. M. Portner

Picture of Oscar on his wedding day.
Courtesy of Peggy E. M. Portner

Mary Amanda "Molly" Dougherty on her wedding day in late May or Early June, 1912. Courtesy of Peggy E. M. Portner

Photo taken in 1912 of Oscar and Molly Portner while on their honeymoon in Atlantic City, New Jersey
Courtesy of Peggy E. M. Portner

Undated photo of Oscar and Molly Portner on vacation in
Atlantic City, New Jersey
Courtesy o f Peggy E. M. Portner

Oscar sitting on the front porch of Windemere with an unknown child in his lap (possibly his niece, Sylvia C. Meredith).
Courtesy of Peggy E. M. Portner

Oscar C. Portner with his family at Windemere in the summer of 1913. Seated left to right are George and Lida Dougherty (brother and sister of Molly D. Portner), Oscar Portner and Molly D. Portner with her newborn son, Robert Joseph Portner in her lap.
Courtesy of Peggy E. M. Portner

Undated photo of John AD Portner sitting on the shoulders of a servant, who was sitting in the shell-shaped basin of the lion's head fountain at Annaburg.
Courtesy of Peggy E. M. Portner

Brothers Robert Joseph Portner (a.k.a. Robert Portner III) and John AD Portner in an undated photo.
Courtesy of Peggy E. M. Portner

Photos of the exterior of Windemere, one of three houses on the Annaburg estate. Date of construction is unknown, but the house burned in the late-1940's.
Courtesy of Peggy E. M. Portner

Photo of one of the bedrooms in Windemere.
Courtesy of Peggy E. M. Portner

Photo of the dining room in Windemere.
Courtesy of Peggy E. M. Portner

Photo of the study in Windemere.
Courtesy of Peggy E. M. Portner

Photo taken of Windemere in 1940. By this time, no one lived in the house and in less than ten years it would burn down.
Courtesy of Henley S. Portner

Herman Henry Portner (1886-1916)

Unfortunately, little is known about Herman's life. For a reason unknown to anyone but Robert, Herman was hardly ever mentioned in his father's diary, so the schooling he received as a child remains a mystery. In 1905, Herman began schooling at the Virginia Military Institute. Enrolling with the class of 1909, he left after only one year. In 1907, he enrolled in the University of Virginia, but only stayed for one semester. Without having a diary or being socially prominent like his siblings, as well as having not married or had any children, even less is known about his life as an adult. It is known, however, that Herman lived at Annaburg from about 1913 until 1916, as well as visiting and staying in Washington and New York on various occasions.

On Monday, February 7, 1916, Herman was involved in a motorcycle accident along the Rock Creek Parkway in Washington. After doctors examined him at the hospital, they felt that he would recover without any difficulty, but before leaving the hospital, Herman contracted pneumonia. With Paul as an escort, Herman was sent to New York to consult with additional doctors. On February 9, one day after his arrival in New York, Herman passed away at the age of 29. His body was returned to Washington and on Thursday, February 11, services were held at All Souls Unitarian Church. After the service, his body was temporarily placed in a vault in Rock Creek Cemetery before being taken to Manassas to be buried in the family plot.

In keeping with the agreement with his brothers, Herman did not leave a will, but instead named Paul as the administrator of his estate. Paul, however, was too distraught over Herman's death to handle the business, so he asked Alvin to act in his place. Once Alvin assumed control of Herman's estate, all of the possessions and interests in the family businesses were distributed between their brothers and sisters.

Herman Portner
Courtesy of Anna Schoellkopf Lacher

Herman & Oscar
Courtesy of Anna Schoellkopf Lacher

Anna Florence Portner (1888-1966)

A few years after graduating from the Holton-Arms school in 1906, Anna, like all notable young women of her time, was presented to society as a debutante. And just as her sisters before her, she quickly became well known for her brunette beauty, which when combined with their German and Swiss heritage gave each sister a unique look all her own. Anna participated in societal events each year, but after her mother's passing, she took to seclusion in mourning. During this time, she met Henry De La Warr Flood, a Congressman from Virginia who was descended from some of the oldest and most respected families there. Despite a difference in age of nearly a quarter of a century, the two found many common interests together. Flood began courting the young woman almost immediately and in the spring of 1913, Anna's engagement to Henry "Hal" Flood was announced.

Throughout the year, rumors ran wild about where the wedding would be held and when the official date had been set for. During the summer, rumors started floating around saying that the engagement had been broken off. What people did not realize, though, was that Anna had not moved from Washington but instead was spending the summer abroad. Upon her return, however, she spent considerable time traveling between Washington and New York, assembling one of the most elaborate and impressive wedding ensembles that Washington society had seen in several seasons.

At 5:00 in the evening of Saturday, April 18, 1914, Anna and Henry were married at All Souls Unitarian Church in Washington. Alvin gave away his sister in marriage while Elsa served as the Matron of Honor and Hilda as the Maid of Honor. Henry's nephew, Harry Flood Byrd, served as the Best Man. The *Fredericksburg Daily Star* wrote about the ceremony, saying:

> For beauty of floral and decorative surroundings, and official and social rank of those in attendance, the wedding surpassed anything seen in Washington in many years. Not even the Mexican controversy [Poncho

Villa] was sufficient to interfere with the presence at the church and later at the reception of President [Woodrow] Wilson, Vice President [Thomas R.] Marshall and Secretary of State William Jennings Bryan. In fact, almost all of those of high official and social importance at the national capital were in attendance.[55]

The wedding itself was quite a 'congressional' ceremony, literally. Included in the bridal party as bridesmaids were Genevieve Clark, daughter of former Speaker of the House Beauchamp "Champ" Clark; Baroness Marie Baumgarten, daughter of Baron Baumgarten, formerly of the Austro-Hungarian embassy; and Lucy Martin, daughter of Senator Thomas S. Martin. Ushers included Congressman Kenneth D. McKellar of Tennessee and H. Garland Dupre of Louisiana; Paul and Edward Portner; and Ensign Richard Evelyn Byrd (U.S.N.) and Thomas Bolling Byrd, nephews of the groom.

At first the wedding reception was to be held at Anna's home in the Highland Apartments. As the guest list grew, however, it quickly became apparent to all that Anna's apartment would not be able to accommodate such a lavish and spectacular reception. An acquaintance of Henry's, hearing of the dilemma, stepped in and offered to help the couple. Henry's friend was the President of the Pan-American Union (now the Organization of American States) and offered to let the couple use their building, located on the corner of 17th Street and Constitution Avenue, for the event. Needless to say, Henry and Anna were eternally grateful to the man.

Being the first time the building was used for such an event, it was certainly done in such a way that would be hard to surpass, if at all. Mr. and Mrs. Flood received their guests in the Hall of the Americas, which had been decorated with palms, various plants, American beauty roses and rhododendron blooms. The *Evening Star* in Washington described the setting of the reception, saying "The building, with its stately marble interior and its broad patio filled with tropical birds and plants and a playing fountain, its broad marble stairways and rooms of massive proportions, formed an ideal setting for the event."[56] Decorated in roses and a color scheme of pink and white, the ballroom served as the beautiful setting for everyone to dance throughout the evening. Guests could step out onto the large first-floor portico or spacious lawns for refreshments or breaths of fresh air.

After their reception had ended, Henry and Anna left for their honeymoon, but because of Henry's position with the Foreign Affairs Committee and the conflict in Mexico, the couple could not travel far since he had to stay in close contact with Washington at all times. Upon their return, the couple continued to reside in Washington, living in the home of Anna's late mother at 1523 New Hampshire Avenue.

Together, Henry and Anna had four children: Bolling Byrd Flood, born on May 22, 1915; Anna Portner Flood, born on March 23, 1916; Eleanor Faulkner Flood, born on August 13, 1917; and Henry De La Warr Flood III, born on October 16, 1920. Unfortunately, Anna and Henry did not survive infancy, both having died within a few days after being born. Each child, however, was buried in the family mausoleum in Appomattox, Virginia.

Like his brothers-in-law, family life was short lived for Henry. He died in the early morning of December 8, 1921 at his Washington residence. His death at the age of 55 had been a result of recent illnesses. For a month prior to his death, Henry had been ill with acute bronchitis and only a few weeks before his passing, Henry developed heart trouble. All of this was added to by overworking as both the Chairman of the Democratic Congressional Committee and the Virginia Democratic State Committee.

Half an hour after Flood died, Congress met for its regular session, but adjourned immediately in respect for Flood, who had been one of their most influential and popular members. House Speaker Gillett appointed a committee of eighteen members to attend the funeral. Services were held at the Church of the Covenant in Washington with the Reverend Dr. Charles Wood officiating. After the services, Flood's body was placed in a vault in Rock Creek Cemetery and later taken to his hometown of Appomattox, where it was placed in the family mausoleum located on the front lawn of the courthouse.

Flood had served in various political institutions since passing his bar exam in 1886, including a number of state government bodies and as a member of the United States Congress from his election on March 4, 1901 until his death. Flood's most influential contribution came when he authored the resolution to declare a state of war on the Imperial German Government and the Imperial Austro-Hungarian Government in 1917, a document which caused the United States to become officially involved in World War I. In later years, Henry's children would unveil a portrait of their late father, which had been presented to Congress by their mother. The ceremony took place in the same room where Flood had sat with fellow members of the Foreign Affairs Committee while considering the resolution of war. After World War I had ended, Henry and Anna attended the peace conference at Versailles, France together.

Throughout her life, Anna Portner Flood impressed many people, even as a child. One evening, as she was preparing for a party, Anna had a conversation with her personal servant, Minnie Jones. As Jones was combing Anna's hair, the child looked at her and said, "Minnie, you're so pretty. You look like an angel." Minnie laughed and the only thing she could say in reply was, "No, Miss Nana, not yet."

As an adult, through both her family name and her marriage, Anna was almost looked upon as a "grand dame" of Washington society. Though she entertained quite lavishly and was of great fame and prominence, she maintained a sense of modesty about her. Two accounts paint quite the picture of Mrs. Flood. The first comes from an article in the *Washington Post*, from a series entitled "These Fascinating Ladies." This particular clipping reads:

> People are tops in her estimation. She likes all kinds, all classes, and she never forgets old friends. It's like turning the clock back to go to a party of hers and find women with grown daughters hobnobbing with men who had been their beaux in their debutante days. She spent her girlhood in Washington, married a Virginian, a member of the House of Representatives…[She] went away after his death, returned a few years ago, and picked up

the threads exactly where she had left off. She's a keen student of politics, an omnivorous reader of newspapers, plays bridge, a little golf, [and] walks a good deal.

[She] enjoys travel more than anything and prefers to travel by motor, enjoys a bit of gossip as well as the next one, but is never malicious and doesn't like anyone who is. Loves flowers but says she never stays long enough in one place to grow them successfully, has an interesting collection of antiques, some of them heirlooms, which give a look of home to her apartment in the Shoreham. A Duncan Phyfe secretary is one of her most prized possessions.

She has a lovely figure, fine dark eyes, smooth, dark hair, entertains a good deal, but more often than not for her son, her daughter or various young nieces and cousins. Her name: Mrs. Henry D. Flood.

A more recent, but equally insightful, account comes from her granddaughter, Mrs. Anna Schoellkopf Lacher. In an email to the author, Mrs. Lacher wrote:

> She had a navy blue Oldsmobile. An older man, who had a bad leg and needed a job, would drive her around. She was in fact providing a job for a needy person. My grandmother was always very generous with others. She very rarely spent money on herself. I remember that she wore the same black suit for many years. She lived a quiet life in her older years. A close circle of beloved friends and family were the focus of her life. One of her favorite activities was to invite a few close friends over to play bridge.

It is no surprise that a woman such as she was involved in many charities, including the Red Cross and the Thrift Shop, as well as attending St. Margaret's Church in Washington. But you can also see the influence that each of her parents had on her, from her generosity toward others to the never forgetting a name or face.

On Saturday, August 1, 1966, Washington society lost one of its greatest and most prized members. The Portner family, one the other hand, lost one of its most vibrant and looked upon kin, not to mention the grand-matriarch, of sorts, for the entire family. Anna Portner Flood, the last living child of Robert and Anna Portner, and the last of the first generation of the American branch of the family, passed away at her home in Washington at the age of 79. Though Anna had been in poor health for a number of years, the same thing that had taken her mother, a stroke, ultimately caused her own death. After services concluded, her body was taken to Appomattox, where she was placed in the Flood family vault with her husband, two infant children, and a brother-in-law.

Anna Florence Portner and Senator Henry De La Warr Flood, along with their attendants, on the day of their wedding, April 18, 1914. Included in the attendants of the bride are her sisters, Hildegarde Rose Portner (to the left of the bride) as maid-of-honor and Elsa Portner Graham (to the right of the bride) as Matron –of-honor. Serving as the groom's attendants included his nephews Thomas Bolling Byrd (3rd man from left), Harry Flood Byrd (4th man from left) and Admiral Richard E. Byrd (2nd man from right).

Courtesy of Anna Schoellkopf Lacher

Anna Portner Flood with her children, Bolling (left) and Eleanor (right), c.1917
Courtesy of Anna Schoellkopf Lacher

Photo of Anna Portner Flood an d Henry De La Warr Flood
c.1920
Courtesy of Anna Schoellkopf Lacher

Anna Portner Flood with her children
Bolling and Eleanor c.1923
Courtesy of Anna Schoellkopf Lacher

Anna Portner Flood with her children Bolling and
Eleanor c.1923 on the Boardwalk in Atlantic City
Courtesy of Anna Schoellkopf Lacher

Dedication ceremony of the late Senator Henry De La Warr Flood's portrait. (March 30, 1928) Back row (left to right) Rep. Linthicum of MD, Mrs. Henry Flood, Gov. Harry Byrd of Virginia, Rep. Stephen G. Porter of Virginia, Senator Claude A. Swanson of Virginia & Rep. Moore of Virginia.
Standing in the front are Senator Flood's children Bolling Byrd Flood & Eleanor Flood.
Courtesy of Anna Schoellkopf Lacher

Hildegarde Rose Portner (1889-1944)

Unfortunately, like Herman, little is known about Hilda's life. Though she lived a fairly long life, dying at the age of 55, her children did not live long and there is little information about her. In 1912, like Anna before her, Hilda graduated from the Holton-Arms school in Washington. On June 15, 1919, Henry and Anna Portner Flood announced Hilda's engagement to C. Palmer Derby, a Lieutenant in the United States Army.

In the engagement announcement, the *Evening Star* said that the ceremony, to take place later in the month, was forecasted to be "one of the most interesting events this season, as Miss Portner is strictly speaking a Washingtonian, being one of several handsome sisters, each of whom made their debuts (to society) in the capital." Like many other romances of the time, wedding engagements were announced only weeks before the wedding date. Though the couples had been engaged for a year or more, weddings were often put on hold because of the bridegroom having to go off to war.

On June 21, 1919, at 5:30 p.m., Hilda and Palmer were married in a quiet ceremony in the Flood's apartment at 2029 Connecticut Avenue. The ceremony took place in a flower-decked drawing room and was conducted by the Reverend U. G. B. Pierce in the presence of closer friends and family. Elsa Portner Humes, married only two months prior, served as Matron-of-Honor while Captain Nelson Page, United States Army, served as Best Man. Guests of the wedding included Oscar and Molly Portner, Paul Portner, and Augustine Humes, as well as several relatives of Henry Flood. After the ceremony, the couple left on their honeymoon. They returned to Washington and made their residence at 2407 California Street. Together, Hilda and Palmer had two children, Palmer Portner Derby, born on May 23, 1920, and Nancy Portner Derby, born on October 19, 1923.

Sadly, Palmer would not live to see the birth of his daughter. On Thursday, May 17, 1923, five months before Nancy was born, Palmer passed away from a sudden heart attack and services were held that Saturday at his residence. Being a veteran of World War I, Palmer was buried in

Arlington National Cemetery. After Palmer's death, Hilda moved her family into the Portner Apartments where she continued to raise her children and live for the next twenty-one years. On Monday, May 22, 1944, Hilda Portner Derby passed away in her apartment. Her death had been a result of an illness that had lasted for the six months prior to her death. Two days later services were held at Gawler & Sons. Afterwards, she was buried in Arlington National Cemetery next to her husband.

Hildegarde Rose Portner (left, age 13) and
Elsa Eugenia Portner (right, age 11), taken in Aldenburg,
Germany in 1903
Courtesy of Anna Schoellkopf Lacher

Hildegarde Rose Portner
Courtesy of Anna Schoellkopf Lacher

Hildegard Rose Portner on her wedding day,
June 21, 1919 to C. Palmer Derby
Courtesy of Anna Schoellkopf Lacher

Photo of Nancy Portner Derby appearing in the
*Washington Pos*t in 1941
Courtesy of Barbara Portner Whitbeck

Elsa Eugenia Portner (1891-1954)

As a young woman, Elsa was educated at the Finch School and the Briarcliff School in Westchester, both in New York, and like Anna and Hilda before her, Elsa graduated from the Holton-Arms school in Washington. On March 3, 1911, Elsa was married to Lorimer C. Graham, a Lieutenant with the United States Navy. The couple had eloped to Baltimore, Maryland, where they were wed in a Catholic church. After returning to Washington, the couple returned to their respective homes before living together as a married couple.

Lorimer and Elsa had two children, Valerie Graham, born on May 21, 1912, and Hildegarde Portner Graham, born on November 1, 1915. Unfortunately, the happiness of the marriage did not last long. On January 4, 1919, while temporarily living in Reno, Nevada, Elsa divorced her husband on the grounds of emotional abandonment.[57] Three months later, on April 2, 1919, Elsa married Augustine Leftwich Humes, a lawyer in New York. After the marriage, the couple, along with Elsa's two daughters, resided at the Plaza Hotel in New York City.

Elsa and Augustine had one child together, John Portner Humes, who was born on November 21, 1921. Carrying on his father's legacy, John, who would later be simply known as "Ambassador," became an Ambassador of the Untied States to Austria. On February 23, 1929, Humes bought a thirteen room, six-bath duplex apartment at 960 Fifth Avenue, an imposing limestone building that overlooked Central Park. The family lived there for the remainder of their lives, as well as owning homes in Newport, Rhode Island and Washington, and having farms in Vermont and Winchester, Virginia.

On September 25, 1952, after a long illness, Augustine Humes passed away at his apartment in New York at the age of 77. In addition to having been a lawyer, Humes' professional career included serving as an advisor to Switzerland on the War Trade Board during World War I and practicing law before the United States Supreme Court.

Humes also served for a time as Director of the International Business Machines Corporation (IBM).

Elsa continued to live in the apartment in New York City for the rest of her life. On February 3, 1954, Elsa Portner Humes passed away. She had taken ill while visiting her son in Mill Neck, Long Island. She died at the age of 62 at North Community Hospital, Long Island, New York. Although Elsa and Augustine both passed away in New York, they are buried side-by-side in the Borough of Brielle, New Jersey, along with Augustine's parents, Andrew Russell and R. Alice Leftwich Humes.

Elsa Portner Humes
Courtesy of Anna Schoellkopf Lacher

Undated portrait of Elsa Portner Humes
Courtesy of Andrew R. Humes

Hildie & Valerie Graham
Courtesy of Anna Schoellkopf Lacher

John Portner. Humes
Courtesy of Anna Schoellkopf Lacher

Photo appearing in a New York newspaper in 1939. The photo accompanied an article announcing her engagement to Charles M. Clarke, Jr. Mrs. Clarke was the first-born daughter of Elsa Portner Graham (later Humes).
Courtesy of Anna Schoellkopf Lacher

Godparents

Edwin	None
Robert Francis Portner	E. Francis
Edward George Portner	B. Edward J. Eils & George Bullen
Alvin Otto Portner	Paul V. Deuster & Otto Portner
Alma Meta Portner	Mrs. Guenther & Mrs. Schandein
Henriette Marie Portner	Felixine Portner & Marie Vernier
Paul Valer Portner	Paul Muhlhauser & Peter von Valaer
Oscar Charles Portner	Richard Guenther & Carl Strangmann
Herman Henry Portner	Henry Bartholomay
Anna Florence Portner	Anna Wilkening & Florence Eils
Clara Loise Portner	Clara Seipp & Louise Muhlhauser
Hildegarde Rose Portner	Hildegarde Hertzog & Louise Rose
Elsa Eugenia Portner	Elsa Seipp & Eugenia Leicht

Endnotes

[48] In 1904, Columbian University officially changed its name to the George Washington University.

[49] It is not known which years Edward did this work, or whether he owned the Magnetic Pigment Company or worked for them.

[50] Peter Valaer's memoirs.

[51] His love of hunting is evident in a newspaper ad placed in the *Fairfax County Herald* in 1905 where he offers a five-dollar reward for a missing hunting dog.

[52] *Evening Star*. December 17, 1908.

[53] Attempts were made to validate this fact, found in the transcripts of Paul's will case, by contacting various departments of the United States Army and United States Government, but no solid proof was ever found.

[54] Peter Valaer's memoirs.

[55] *Fredericksburg Daily Star*, April 20, 1914.

[56] *Evening Star*, April 19, 1914.

[57] Lorimer later remarried to a woman named Elzina K. and retired from the United States Navy as a Commander. He died in 1969 and is buried beside Elzina (1887-1968) in the Hillside Cemetery in Ormond Beach, Florida.

Undated photo of Anna von Valaer Portner taken in France
Courtesy of Edward M. & Vivian S. Portner

Photo of Robert & Anna Portner in formal attire, presumably around turn-of-the-century. Courtesy of Anna Schoellkopf Lacher

Photo taken c.1887 of the Portner children.
Left to right: Robert, Edward, Alvin, Alma, Henriette (Etta), Paul, Oscar and Herman
Courtesy of Anna Schoellkopf Lacher

Photo of an oil painting of the Portner family.
The painting was done on April 16, 1890 (the infant Anna is holding a calendar with this date on it).
Left to right are: Alma, Oscar (seated), Henriette (Etta), Robert, Clara, Anna von Valaer Portner, Hildegarde (Hilda; being held by her mother), Paul, Clara, Herman, Robert Francis (at the piano), Edward (holding the flute), and Alvin. The original painting measured twelve feet wide by nine feet high.
Courtesy of Anna Schoellkopf Lacher

Photo of the six oldest Portner children, Taken c.1892/3.
Left to right are Paul, Henriette (Etta), Alma, Alvin, Edward and Robert.
Courtesy of Anna Schoellkopf Lacher

Photo of the six youngest children, taken c. 1892/3.
Left to right are Elsa, Hildegarde (Hilda), twins Anna and Clara, Herman and Oscar.

Courtesy of Anna Schoellkopf Lacher

The last known photo taken of the entire Portner family, taken in 1898. Standing left to right: Oscar, Henriette (Etta), Edward, Robert Francis, Alma, Alvin, Paul and Herman. Front row, left to right: Anna, Anna von Valaer Portner, Elsa, Hildegarde (Hilda), Robert and Clara.
Courtesy of Anna Schoellkopf Lacher

Robert "Robbie" Francis Portner, Jr.
Courtesy of Anna Schoellkopf Lacher

Clara c.10 years of age, 1898
She died of typhoid fever shortly after this picture was taken.
Courtesy of Anna Schoellkopf Lacher

Unidentified child sitting on a motorcycle at Annaburg
(estate, not the house). Date unknown
Courtesy of Peggy E. M. Portner

Photo of the Portner family plot in Manassas as it appeared sometime in the 1960s
Courtesy of Barbara Portner Whitbeck

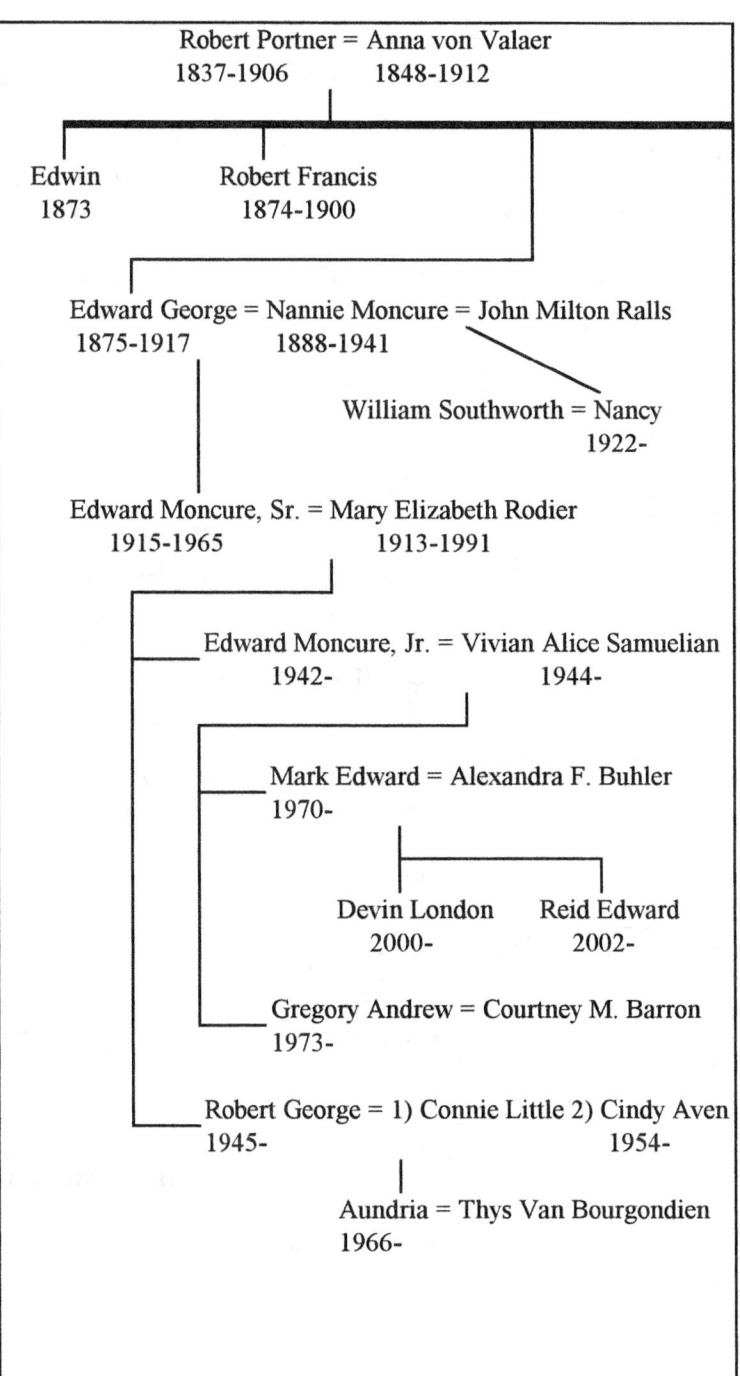

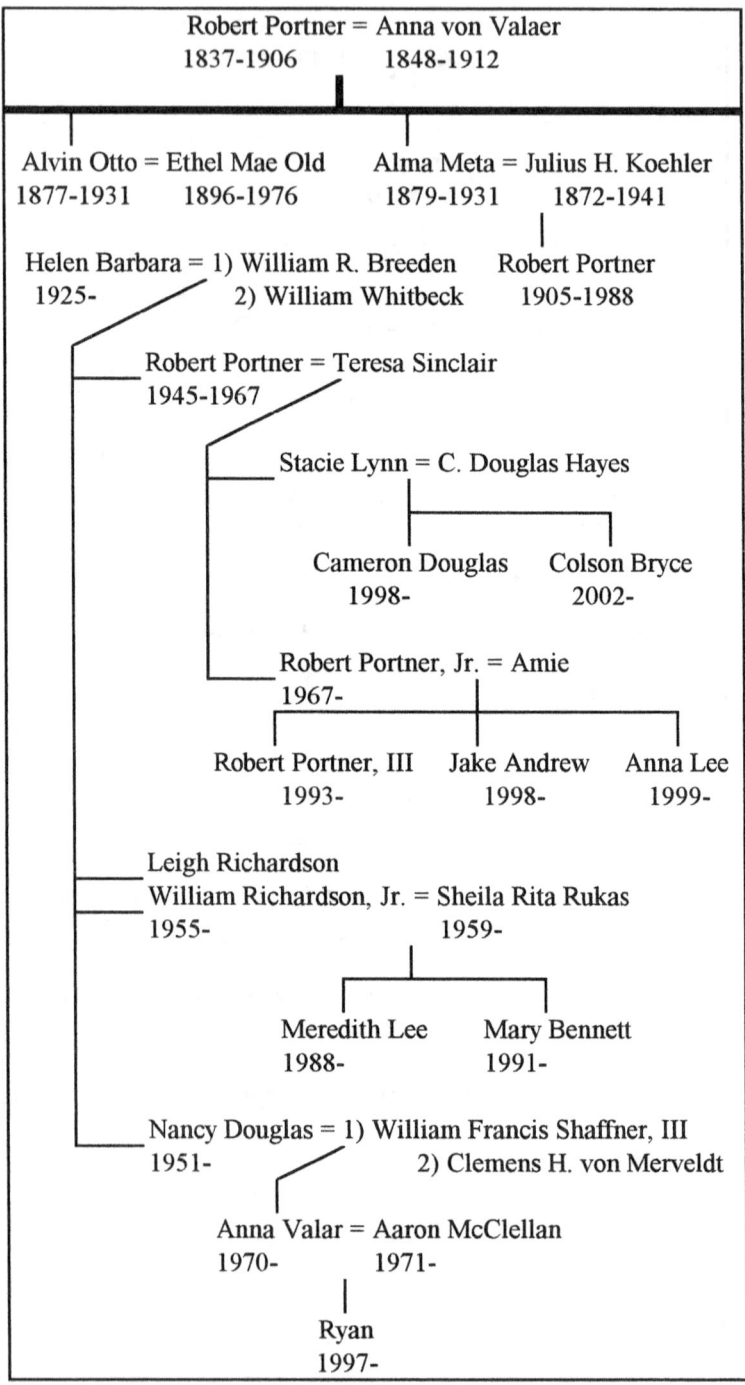

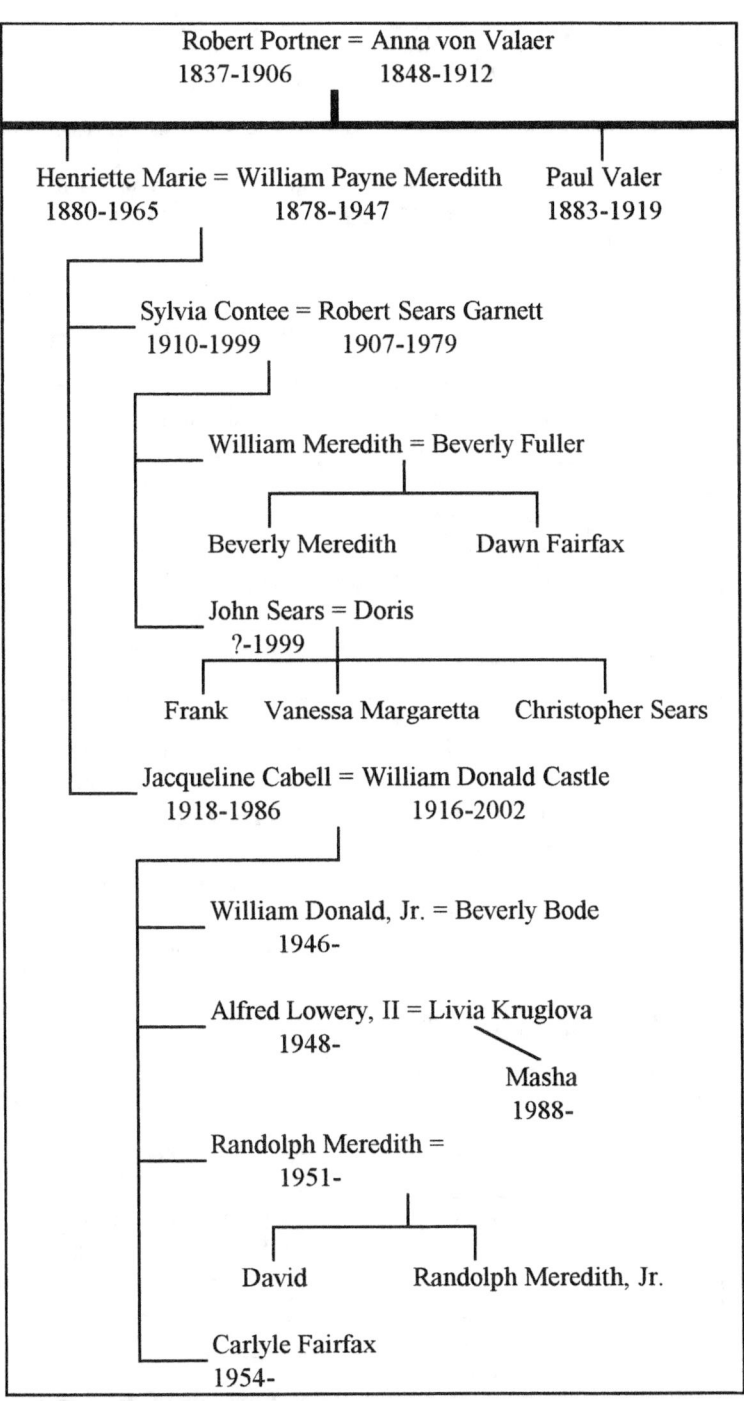

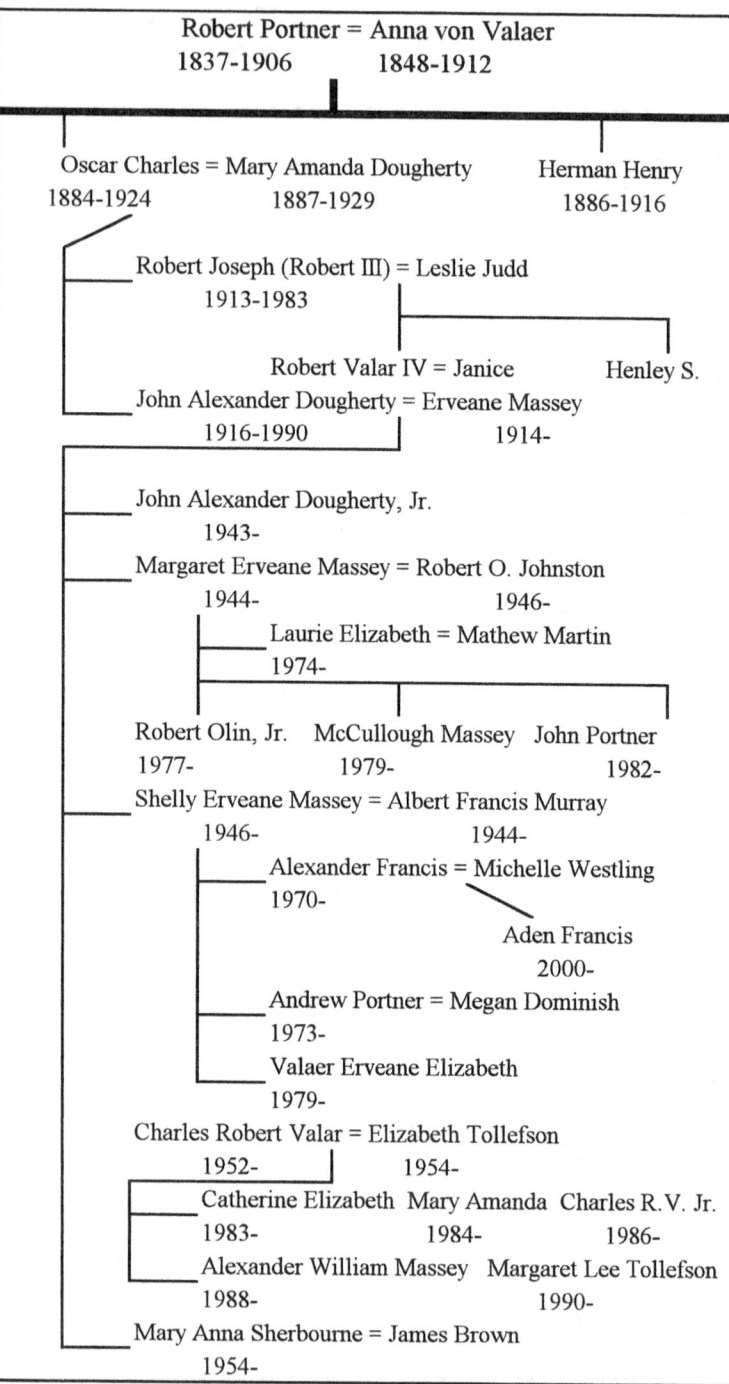

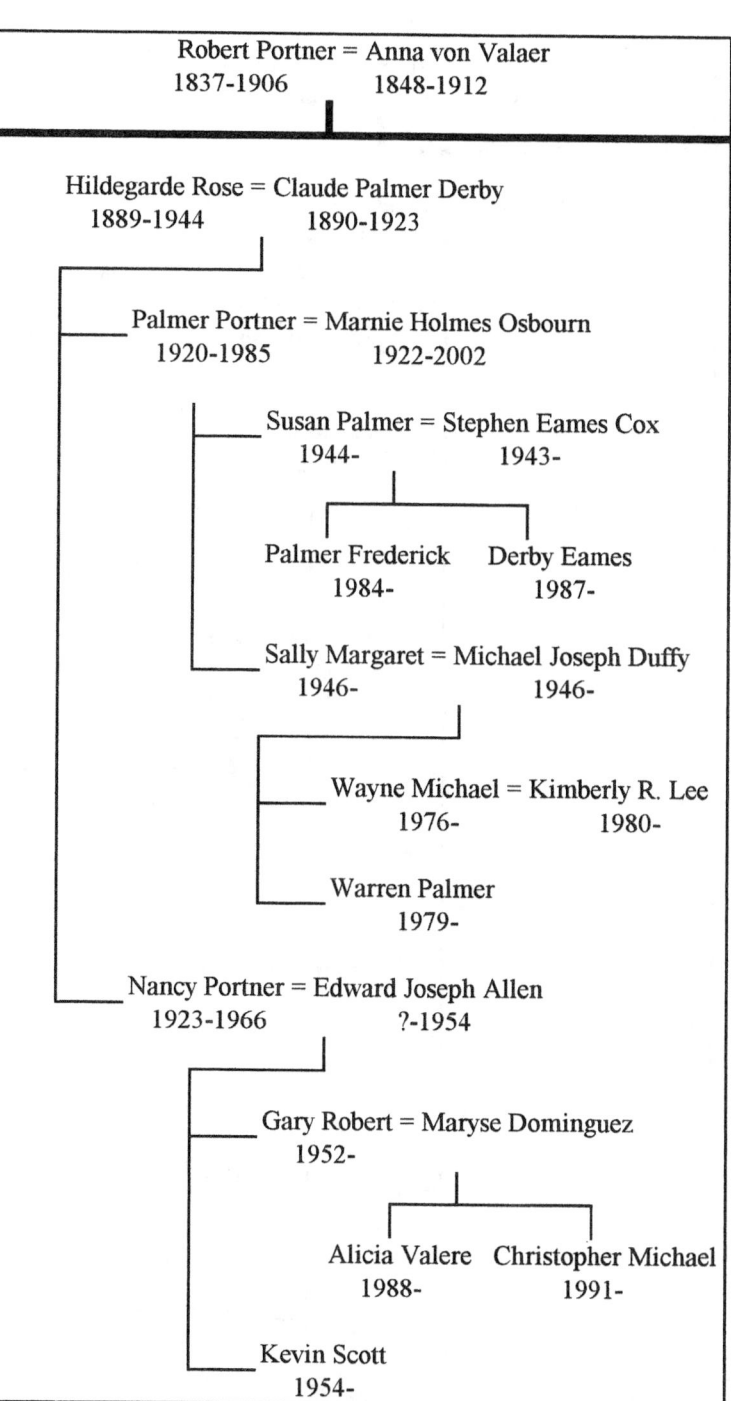

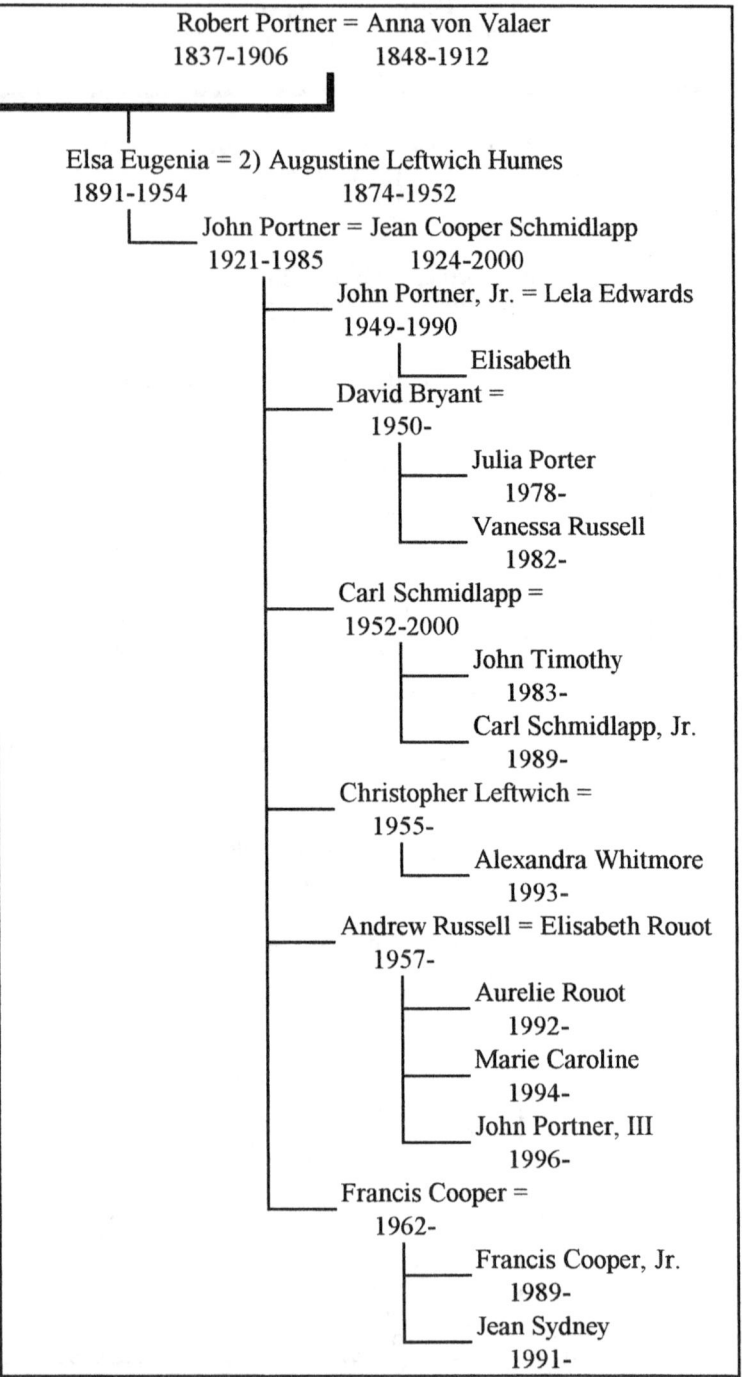

Annaburg—1887

Photo of the Portner family at Annaburg in 1887. Seated on the balcony are Robert & Anna, and standing below are their children (from left to right): Robert, Edward, Alvin, Alma, Etta, Paul and Oscar. Baby Herman is in the carriage. This house would be replaced in 1892 by a new, larger structure.

Courtesy of Anna Schoellkopf Lacher

7

A Palace in the Countryside

In 1868, Swiss immigrant-turned New Jersey businessman Christian Mathis was forced into retirement due to of poor health. Wanting to retire in comfort, he chose to move to Manassas, where he bought a 1,868-acre farm, located one quarter of a mile outside of the town. On May 23, 1868, Mathis paid Robert Carter Weir $800 for the land. Within a matter of days, Mathis contracted John and Ira Cannon, a father-and-son team who built many of Manassas' buildings, to build a new home for him and his family. Unfortunately, Mathis' retirement lasted less than ten years. After continued health problems, he passed away on October 28, 1875, leaving behind $10,000 in real estate and $5,400 in personal property. After his death, Mathis' widow continued to live on the farm along with a gardener, two farm laborers, and two general laborers.

By 1883, Robert Portner came to realize that he needed a place where he could relax and escape the chaotic city life and troubles of his businesses. As soon as she had first laid eyes on it, Anna Portner fell in love with the Mathis farm in Manassas. With its native trees and splendid view of the mountains, the estate reminded her of her homeland. Because she loved it so, and with its close proximity to Washington and Alexandria, Robert felt the farm was just the place he was looking for. On January 4, 1883, he bought 191 acres of the farm, including the ten-room house, from Anna C. H. Mathis and John D. McPherson, executor of Christian Mathis' estate, for $6,000.[58] "I bought Annaburg, because Mamma liked it so much. I started to build there too, [and] had everything repaired, and we were able to move there in the spring of 1883. We all liked it there very much." (16)

During the time that the Mathis family lived there, the farm had no fixed name other than the Mathis farm. Once Portner bought the property, though, he chose to name it Annaburg. Over the years, many people have speculated as to where the name Annaburg came from and why he chose that particular name. Some people believe that he named it after the military academy he attended as a youth while others feel that he named it for his wife (translated from German, Annaburg means "Anna's place"). Some even believe that Portner, as a matter of convenience, named his new home for both of these reasons. In an interview with Robert Portner Koehler, a grandson of Portner's, Koehler was adamant about the fact that the estate was named for the military academy and <u>not</u> his grandmother. Whatever Portner's reasoning, it was fitting as the beauty of the estate certainly complemented the beauty of both his wife and Castle Annaburg.

As with many other properties, Annaburg was considerably different when Portner bought it compared to what people know it as today. More specifically, the Mathis house itself is not the one currently present on the property. The original three-story house was built as a combination of the Italianate and "Steamboat Gothic" Victorian styles, a rarity in northern Virginia. Built in a cross shape, the house had a two-story porch that surrounded the entire house as well as a square cupola on the roof, which gave the building its "steamboat" appearance. The exterior was painted a light color, most likely pink since it was later known as the Pink House. It also featured shutters and trim that were said to be dark green, which would have complemented the light pink quite nicely. The Cannons gave the house quite a bit of decorative trim, both inside and out, including two dark marble mantles, chambered and bracketed porch posts, jigsaw porch railing, and floorboards crafted out of local pine.

The ten-room house served as the Portner family's summer retreat for many years. In his memoirs, Portner wrote: "I kept buying real estate adjacent to Annaburg, especially when it was very cheap. This will also be a good investment for you children, and I like to do it." (17) After buying the original land from Mrs. Mathis, Portner bought an additional 57 acres from her as well as an unspecified amount of land from George and Harriet Hixson. In August and September of 1884, Portner bought land from John D. McPherson and George Black, and on August 11, 1885, he bought 302 acres from Virginia B. McLean for $2,700, which contained the Confederate Civil War earthworks of Fort Beauregard. Two months later, on October 22, he bought some additional land from Hixson. On December 7, 1886, he bought one and a quarter acres from the heirs of William J. Weir for $1,000.[59]

As early as 1887, Robert was already receiving accolades for his estate in Manassas. In a letter to the *Alexandria Gazette*, dated September 26, 1887, the corespondent wrote:

> During a recent visit to Mr. Robert Portner's farm we find he has made many improvements. The old fortifications [Fort Beauregard] there are still undisturbed (because they were built by Alexandrians) and he has bestowed considerable care and attention to it, beautifying it in various ways. In this connection we are glad to see that one of Alexandria's industries, Portner's beer, is

becoming one of the institutions of this enlightened age.

As his property continued to grow, the need for more servants at Annaburg grew as well. These employees included a horse trainer from England, attendants for the children, a cook, and locals from Manassas to assist with various tasks around the estate. Being a man of good conscience, he could not provide those employees brought in from long distances a job without offering them a place to reside. Many of the tenant houses that Portner had built on Main Street for this purpose still stand today.

Though the Portner family was considerably higher on the economic and social ladder than any citizen of Manassas, the family treated their neighbors as no less than equals, being very hospitable and entertaining lavishly. The late Adra Lion Hall, a Manassas native, once recalled this about the Portner family:

> Every Fourth of July the Portners would invite a certain number of people to see the fireworks. And they served watermelon and ice cream and cake, and the whole place was just full of visitors. Mr. and Mrs. Portner were...very

> sociable and very nice...they didn't have any airs about them in any way.[60]

Three other natives of Manassas each recall stories from their youth regarding various aspects of the Portner family. The first two stories were recorded and published by Charles A. Mills in a book titled *Echoes of Manassas* in 1988 while the second comes from Byrd's own book titled *Town of Manassas and Old Prince William*.

> Walser Conner Rohr:
>
> The Portner's built a beautiful estate. They had two thousand acres and it went from Main Street all the way to Bull Run. Besides the huge home and the surrounding beauty, they had trees from every country they could get trees from. They had a large pond with swans on it. They had a small pond with ducks on it. They had a swimming pool, which was almost unheard of then. They had driveways around the estate. They had a deer park where the men used to go hunting. There was a little hunting lodge in the deer park. It was fenced and they had deer there. They had several farms to sustain the house and raise crops and cattle.

They had beautiful horses... I particularly remember the little pony carts the Portner children rode around in. My Uncle Eppa Goodwin helped take care of the horses and he drove the pony cart when the children wanted to go for a ride.[61]

Marion Lewis Lewis:
I was very envious of a beautiful pair of ponies and a cart that the Portner children had. They'd drive up and down town. I lived on the farm and we had horses and buggies and things like that, but they weren't appealing. The children were older than I. One thing I remember about the Portner boys was that they were kind of wild. [Mr. Portner] was very devoted to his wife...Mrs. Portner was a very nice, friendly person. She didn't get out much; she had a large family. She had her servants. She was a busy person. I never visited the home. Of course, I was younger. I wasn't too impressed by anything about it, but I was a bit envious of that pony cart.[62]

Ethel Maddox Byrd:

I became acquainted with some members of the Portner family through my friend, Bettie Simonds whose father John T. Simonds was overseer of Annaburg for many years. The Simonds lived on North Main Street across from the main entrance to the estate, so Bettie and I found it entertaining to keep in touch with the goings and comings of the Portners and occasionally we visited the twin girls, Anna and Clara Portner. Then too Oscar, one of the younger boys was sociable with the town boys and girls. Upon one occasion I now recall, Rena Merchant, daughter of Robert W. Merchant, a local merchant had visiting her a friend from Baltimore and one feature of entertainment was a hayride. So Rena invited Oscar and also invited him to furnish the wagon, horses and straw. Oscar drove the horses and was escort of the visiting girl who occupied the honor seat on the straw. Phillip Lipscomb was my escort, the others invited not now remembered. The time was summer and the soft moonlight added glamour and romance to the occasion. Such was the diversion in the early 1900's.

Before long, Robert came to realize that he needed a larger house for his growing family. Having the option of designing a brand new house, he spared no expense in its design. Portner was aglow with ideas, yet he had an ambition for efficiency. For example, his home was insulated. To have insulation, however, one must have something that would require insulation. Knowing how sweltering Virginia summers tended to be, and being the creative person that he was, Portner soon designed something that would lead to a revolution in home comfort many years later. Modifying the beer cooling and air purifying systems he had received patents for, Robert designed a system of copper pipes to be installed within the walls of Annaburg. Using a mechanized system, the pipes would circulate ice-cold water through them. Robert had thus turned Annaburg into what is believed to be the first air-conditioned home in the country. In 1975, Robert Portner III was quoted as saying, "You noticed it as soon as you stepped in the front door, it was like an icebox."[63] Ice used for this process was taken from the estate ponds each winter and stored in an icehouse near the house.

Robert wanted only the best for his family, and in so doing, ended up creating one of the most impressive homes in northern Virginia. He hired Oscar Vogt, a German architect who worked in Washington, as the architect for the project. Vogt combined the styles of several of Portner's favorite European mansions to create the floor plans and façade of the new house, the plans of which were completed shortly after Christmas of 1891.

Portner did not want to tear down the existing house, so to make room for the new house, the original had to be moved. To do this, the house was divided into two sections and moved to a new location nearby on the farm, which allowed Portner and his family to continue using the house while the new one was being built.

Once the original house was moved, Portner was able to begin work on building his new home. On April 28, 1892, the cornerstone was laid, which bore the inscription "R. P. 1892." For the construction of his new home, Portner employed over one hundred men. The Cannons were once again called out to the property to oversee construction. Masons, bricklayers, painters, plasterers, plumbers, carpenters, and several other types of workers, each of whom would take a train to and from Manassas each day, received one to three dollars a day for a ten-hour work day.

Portner had the best materials used in the construction of his home. With the exception of the sandstone, which came from two local quarries Portner operated, most of the other materials came from Europe, including marble fireplace mantles from Italy. Like the sandstone, the brick used in construction was made locally. "The brick yard on the property of Messrs. Weir & Bro., of Manassas, is in operation [and] within a few weeks will have 200,000 bricks ready for use. 150,000 of these will be used on Mr. Robert Portner's new residence."[64]

Knowing the size of his new home and the land he already owned, as well as that which he intended on later purchasing, Robert was forced to think ahead about conveniences for the home. He already had access to a number of artesian wells on the property, but knew that his family would require more than that which was provided.

> For the purpose of obtaining a larger supply of water a dynamite cartridge was exploded in one of Mr. Robert Portner's artesian wells at "Annaburg" on Thursday of last week. The experiment, which was witnessed by a number of persons, was attended with satisfactory results in opening up the fissures in the bottom of the well. When the dynamite was first exploded water spurted into the air to the height of forty feet and an abundant supply of

the sparkling fluid continues to flow from the well.⁶⁵

Once the cornerstone was laid, construction proceeded at a fairly rapid rate and the beauty of the new house quickly became evident. Only six months after the cornerstone was laid, the house began receiving praise by local newspapers. "Mr. R. Portner's country residence is progressing quite rapidly and will when finished be a decided credit to this section, if indeed not the whole State."⁶⁶ As construction of the home proceeded from the exterior to the interior, Portner was on hand as often as possible to make sure everything was being done to his liking. He was so particular about details in his new home that he did not even want any nail heads to show. To prevent this, he had workers cut out a small sliver of wood, drive the nail in, and then glue the sliver back over top of the nail.

By all accounts, construction of the new house proceeded without a hitch, with one exception. After the original house had been moved, workers began digging a basement for the new house when they made a startling discovery.

"Speaking of the battle [First Battle of Manassas]," said Mr. Portner, "when my house was being built, the workmen dug into the grave of an unknown soldier. There was nothing to mark the spot; no one knew that a grave was there. It was discovered in the digging. I had the bones collected and reburied in the graveyard at Alexandria."[67, 68]

Towards the end of 1893, construction had progressed to a point where Portner knew that the original house had become obsolete and was no longer needed. He sold the Mathis house to Richard S. Hynson, who moved it off the property to a lot on the corner of East Street and Old County Road (known today as Quarry Road), where it still stands today. For the house to be moved a second time, it had to be dived into two sections once again and moved with a winch and horses.

The original two-story annex, however, was not moved with the main house. For reasons not known, the annex was sold and moved to a different location before being moved to its present location on Centreville Road, across from the fire station. A few years after the Mathis house was moved, a new second-story addition, which contained a kitchen and dining room, was built on the rear of the house. Under new ownership, the house was most likely remodeled, and it can be assumed that this was when the house's trademark square cupola was removed.

In time, the house passed down through the Hynson family, which earned it a new nickname as the "Hynson House." In 1982, Luke Barzegar, a local merchant in Manassas, bought the then-vacant house. Over the course of the next two years, he converted the house from a vacant, run-down structure into a building that contained four efficiencies, a one-bedroom apartment, and a two-bedroom apartment. In December of 1984, the first apartments were ready to be rented. To this day, the house still remains a converted apartment building.

ooo

In December of 1894, after nearly two years of construction and a cost of $150,000, the house was finally finished. Because the style of Annaburg was achieved through the combination of several European mansions, it is difficult to assign one particular style to the house, although Colonial Revival (with Neo-classic elements) and Renaissance Revival certainly are the more predominant styles. The house contained thirty-five rooms over three floors and a basement.

In addition to this, Annaburg featured two other luxuries, electrical lighting and indoor plumbing, in a time when only the affluent could afford such indulgences. Robert Portner III once said, "Annaburg featured three different sized bathrooms, each one at a prominent location to show it off. The largest featured a ten-foot tub, the second largest a four-foot tub, and the smallest a water closet and sink."[69] To furnish his home, Portner used only the finest accessories and pieces of furniture he could find. Like many of the materials used in the construction, furnishings for Annaburg were shipped directly from Europe.

When Portner hired employees at Annaburg, he requested that they speak German, the only English spoken in the household being reserved for guests. On one particular occasion, Portner placed an ad in a Manassas newspaper seeking a German-speaking butler and chauffeur. Much to his surprise, a colored man answered the ad. After being led into the house, Portner reminded the gentleman that the ad was for a German speaking person. In response, spoken in German, the man told Portner that he had learned the language from his mother who had been a cook in a German orphanage in Pennsylvania. Needless to say, the man was hired. "Always at the table was a special "German butler" who expected you to ask for things in German."[70] Many citizens of Manassas would be easily amused watching the chauffeur drive the Portner's around town. He always sat so tall in the front seat that the Portner's, most of whom were small in stature, looked like little children sitting in the back compared to the driver.

Whenever painting was needed at Annaburg, whether it was touch ups on the murals or a wall being repainted, the Portner family employed Oliver Newman, a family friend and nephew of Christian and Anna Mathis. An employee of the Pullman Company, Newman performed side work for the Portner family for nearly thirty-five years, from the time the house was built up to the mid-1920's.

ooo

To look at pictures of Annaburg shortly after Portner had it built one can see how impressive the home looked. Unfortunately, pictures cannot begin to do justice to what this house must have looked like in person.

Imagine that you are one of Robert Portner's close friends and trusted employees. It is July of 1895 and you have been invited by your friend to attend a Fourth of July celebration at his new summer home in Manassas. After taking the train to Manassas, you board a carriage waiting for you at the station. The carriage heads through town down Battle Street. You come to an intersection with the newly completed Portner Avenue, where your carriage turns right. You travel for one block before coming to an intersection with Main Street and directly in front of you is the entrance to the Portner estate.

Standing before you are two large sandstone columns, each measuring seven feet in height and two and a half feet across, supporting a wrought-iron gate. Below the cap of each column is a six-inch section containing an inscription. Looking closely at each one, you see that the left column reads "R. Portner" and the right column reads "Annaburg." Flanking the columns and gate are lush, carefully manicured foliage of various kinds, which did not allow visitors much more than a glimpse as to what lie on the other side. Through the shrubbery and foliage you can see the gatehouse.

> On each side of the Main Street entrance to Portner Park is a Linden or lime tree which is delightfully fragrant when in full bloom as is the case this week. The linden is one of the common shade trees of European countries and, according to Mr. Thwaite, the gardener of the Portner premises, furnishes the best bloom known for fine honey.[71]

The shrubbery and gatehouse come together in such a way as to create a sense of intrigue and aura of mystery, causing any visitor to wonder what was hidden behind this screen. As a visitor, though, any curiosities you may have would soon be answered after passing through the gates. Your carriage travels along a crushed gravel drive, following it as it slowly begins to curve to the left. Soon, you see Annaburg slowly rise above the trees to the right of the drive while a large sandstone tower rises above the trees to your left.

After clearing the trees, you finally are able to see the breathtaking beauty of Annaburg up close. The dark red sandstone used in its construction gives a creative and decorative accent to the light-colored brick. Because of its durability, sandstone was used in key areas of the house, including the middle of the front façade, the columns of the front porch, window ledges, and the four corners of the house. All of this blended artistically and architecturally to make a very pleasing contract.

As you look at the house, your eyes begin to take in the details, from the Palladian window on the left side of the first floor to the one-over-one windows on the right side and across the second floor. In the center is a large porch, featuring three sets of doors leading from the house, and Ionic columns holding up a circular porch off of the second floor. Large wooden verandas, coming off the sides of the porch, sweep around both sides of the house and feature Tuscan columns and urns with potted plants on the railings. Looking up you see large dentaled brackets with crenalization running across the underside of the roofline that separates the second from the third floor. Across the third floor, partially hidden by a hipped roof, a large dormer punctures the roof in the center of each side, and each dormer is topped by its own gable roof. Five chimneys pierce the roof while a widow's walk runs along the peak.

After taking in the house as you came up the drive, you finally arrive. The drive splits with one path going beyond the house and another going under the porte-cochere. The driver pulls under the porte-cochere and you step out of the carriage. As you ascend the steps, the front door opens and the butler welcomes you to Annaburg.

After entering the house, you find yourself in the main hall, which stretches the length of the entire house. Walking across the stained and polished hardwood floors you admire the pilasters along the walls and the decorative plasterwork adorning the cornices. Having been built as a summer home, you see that the interior has been designed for easy cleaning. Mats, rugs, and Persian carpets can be found in various locations and as you pass by rooms, you see they are adorned with green or white wicker furniture.

As you proceed down the hall, you notice an alcove mid-way down the hall. Carved spindles along its curve stretch toward the ceiling where they stop at a large seashell carved into the top. The alcove features minimal decoration; it contains a marble pedestal and atop it is a statue of Venus rising from the half shell carved from limestone. Across the hall from the alcove is a large fireplace. It is simple in design and features three silver-plated mirrors built into the wall above it.

You pass the grand staircase and the butler leads you into the last room on the left of the hall, the study. The butler excuses himself, telling you that Mr. Portner will be down momentarily. After the butler has left, you begin to look around the room, noticing that it is tastefully decorated and lit by four windows, each a one-over-one with a transom window above. Three of these widows are along the side facing out onto a veranda while one window looks out upon the back yard.

As you are looking upon the back yard, Robert enters the room. He greets you warmly, happy that you are able to attend his celebration. After having exchanged pleasantries, Robert tells you that while waiting for the other guests to arrive he would like to show you around the rest of the house.

Upon leaving the study, he takes you across the hall into the east parlor. Here, two windows along the front wall light the room while additional light flows in from the ballroom to the right. To your left is a fireplace beside the doorway, which features intricate carvings and a single-pane mirror built in above. Gazing upwards you see that the ceiling has been adorned with murals: lively scenes of angels, cherubs, and landscapes in each corner and a large elegant circle in the middle.

And then you see it. Your eyes fall upon an oil painting of the Portner family. Immediately, you are in awe of the shear size of it, measuring twelve feet across and nine feet in height. Because of the size of the portrait, the wall does not have any windows and you later find out that the exterior of the wall is decorated with a large sandstone cutting of the Valaer family coat-of-arms, measuring approximately four feet wide by five feet tall. As you look at the painting closer, its beauty captures you. Painted in dark, rich colors, you see the three older sons with various musical instruments off to one side while the rest of the family, including Robert, flanks Anna, who is sitting holding the newborn Hilda. One of the twins, just shy of two years old at the time, sits on the ground at her mother's feet and holds a calendar that reads April 20, 1890.

After complimenting Robert on the portrait, he leads you into the ballroom. Looking around, you notice the three solid wood doorways you had seen when approaching the house, each one opening onto the large porch and overlooking the front lawn. A fireplace is situated on the opposite side of the room from the doors, but unlike the one in the east parlor, the ballroom fireplace has a large, mahogany-framed mirror above it and separate from the fireplace. Also, you notice that the ceiling features murals similar to those painted in the east parlor.

Rather than go into the drawing room immediately, Robert leads you out onto the front porch. As you stand in the shade of the second story porch, Robert tells you about the various species of plants he has brought to Annaburg. As you walk further out onto the porch you notice small, circular drains and make a point to ask Robert about it later.

In front you see a circular garden area surrounded by small boxwoods. Robert takes you down into the garden area where paths lead from the porch to the center. Here, you see a fountain with a statue of a boy riding a seahorse situated in the middle. A low sandstone wall surrounds the garden area and meets in the middle where a sandstone fence sits between some boxwoods. Trees and assorted potted plants decorate this area as well.

As you head back to the house, you see a sculpture of a lion's head that has been built into the front of the porch. When you ask Robert about it, he tells you that it is a fountain that runs off of rainwater. Water flows into the grates you had seen on the porch and through pipes built into the porch before flowing out of the lion's mouth into a seashell-shaped basin below.

Back inside, Robert leads you into the drawing room. Here you see an upright piano, similar to that in the portrait, and a number of other furnishings. With two windows on the side wall and a large Palladian window on the front, the room is flooded with sunlight. One striking feature to this parlor is the beautiful fireplace with its Italian marble mantle and large, silver-plated mirror above it, the same as in the east parlor.[72]

Robert then takes you upstairs to the second floor. Though this is considered the family's private area, being one of Robert's closest friends allows you the privilege to see this area. As you head up the staircase, you come to a landing. A large window allows you to gaze out onto the backyard where you can see the children riding their pony carts around a track. From this view, you begin to understand just how big Robert's estate really is. His property stretches for as far as you can see, literally. You ascend a few more stairs and Robert points out one of the home's bathrooms to your left.

When you walk onto the second floor, you see that there are nine rooms. Three line the front of the house, including the master bedroom in the center, and four smaller rooms are along the back. At each end of the hall is another room, each of which has its own porch. Robert tells you that in addition to him and his wife, his daughters stay on this floor as well.

You head back to the stairs and ascent to the third floor. Again, as you are climbing the stairs, you come to another landing which has another window looking out onto the backyard. When you reach the third floor, Robert points out another bathroom beside the stairs. On this floor there are eight rooms, seven of which are used as bedrooms. Like the floor below, three rooms line the front of the house and one on each end of the hall, but the back has three rooms instead of four. None of these rooms, however, have exterior porches. This is where Robert and Anna's sons reside, leaving one additional room for guests. The large room in the middle of the front is a game room, which contains a pool table.[73] You also notice a door between two of the bedrooms on the back wall, which you learn leads to a spacious attic.

Being a close friend of Robert's, you are able to ask him questions other people are not. He informs you that some of the servants, including the butler and cook, live in homes across from the estate on Main Street. When you ask about the family's personal servants, he tells you that they reside in the seven-room basement. You marvel at all of the modern efficiencies the house has and he tells you that he also had a series of bells installed that can be used to summon anyone in the house at any given time, be it a child or a servant.

Just then the butler arrives to tell Robert that more guests have arrived. The two of you return to the ground floor and greet everyone, some of whom you know from the brewery and others you find are friends of the family. Before long the dinner bell sounds and everyone retires into the dining room.

Upon entering the dining room, a wonderful feast lays before you on the table. Unlike the dark wood furniture throughout the upper floors, at the center of the dining room is a large, Golden Oak table with matching chairs. A fireplace, as decorated as any other in the house, is to your left while a Palladian window on the side wall and two large windows on the back wall allow plenty of light for a soft summer evening glow. To your right is a large china cabinet that has been built into the wall. All of the walls are adorned with decorative wood paneling that stretches from the floor up to a chair rail. Above the chair rail, the walls are papered and a mural flows across the ceiling.

As you take your place at the table, you notice the place settings are all equipped with all of the amenities any well to do family would have. The china, upon close inspection, is of a simple design. A large pink stripe is at the edge of every plate with a crest at the top. When you ask Robert what the crest is of, he tells you that it is the new Portner family crest, which he has designed himself. It features a shield with an American flag pattern upon it with two flags crossed behind it, the German and Swiss flags. After a sumptuous dinner, Robert invites you and the rest of his guests to the parlor while Anna entertains the wives in another parlor. Before long, the evening comes to an end, and after everyone has left, Robert shows you to your room.

ooo

Once construction of Annaburg was finally completed, Robert began to create the finest estate possible. He took the twenty acres of land that surrounded the house itself and planted a wide variety of species of both bushes and trees. In addition to any native trees already on the property, Portner had fir and pine trees shipped from the Black Forest of Germany and planted on the grounds. It has also been said that he had the state tree from all forty-four states in the Union in 1894 sent to Annaburg, providing that each variety could grow in Virginia's climate. At the center of all of this was a large duck pond. To the citizens of Manassas, this area was affectionately known as "Portner Park."

As time progressed, Portner continued to purchase even more land surrounding his estate. The fence line for his front yard was on the boundary between Manassas and Prince William County but of all the land that he purchased for Annaburg he never ventured into the town; he just continued to stretch further and further into the county. When he died in 1906, Annaburg totaled nearly 2,000 acres of land, beginning at Main Street and extending all the way out to Bull Run Creek. Given the size of his estate, it is amazing to think that he was able to utilize it all without repeating himself. Robert Portner must have been a man of incredible mental capacity!

Just to the west of the house, no more than fifty paces away, Portner had a large three-story sandstone tower erected. Though the origin of the tower design is not known, it is believed to be based off of the Tower of Rahden. According to Tim Dennee, this particular tower, located in the center of Portner's hometown, is a ruin today, but was originally a square in plan. Portner's tower, however, was circular. Though he only mentions it once in his diary, Robert tells of his joy upon seeing the tower for the first time since leaving Prussia. "Never in my life have I experienced such emotion and joy as when I saw the tower of Rahden [...]" (5)

It has never been determined what, if any, purpose the tower was built for. When Secretary Morton of the Department of Agriculture visited Manassas in 1895, he was given a tour of Annaburg, which included visiting the top of the tower. The *Washington Post* article declares the tower having been built as an observatory, "modeled after those strongholds of the Rhine [...] and from its turrets a wide view of the country for a sweep of full twenty miles can be seen."[74] Peter Valaer's commented on the tower in his memoirs, saying "Near the home was a stone castle resembling the castles on the Rhine, [it] was used mostly as a museum. Bits of cannon and cannon balls and other residue of the battlefield nearby which had been dug up by farm machinery."

Three years after construction on Annaburg began, and less than a year after it was finished, the estate was already being lauded for its beauty and many attractions. In May of 1895, a reporter for the *Fairfax Herald* wrote a column in the *Alexandria Gazette* telling about Portner's summer home.

> During a recent trip to Manassas we had a pleasant drive over Robert Portner's splendid estate. Mr. Portner has one of the finest estates in Virginia, which has been beautified and adorned beyond comparison with anything in this part of the State. Among other adornments he has made a number of lakes including a bathing pool upon the edge of which is a bathhouse. A number of swan gracefully move around one another, and there is a much larger lake upon which Mr. P. will shortly place a beautiful little steam yacht.[75]

It was on this larger pond that citizens of Manassas would go ice-skating in the winter months.

In addition to all of this, Annaburg featured several attractions at the rear of the house, including a small brick building, which measured twenty-five feet by twenty-five feet. This building served as the powerhouse, providing the estate with all of its electricity. Beyond that and to the right was the icehouse. Like the ones built for the brewery, though on a much smaller scale, the icehouse was an insulated building used for storing the ice used in the home's air-conditioning machine. During the winter months large blocks of ice were removed from the ponds and stored here for use during the summer months.

Behind Annaburg was a large stable and carriage house, which had an apartment above it where the horse trainer lived. It has been said in the past that Portner had a large variety of horses on his farm, which included Shetland ponies and "blooded horses, "mostly of the hunter type."[76] In keeping with his generous nature, Pornter would often host horse shows at Annaburg each year, of which he won his fair share of cups and medals.[77]

Near the stable was the kitchen garden, two acres of gardens that were surrounded by a large thorn hedge. Directly behind the powerhouse was a large rose garden, which had a heated greenhouse at its center. Annaburg also featured a 40-acre vineyard. On average, the vineyard would yield 100,000 pounds of grapes per season. Whatever Portner did not sell, he would use to make his own wine with. Some of his wine even won gold medals in competitions in Paris, France, and one at a World's Fair.

In addition to the vineyard, rose garden, and kitchen garden, Annaburg also contained a pear orchard. Like the vineyard, the pear orchard was very productive. When Secretary Morton visited Annaburg, one of his first comments was in regards to the orchard.

"Look there. Look at those pear trees. Did you ever see anything like it?" Here the Secretary led the way to a pear orchard, where the boughs of the trees were supported and propped to prevent them being torn limb to limb by the bending burdens of their own fruit. [...] Not only were the trees loaded, but the ground beneath them was strewn thick with those which had fallen.

"What will I do with them?" said Mr. Portner. "Nothing. There's nothing I can do this year, but use what I need, give away what I can, and let the rest rot on the ground. Some coming year I may be fixed to do something."

"What should be done," remarked Secretary Morton, as he gazed dubiously at the rich crop going to waste and loss, "is to take this fruit and evaporate it. Not dry it, mind you; but use these new fangled evaporators that preserve fruit as it were in a state of suspended animation. When you cook it months afterwards it is as if you cooked fresh fruit."[78]

It is not known whether or not Portner bought one of the "new fangled evaporators" Morton told him of, but being a man constantly intrigued by new technological advancements, one can easily assume that he did.

When traveling down Portner Avenue toward Liberia Avenue, there is a row of pine trees on the left-hand side. According to family members, this was known as Pine Row or Pine Mile, which led to a 30-acre fenced in piece of land. Heavily wooded, Portner kept many deer brought from Germany, in addition to those of the local variety, as well as quail, wild turkeys, and other various animals. The park also featured a small lake, stocked with bass, and a hunting lodge. Robert was known to host a number of deer- or quail-hunting parties here.

Liberia

Whenever Portner purchased land surrounding his estate, he would receive whatever amenities the land held. Most times there were no structures on the land as it was all farmland, but occasionally a house or other building would be included. One purchase yielded the farmhouse Windemere while another purchase included Fort Beauregard, one of the many Civil War fortifications scattered throughout the area surrounding Manassas. Every time he purchased a piece of land containing a historic site on it, Portner was sure to preserve the site as best as he could.

On April 30, 1890, Portner bought 377 acres for $10,000. He had bought the land from Elisha E. Meredith, a special commissioner in a chancery suit between the guardian of the Liberia estate and its administrator. Liberia, the family home of the Weir family, was of considerable historic value. In addition to the house, the land also contained the Weir family cemetery, which the family was able to retain control of.

Unlike most other buildings in Manassas, Liberia's history goes back far beyond the Civil War. Its origins can be traced back to 1724 when the land was a part of the vast amount of land patented by Robert "King" Carter. Carter owned as much as 90,000 acres in the present day counties of

Prince William, Fauquier, and Fairfax in the names of his sons, grandsons, and other family members. The 6,730-acre lower tract, called Lower Bull Run, was divided into twelve plantations, each of their names taken from a sign of the zodiac. Carter patented the "Libra" tract in the name of his son Robert. Later he would will the land to his own son, Councilor Robert Carter. Eventually, a 1,660-acre portion of the Libra tract ended up in the possession of Harriet Bladen Mitchell, a granddaughter of Councilor Carter's, who had married William J. Weir. Liberia, the only home from this tract that still retains its name, was built sometime around 1825 by Weir.

When the Civil War began in 1861, the first land battle was in Manassas. Though the actual battle took place several miles from Liberia, the house was seized in June by General P. G. T. Beauregard, Commander of the Confederate Army of the Potomac, and used as his headquarters. Beauregard kept his headquarters here through September of the same year. President Jefferson Davis visited the house on July 1 and, after the First Battle of Manassas, met with Generals J. E. Johnston and Beauregard for a Council of War.

A year after it was first taken over, Liberia was seized again for use as a headquarters, this time by Union General Irvin McDowell. President Abraham Lincoln and Secretary of War Edwin Stanton visited McDowell at Liberia on June 19,

1862. Two days later, Secretary of State William Seward visited Liberia as well. In November of the same year, Liberia was used one last time as a headquarters, this time by Union General Daniel E. Sickles as his troops guarded the Orange and Alexandria Railroad, a major supply line for Union forces. Throughout the course of the War, Manassas was burned twice, the first time in March of 1862 by General J. E. Johnston, and the second in August of the same year by General Stonewall Jackson. Liberia was the only house in the immediate area to survive both attacks.

Given these facts, one can understand why scholars believe that Liberia is the only building in the state, and quite possibly the country, to be visited by both Presidents during the war. After the Civil War ended, the house continued to pass down through the Weir family until it was sold to Portner.

Once Robert had bought the land, he converted it into a dairy farm, called the Valaer Creamery, by adding a large barn and several related outbuildings. It was near here that Portner also had a large stock farm. By the early twentieth century, Portner dairy products from Liberia had become quite common in Manassas. So as not to let the house sit empty, Portner allowed his farm manager to live in Liberia. With an area so rich in history and the sight of such extensive battles, the farm must have provided hours of enjoyment for the

Portner children. It is easy to image the kinds of souvenirs they found while playing here! Through the use of tenant farmers, dairy production continued at Liberia until 1947.

Later Days of Annaburg

As the Portner family continued to grow, they enjoyed many good times at Annaburg. In 1903, the family moved to the estate and converted it into their full-time home. In converting the home, Portner added yet another improvement of "modern technology," steam heat. The family continued to live in Annaburg for three more years before Robert's death in 1906. Afterwards, Anna continued to live in the house while most of the children lived in Washington.

During the last six years of Anna's life, there was one event that comes to mind as one of the most memorable in the recent history of Manassas. In June of 1911, Manassas celebrated the 50th anniversary of the Battle of Bull Rub, as the Union called it, or the Battle of First Manassas, as the Confederates knew it. That year, George Carr Round, a veteran of the war who had relocated to Manassas, organized and chaired the Peace Jubilee of 1911. For the event, President William Howard Taft and other dignitaries came to Manassas to speak. At noon, both Union and Confederate veterans lined up on the Manassas Battlefield facing one another and, on a given signal, approached the other side and shook hands. This historic event is believed to be the only organized event where survivors of both sides of a battle met and exchanged friendly pleasantries.

President Taft was supposed to speak outside of the Prince William County courthouse that afternoon, followed by a luncheon at the Round home and dinner at the Portner home. Unfortunately, due to inclement weather, Taft and only a fraction of his entourage arrived in Manassas several hours late. Taft did give his speech to the crowd, but unfortunately, had to leave shortly thereafter to return to Washington.

After Anna died in 1912, the house continued to be used as a permanent home. Paul and Herman used Annaburg as their residences while retaining their own apartments in Washington. In 1912, a month before his mother's passing, Oscar and his new bride moved into Windemere, where they continued to live through the early part of 1920. With Anna's death, the children now had control over Annaburg and other land holdings in Manassas.

Rather than risk conflicts over what to do with the land, they created the Portner Realty Company in that same year. On September 10, 1912, a charter was signed creating the company, which named Paul Portner as the President and Robert M. Heth as Secretary and Treasurer. It also named Alvin, Paul, Oscar, David M. Pitts, and Heth as members of the Board of Directors. According to the charter, the corporation's offices would be located in Manassas and that the purpose of the corporation was:

> [...] to buy, sell, exchange, operate and develop farm and other lands; all kinds of livestock, poultry, crops, dairy and general produces of every description; all kinds of farming machinery and implements and also to manufacture, buy, sell, and trade generally in such articles as may be manufactures from any raw materials which may be handled in carrying on the business therein described.[79]

The charter also set the capital stock for the corporation at $30,000, maximum and minimum, and to be divided into shares of $100 each; the duration of the corporation to be unlimited and "the amount of real estate to which the holdings of the corporation at any times is to be limited to five thousand acres."[80]

In 1913, the ten surviving Portner children took the first step towards dissolving private ownership of their father's real estate holdings in Manassas. On December 8, the heirs signed a deed, which conveyed six lots in the town to the Portner Realty Company. The six lots were located on Main

Street, across the street from the Annaburg estate. While most of the land was vacant, two lots did have buildings on them. As time went on, the heirs continued to convey more land to the Portner Realty Company, which would later sell the land to various people in town.

By 1920, James F. Birkett served as the farm manager for the Portner estate. Once is had become apparent that Oscar's family would no longer be using Annaburg as a full-time residence, the task of finding Birkett additional help was set about. By March 12, 1920, Albert Roseberry had sold his farm in Brentsville to move to the Portner estate and become the assistant manager under Birkett. By April 2, Roseberry had moved onto the estate and had assumed his duties. In later years, when Annaburg was abandoned, Roseberry became the manager and caretaker of the estate.

After Oscar moved his family to Washington, no one used the estate full-time anymore. As a result, Annaburg was once again outfitted as a summer home. From here on out, Annaburg was used for one week each summer and left in the hands of the caretaker for the rest of the year.

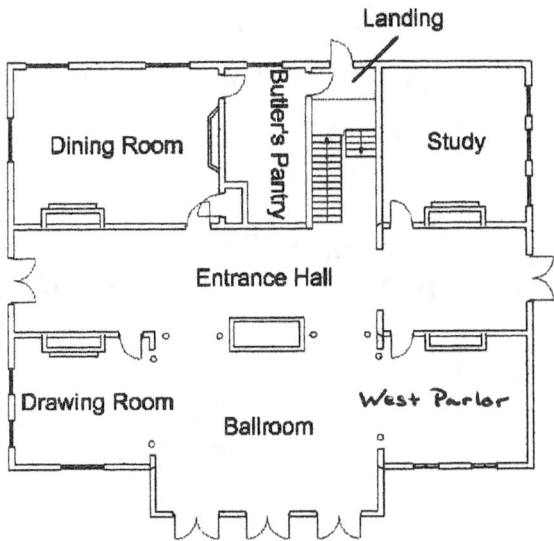

Annaburg - First Floor

Inventory of Annaburg

From October 27, 1904 to March 17, 1917, inventories were taken of the possessions at Annaburg, Liberia, and Yorkshire, and recorded in a leather-bound book. The inventory was not limited to just furnishings, but to land holdings, equipment, farm animals, and other related items. Below is a partial listing of the book's contents, as provided by the descendant whose possession the book now lies within. The list is the inventory taken for Annaburg on March 17, 1917. The meaning behind the numbering system used in this inventory is not known, so it has been recorded as it appears in the book.

First Floor

Entrance Hall	Study
Mirror	Portrait of Rbt. Portner
Rugs/mats (9)	Portrait of man
Carved suite (3pc)	Small pictures (2)
Brass Stand	Ornaments (2)
Wicker chairs (2)	Desk & chair
Portieres	Typewriter
Upholstered suit (5pc)	Waste paper basket
Inlaid stand	Table
Victrola	Cloth
Records	Carpet
Carved stand	Covered chair
Bronze bowl	Roll-top desk
Clock	Chair

Entrance Hall cont'd
Brass lamp
Vases & pots (5)
Round table
Fire guard
Marble clock &
　ornaments
Photographs
Marble shell &
　figurine
Round table
Hat rack
Seat
Painting by Boker

Drawing Room
Ornaments (3)
Music closet
Marble of child
Quilt furniture (20pc)
Fender brass
Piano & stool
Ornaments, photos (23)
Clock
Box
Rugs, mats, etc. (8)
Embroidered tablecloth
Leopard
Carved writing table
Pictures:
　Woodland
　Mountains
　Baby

Dining Room
Table
Chairs (5)
Chairs (9)
Fire guard
Dining wagon
Sideboard
Screen
Glass closet & contents
Carpet
Silver
Glass closet & contents
Oil painting (large)
Oil painting (small)
Candlesticks, soup
　tureen, tray, etc.

Ballroom
Silver cups
Green furniture (9pc)
Table
Carpet
Clock & bronzes
Fire iron & fender set (2)
Table

Butler's Pantry
Silverware
Icebox
China
Table
Sundries
Chair

Drawing Room cont'd
Girl
Woman's head
Portrait of lady
Portrait of family
Pedestal
Portieres (4 sets)
Brass stand
Foot stools (2)
Marble stand
Pillows (3)

Kitchen (basement)
Utensils, etc.
Range

First Landing
Mats, carpets, etc. (4)
Furniture (6 pieces)
Chair
Bookstand
Music stool
Piano
Pictures (7)
Bookcase

Second Floor
(Beginning of unidentifiable numbering system)

Room 1
Mirror
Vessel
Brush

Room 2
Portiere
Towel rail
Chair
Mat
Corner cupboard
Folding chair

Room 3
Basket
Towel bar
Mat

Room 10
Mats (4)
Carpet
Bookcase
Chairs (4)
Basket table (2)
Couch
Dressing table inlaid
Dressing table
Working desk
Double bed
Clock

Room 11
Chairs (2)
Couch
Bureau

Room 3 cont'd
Mirror

Room 4
Brass bed
Sewing machine
Chairs (4)
Bureau
Carpet
Folding chair

Room 15
Chairs (5)
Carpet & rugs
Settee
Working desk
Table
Table
Dressing table
Basket
Ornaments (4)
Pictures
Dressing table
Bed
S_____ table

Room 23
Mat
Crib
Chairs (3)
Small tables (2)
Wicker stand
Dressing table

Room 11 cont'd
Dressing table
Bed
Pictures (2)
Clock

Room 12
Pictures, photo, etc.
Ornaments (4)
Wicker box
Screen

Room 18
Chairs (2)
Carpet
Dressing table
Wardrobe
Writing table
Bed

Room 20
Chairs (4)
Bookstand
Dressing table
Writing desk
Couch
Bureau
Pictures (16)
Table
Mat, carpet
Drawing by Hurlburt
Bed

Room 23 cont'd
Bed
Pictures (11)

Third Floor

Bathroom
Chair
Mirror
Towel rail

Bedroom
Bed
Mats
Dressing table
Bureaus (2)
Chairs (2)
Mirror

Room 2
Dressing table
Chairs (2)
Working desk
Pictures (5)
Mats

Room 6
Dressing table
Chair
Single beds (2)
Wash stand
Hat rack

Room 3
Chairs (3)
Dressing table
Beds (2)
Wash stand
Table
Writing desk
_____ (closet)
Chair
Hat stand
Pictures (5)

Store Room
Hopeless, ens--- (void)

Room 5
Bed
Bureau
Chair
Wardrobe
Bookcase

Room 7
Suite (4pc)
Settee

Chairs (14)

Attic
Chairs (14)
Pedestals
Ornaments
Desks

Grounds

Outside
Dog house

Green house
Plants

Engine House
1 pump

Strickler House
Tenant House (Nailor lot)

Annaburg
Main house
Engine house
Greenhouse
Automobile house
Lodge house
Tower
_____ barn
Horse barn
_____ house
3 dwelling house
Barn
  Horses
  2 sets single
  2 sets div.
  2 _____ Phaeton
  3 wagons
  8 ponies

Liberia
Brick house
Large barn
Back barn
Silo
Horse barn
Corn house
Boarding house
Sheep _____
Dairy house
Small out buildings
Tenant house

Yorkshire
1 barn
1 corn house
1 tenant dwelling
1 dwelling house
1 dwelling house

Weems (Windemere)
1 dwelling house
1 barn

Mill, corn house, barn
Out buildings

Endnotes

[58] Prince William County Deed Book 33, page 557.
[59] William J. Weir was the son of Robert Carter Weir.
[60] June Rabatin, *Count the Ties to* Manassas, 25.
[61] Charles A. Mills, *Echoes of Manassas*, 26.
[62] Ibid. 26-7.
[63] *Potomac News*, Friday, April 25, 1975: C-1.
[64] "Prince William Notes." *Alexandria Gazette.* 9 July 1892.
[65] "Manassas Notes." *Alexandria Gazette.* 25 July 1892.
[66] "Manassas Notes." *Alexandria Gazette.* 8 October 1892.
[67] *Washington Post*, 22 Aug 1895.
[68] The discovery of Civil War graves in and around Manassas within thirty or forty years of the Civil War was not uncommon. When the Manassas Agricultural School was built in 1908, several Civil War graves were discovered.
[69] *Manassas Journal Messenger*
[70] Peter Valaer memoirs.
[71] *Manassas Democrat.* June 20, 1912.
[72] There was an extensive use of leaded and stained glass in the windows, so curtains were not necessary on the ground floor, though it has been said by some that the house did indeed have them. The woodwork throughout the house, like the floors, was stained while the walls and ceilings, in order to help lighten the rooms and make them appear larger, were adorned with bright, vibrant colors. Judging from family photographs, some of which showed partial interiors of other Portner residences, it can be assumed that the walls of Annaburg featured textured wall coverings, commonly used in decorating Victorian-era homes.
[73] In Peter Valaer's memoirs, he recalls staying at Annaburg one summer and one evening he and the Portner sons all went to sleep in the game room.
[74] *Washington Post*, 22 Aug 1895.
[75] *Alexandria Gazette*, 31 May 1895.
[76] Peter Valaer memoirs.

[77] Starting in the 1940's, the Bull Run Hunt Club would host their own horse shows, which would be held on the grounds of Annaburg.
[78] *Washington Post*, 22 Aug 1895.
[79] Prince William County Charter Book 1, p. 193
[80] Prince William County Charter Book 1, p. 194

A sketch of Annaburg, the tower and the gatehouse as appeared on the front page of a Manassas newspaper in September 1904

A colored postcard view of Annaburg, postally used in 1910.
The text reads
""Annaburg" residence of Mrs. Robt. Portner, Manassas, VA"

A photo of the front circle of Annaburg taken from the second floor porch. The photo originally appeared in a 1915 Manassas high school yearbook, and was reprinted in a Manassas newspaper.

A postcard view of a snow-covered Annaburg during the winter, looking up the front drive towards the house. Date is unknown.
Courtesy of Anna Schoellkopf Lacher

Photo of a statue that graced the steps of the front porch of Annaburg. It has been said that these statues held "torches" that were lit by electricity.
Courtesy of Peggy E. M. Portner

A view of the back corner of Annaburg. Seated in the horse-drawn cart are Molly D. Portner with her infant son, John A. D. Portner in her lap and an unidentified boy beside them.
Courtesy of Peggy E. M. Portner

Annaburg in its prime, complete with potted plants and trees on the front lawn. Here, Molly Portner and two other unidentified women watch over Molly's son John.
Courtesy of Peggy E. M. Portner

Louis Allwine with a pony cart in front of Annaburg sometime in the 1930's.
Courtesy of Barbara Portner Whitbeck

The carriage port on the side of Annaburg. This piece was removed when the house was converted into a nursing home.
Courtesy of Peggy E. M. Portner

A view of the front of the fountain in the front lawn of Annaburg. It appears to be a boy riding a sea horse. Behind it is John AD Portner and his mother, Molly.
Courtesy of Peggy E. M. Portner

Fountain-Side View
Courtesy of Peggy E. M. Portner

A close-up of the lion's head fountain located on the front of the front porch of Annaburg.
Courtesy of Peggy E. M. Portner

Postcards of the Portner Tower, a three-story sandstone structure located in the front yard of Annaburg It was built the same time as Annaburg (1892) and torn down in 1979.

View of the pond within the 30-acre fenced in deer park at Annaburg.
Courtesy of Peggy E. M. Portner

Postcard of the Annaburg Gatehouse. Given the attire of the workers and the lush foliage, it can be assumed that this was taken sometime between 1895 and 1920 while the family still lived there.
Courtesy of Henley S. Portner

Robert Joseph Portner (a.k.a. Robert Portner III) and his brother, John A. D. Portner (sons of Oscar and Molly Portner) standing at Fort Beauregard. The fort was one used during the Civil War and was part of the Annaburg estate.
Courtesy of Peggy E. M. Portner

Photo taken of Liberia in 1941. When Portner bought the estate, he converted Liberia into a dairy farm and the caretaker of the estate would live in this house. After it was sold, the new owners (Jack and Hilda Breeden) demolished the farm buildings and converted Liberia into their own home.
Courtesy of Henley S. Portner

A child sitting in a chair on the front porch of the hunting lodge. This lodge was located within the deer park at Annaburg. In the distance can be seen structures at Liberia, which Portner converted into a dairy farm.
Courtesy of Peggy E. M. Portner

8

A Dynasty Ends, A New Era Begins

By 1920, the Portner children had married and moved away from Manassas. Being involved in busy social lives, they had lost interest in the family farm, with the exception of occasional weeklong visits in the summer. When Molly Portner returned from Europe in 1928, she found an Annaburg she barely knew. During her absence, nearly all of the furnishings at Annaburg had been sold at public auction. The family had come down before the auction to remove any personal items that they wanted, though no one had informed Molly of this. The auction marked the last time that the family would gather at Annaburg as a whole. Once the furnishings had been sold, the house sat vacant, its doors and windows unlocked, and left to fall into disuse and face the wrath of vandals and nature. In 1931, however, the estate received a temporary reprieve.

The Piedmont Dairy Festival

During the Depression, local diary farmers and businessmen began thinking of a way to advertise and promote the dairy industry of the Piedmont region. In the autumn of 1931, businessmen of northern Virginia unveiled the Piedmont Dairy Festival. Sponsorship came from eleven nearby counties, Washington, D.C., and the cities of Alexandria and Fredericksburg. Since Prince William County was located in the "heart" of the participating municipalities, and since Manassas was one of the more prosperous towns therein, it was decided that the festival would be held there.

Over the next five years, Manassas resident Catherine "Kitty" Arrington would lead spectators through the festivals as the emcee. Although the schedule varied slightly from year to year, each festival followed the same basic format. Taking place on a weekend in late-September or early-October, the festivities would begin on Sunday morning with a performance by the United States Marine Corps Band. The coronation of the Queen of the Piedmont Dairy Festival, crowned by the Governor of Virginia or another dignitary, followed. Upon being crowned, each Queen assumed the successive title of Regina (I, II, III, etc.).

Following the Queen's coronation, a pageant was performed, followed by a luncheon for the Queen and her court. Ellen Turberville, a native of Manassas, would perform a dance to open and close the pageant each year. After lunch, the grand feature parade, "The Milky Way," made its way through the streets of Manassas. The parade featured magnificent floats, displays of all kinds, and bands. The day culminated with the Queen's Ball, located in the Manassas High School gymnasium, and was attended by the Queen, her court, and anyone who could afford the price of a ticket. When the festival had been created and planned, it was decided that the grounds of Annaburg, specifically in front of a then ivy-entombed Portner Tower, would be used for the coronation of the Queen, the Marine Corps Band performance, and pageant. Annaburg itself was used as a staging and dressing area for many of the performers and maidens within the pageant.

Unfortunately, the Great Depression affected things in ways greater than anyone could have ever imagined. Because of the economic strains caused by the Depression, the Piedmont Dairy Festival was forced to discontinue after only six years. Each year, the festival would bring large crowds and publicity to the area, the likes of which this small farming community had not seen since the 1911 Peace Jubilee. While the concept was a good one, the Festival did not yield a sold enough base during the Depression-era years to build such an event upon.

Because the actual Festival took place in Manassas, the town covered almost all of the expenses, incurring a debt of nearly $3,000 each year. A few weeks after the 1936 festival ended, the local newspaper announced that the 1937 Piedmont Dairy Festival had been postponed because Manassas could no longer afford to carry the burden of the expenses and no one else had come forward offering to host the festival. Organizers had hoped to continue it in 1938, allowing Manassas time to recover from its debt from the prior festivals or to allow time to find another city to host the event, but again, no one came forward.

By the time the Depression came to an end and money was available to resume the festival, the dairy industry was not as prominent as it had been in the past. More importantly, though, too many people were preoccupied with the United States' participation in World War II. Though it has been over seventy years since the festival was discontinued, many people can still remember the Queen's court, the crowning of the Queen, the lavish setting of the festival with large trees in the background, and the Portner Tower covered in ivy as it loomed over the trees. Etta Portner Meredith, whose daughter Sylvia was a maiden in the 1932 festival, once remarked to Ethyl M. Byrd that her father "would be happy to know that some use was being made of the Mansion by the Town's people."[81]

Religion & Ceremonies

While there has been no concrete evidence as to what religion the Portner family practiced, items such as marriage records and burial places suggest that the family was most likely Episcopalian. There is no proof that the family was a member of any particular church in Manassas, but records of their contributions to and participation in the community are plentiful.

The family's beautifully sculpted land was a favorite strolling place for local citizens, especially on Sundays after church. Years after Annaburg had been abandoned, Pastor John D. Edens of the Manassas Baptist Church used the farm in a sermon, comparing the empty and desolate building to that of a wasted life. Several people visited Annaburg later that afternoon just to see what Edens had been talking about.

Additionally, flowers and greenery from Annaburg's greenhouse were used in various events throughout the community. For example, when Effie Nelson and Albert Spieden were married, the floral decorations for the service came from the Annaburg greenhouse. The Portner family even opened up the use of their estate to the religious community. While the ponds at Annaburg were a favorite spot for ice-skating and swimming, the Deer Park pond was a popular place for baptisms, including the First Baptist Church, Manassas' oldest African American congregation.

The Last Years of Annaburg

The end of the Piedmont Dairy Festival in 1936 brought about the end of any organized or civil activities at Annaburg. Since the house was empty and the family scattered, no one wanted to use the estate anymore. Kenneth Lyons, a local resident of Manassas, can still vividly remember playing on the estate as a child:

> By this time I don't think any member of the family was still in residence. I hope not, for any number of times I entered the house through the vents at basement level (I think these were vents of an early type of air-conditioning!) and as Uncle Jared (caretaker) had told me many times, "Kenneth, you can play on the grounds, but don't go in the house and stay off the tower!" But the fascination was too great. I remember the huge family portrait in oil – it must have been nine by twelve feet in size – in the magnificent gilded

frame, hanging on the south wall of the dining room, the room on the extreme right of the first floor. The interior was then still very sound and the ceiling art, so very beautiful, was intact. As the picture of Annaburg shows, the life-size statues are in place, still holding their lamps. I can recall only once seeing the fountain in full display. The gravel driveways of tiny, white stones were in excellent condition and the north portico for the carriages was waiting for someone to arrive. I try not to remember what the condition of the house was when I came back from World War II.[82]

From 1936 to 1947, Annaburg was subjected to vandals, the pranks of teenage children, and weathering. While the estate did have a number of caretakers over the years, it seemed that only minimal upkeep was performed during this time. Since all of the doors and windows sat wide open, there was no need for anyone to break into the house. Local teenagers would enter it and remove anything and everything of interest, including brass hinges, locks, and old books. During World War II, a time when copper was particularly scarce and valuable, Annaburg suffered her greatest damage. Vandals went in and ripped the copper piping from Portner's air-conditioning system out of the walls.

Since no one used the estate anymore, the Portner family considered Annaburg to be more of a liability than an asset. Aside from creating the Portner Realty Corporation, not much else was done with the farm until the mid-1940's. In late 1946, Manassas businessman I. J. "Jack" Breeden approached the family and offered to purchase the estate from them.

Over the next four months, negotiations over the sale took place and on February 7, 1947, the *Manassas Messenger* announced that the last Portner heir had signed the contract of sale. The transfer of property took place on May 20 when Breeden and his wife Hilda, Portner heirs, and representatives from trust companies in lieu of deceased heirs and minors, all signed a deed.[83] Breeden bought Annaburg from the family for the price of $215,000. Heirs involved in the transaction included Elsa Portner Humes, Anna Portner Flood, Etta Portner Meredith, John A. D. Portner, Robert J. Portner, and Robert Portner Koehler. Breeden did not have all of the money to pay the Portner's immediately, but as soon as he gained control of the estate, he sold the 377-acre Yorkshire tract for $75,000 to pay the family the rest of what he owed. Thus the dissolving of Annaburg had officially begun.

With the sale of the family estate, the heirs dissolved the Portner Realty Corporation on September 1 of the following year. On April 1, 1949, the remaining land the family owned in Manassas was sold. All of the land involved in this sale, four lots total, was sold to C. Lacey Compton, a local attorney in Manassas.

The first lot consisted of land bounded by Main Street to the east, Portner Avenue on the north, Battle Street to the west, and land owned by Mr. Sigman on the south. This piece of land was composed of the "Slaugh Lot" as described in the deed from James Birkett to Anna Portner dated on October 6, 1906.[84] The parcel also consisted of portions of land acquired by Robert Portner from Arthur Robinson[85] and Rebecca M. Weir.[86]

The second lot was situated on the northwest corner of the intersection of Portner Avenue and Main Street. Main Street bounded it on the east, Portner Avenue on the south, Battle Street on the west, and the "Penn Land" on the north. On Occasion, the parcel had been known as the "Arthur Robinson Lot."[87]

The third lot, known as the "Weir Lot" was bounded by Portner Avenue on the south, Battle Street on the east, West Street on the west, and the "Stover Land," later known as the Northwest Manassas Subdivision, on the north. Portner had bought this land from E. Wood Weir.[88]

The fourth and final lot was known as the "Capital Construction Company Lot." The deed did not give street boundaries, but rather listed the boundaries by specific coordinates as follows:

> Beginning at a point south of Railroad and east of Grant Avenue, thence with said avenue S. 2 ¼° E. 206 feet to a point on the north side of South Street [Prince William Street today], thence with said street N. 86° E. 89 feet to the corner of Tillett (not Town of Manassas) thence with last mentioned line N. 3 ¼° W. 207 feet to the south side of Railroad, thence with said railroad S. 84° W. 86 feet to the beginning [...]"[89]

This particular lot contained approximately 18,062 square feet and had been sold by John W. Wilconxin to Robert Portner through a deed dated July 8, 1902.

Now that Breeden owned Annaburg he began to divide the land into individual parcels, each with no less than a seventy-five foot frontage. Sales typically went to private investors who soon began to build housing developments, shopping centers, and other structures across the vast landscape. Through this process, the subdivisions of

Annaburg, Yorkshire, Yorkshire Acres, Liberia, Deer Park, Landmark Square, and Musket Hills began to emerge. Aside from these subdivisions, the City of Manassas Park also began to emerge and was incorporated into a city in 1957.

Before long, traces of Annaburg's beautiful and glorious past began to slowly disappear. Windemere had burned down sometime in the late-1940's and its lot was soon cleared to make room for another housing development. The estate's lush rose and vegetable gardens, now dead and weed-infested, were torn out and covered with a shopping center that now includes a Hollywood Video store. The carriage house was sold, razed, and until recently, a Texaco station occupied the site. Even the Civil War earthworks of Fort Beauregard, which Breeden promised would remain untouched, were destroyed to make way for the Manassas Shopping Center. Today, a Bowl America sits atop the site of the actual fort.

As the Breedens sold off the estate, they kept two particular parcels for themselves. After buying the estate, the couple had their choice of where to live. While Annaburg had been a much bigger and nicer home than Liberia, it had been vacant and heavily vandalized, thus needing many repairs. Liberia, on the other hand, had been continually lived in by the estate caretaker. Even if the Breedens had decided to repair Annaburg for their use, the house was simply too large for just the two of them. Once they moved into Liberia, they began renovating the house and grounds for their residence, including the installation of modern conveniences such as hot water, heat, and air conditioning.

Mr. and Mrs. Breeden continued to live in Liberia until 1986, at which time they donated the historic house and its five surrounding acres to the City of Manassas. When they donated it to the City, the Breedens made an agreement with the City that should it ever decide to sell the house, a member of the Breeden family would have the first option to buy it. The house is currently a part of the Manassas Museum system and is currently being restored for use as a house museum. As early as 1994, the first steps were taken towards achieving this goal when the front portico, added by the Breedens in the early 1950's, was removed.

After deciding to keep Liberia for themselves, the Breedens also chose to keep the site of the deer park. Mr. Breeden had the pond filled in and removed any remaining traces of the burned hunting lodge from the land, and from here construction soon began on what would become the Deer Park Apartment complex. The first sectioned opened in 1965 as the other sections continued to be built, the last one opening in 1968. After the Breedens donated Liberia to the City, they moved into Deer Park and concentrated on running the complex. After I. J. Breeden's death in 1991, Mrs. Breeden continued to live in and run the complex until her own death in 2000.

As the former Portner estate was subdivided and sold, and new homes built, it was only a matter of time before new roads were built. The three ponds in front of Annaburg were filled in and paved over. Today, Irving Street runs across what used to be the middle of the three ponds. As new roads were built, Breeden picked names which reflected the history and its people of the area, including Portner Avenue, Mathis Avenue, Irving Street, Jackson Street (both named for Mr. Breeden), Maple Avenue, Reb Yank Drive, Carriage Lane, and Weir Street.

The Portner Gatehouse

During the time the Portner family lived at Annaburg, the gardener, Mr. Bouffet, lived in the gatehouse with his wife and two sons, Albert and Julius. When it was built, the gatehouse contained four rooms, but no solid walls (each interior wall had a doorway). The four rooms consisted of a bedroom, sitting room, living room, and dining room. The Bouffet family continued to live here during his tenure as gardener, and it can be assumed that successive gardeners lived here until the family stopped using the estate.

By the 1940's, Albert Roseberry was still serving as caretaker of Annaburg, residing in Liberia as previous caretakers had done before him. By this time, however, a full-time gardener was not needed, thus leaving the gatehouse vacant. When Albert's son John married, he and his new bride had nowhere to live, so Albert let the new couple move into the empty building. Here, John and his wife raised their first two children, Jackie and Jean. Before long the house became too small for the family and they moved in 1945. From then until 1947, the gatehouse sat empty once again.

As Annaburg was being divided up, the gatehouse became separated from the manor house. Two years after Breeden acquired the Portner estate, the gatehouse and the half-acre of land that it sat on was sold to Grace Bradford, who moved into the house with her sister. As the Bradfords continued to live there, they saw many changes to the area around their little home. To extend Portner Avenue beyond Main Street, the posts and front gates had to be removed as well as the shrubbery and greens surrounding them. The large columns holding up the gates were moved to the Manassas City Cemetery and places at the entrance to the Confederate plot. It was at this time that the six-inch sections, which bore the inscriptions "R. Portner" and "Annaburg" were removed. One set of smaller columns was moved, though only slightly as they remained at the intersection of Portner Avenue and Main Street, while the other set was presumably disposed of.

Once Ms. Bradford bought the gatehouse, she continued to live there until 1975, at which time the property was sold to William and Mary Jo Detwiler of Manassas. At the time of the sale, the house was in need of some dire repairs and upgrades, and the Detwilers saw that the best job was done. A back porch added in 1900 had since been enclosed and had a kitchen and bath added, but had become rotted and was in need of immediate replacement. Through Carter & Sons of Manassas, the Detwilers had the old addition removed and a new one put on in its place. This new addition contained a new kitchen, bath, and walk-in closet. Restoration Services, Inc. of Maryland was asked to come in and replace and re-point the mortar that had worn down between the brick joints.

In addition to making structural improvements, the Detwilers had to make the house habitable by modern standards. Wall-to-wall carpeting was installed as well as central air conditioning and heating, and electrical rewiring. Prior to this the house was fitted with the original five amps of electricity first installed in the house. Presently, Mr. and Mrs. Detwiler continue to own and rent the house, though they have since moved from Manassas.

Unlike Annaburg, however, the exterior of the gatehouse has never been painted or altered, with the exception of the addition on the back. The house even features original locks and weight & pulley systems on the windows, as well as two original miniature chandelier light fixtures from 1892. The gatehouse, along with the small original columns on the southwest corner of Portner Avenue and Main Street, help to serve as a constant reminder to those who can remember that here is where the Portner family's estate began.

Annaburg: A New Beginning

From 1947 to 1960, Annaburg continued to sit empty as the land around her slowly began to be developed. Sitting vacant, the house continued to be subjected to constant vandalism. With a new era of children growing up, Annaburg began to suffer a new kind of abuse. Rather than having pipes ripped from her walls and possessions and fixtures stolen from the house, it started to see graffiti written on the walls, some of which still remains in the attic today. Teenagers would often use the house as a refuge for underage drinking and smoking, and vagrants often sought shelter in the vacant structure. Some people can remember going in as young children and finding the remnants of such illegal activities: cigarettes, beer bottles and cans, and even small circles where homeless people had attempted to keep warm by lighting a small fire. With wooden floors throughout the house, as well as significant wood paneling, it is a wonder and a miracle that the house never burned down!

In 1960 Annaburg received a new lease on life. Breeden sold the house and the seven and a half acres of land surrounding it to a private investor, John Kennedy Sills of Alexandria, who had plans to turn the house into a nursing home. For two years, the house and land continued to sit empty, but in 1962 construction began to convert the mansion into what would ultimately be the center portion of a nursing home facility. Supervised by J. Richard Waddell of Manassas, construction continued over the next three years as portions of the house were modified, torn down, or built upon. At a cost of $2.6 million, three-story brick wings were built on either side of the house. Sills felt that the bright red brick of the extensions did not fit well with the tan brick and red sandstone of the house, so he had the mansion painted white. Unfortunately, people of Manassas would never be able to appreciate the house for its real beauty or see its original colors ever again.

Windows on either side of the house were closed and turned into bookshelves and the porte-cochere was torn down to make way for the west wing. The wooden verandas that had swept across the sides and front of the house were also removed for the wings, as well as the two porches on the back. The builders did preserve one part of the house, though. On the wall in which the large family portrait hung, the outside featured Anna Valaer Portner's family crest, carved in sandstone. When the east wing was built, plans for the hallways that ran between the wing and the house allowed for a portion of the wall to show the crest, which can still be seen today.

The interior of the house underwent drastic changes, as well. One of he most noticeable changes to the first floor was a new wall that was built to close off the staircase. Less noticeable changes were two new bathrooms added off the hall beside the staircase and the removal of the dumbwaiter from the dining room. The basement was, by all intents and purposes, gutted and redesigned to feature a modern staff kitchen and snack room, beauty parlor, and pharmacy. Beneath the east wing, a large industrial kitchen was built to accommodate the residents of the new facility, as well as a dining room. Beneath the west wing, physical therapy facilities were built, along with maintenance and laundry services. The second floor of the mansion was redesigned to allow for small apartments, which included individual bathrooms, while the third floor was designed for offices.

Aside from structural changes, other alterations were made as well. Because of the damage to walls when the copper pipes were torn out during Annaburg's vacancy, the walls had to essentially be rebuilt. On the ground floor, most of the new walls were wallpapered, though those in the dining room were painted. The interior columns that separated the parlors from the ballroom were painted blue to compliment the cream colored walls. The hardwood floors within the parlors and ballroom were left alone, but the flooring in the main hall was covered in faux marble tiles. Additionally, of the three sets of doors that led to the front porch, only the center remained as a doorway; the other two were redesigned as large windows.

Louis B. Armstrong, a graduate of the University of Georgia's School of Hospital Administration, was hired to lead the facility as its Head Administrator. His wife Margaret, a graduate of the same school, was hired as the Director of Nursing. Before coming to Manassas, Mr. and Mrs. Armstrong had designed nursing home facilities in Weston and Smithers, West Virginia.

On February 18, 1965, the nursing home officially opened, though only a portion of one wing was actually completed. With 29 rooms available, the Manassas Manor nursing home admitted its first patient, Robert C. Morrow, an 83-year-old veteran of the Spanish-American War.

Hailed as one of the most modern facilities in the area, Manassas Manor was able to serve and house nearly two hundred fifty new residents. To serve and aid so many people, between 95 and 120 new employees were hired. The facility also featured some of the most modern treatment methods available for disabled or injured persons, including occupational basic therapy departments. For the residents, a beauty salon and barbershop, a party room, auditorium, and six solariums were added. Two elevators were installed in each wing to eliminate stairway hazards and make floors accessible to the disabled. Later that fall, construction was completed on the entire facility.

Over the next fourteen years, Manassas Manor continued to function without any apparent troubles. In the 1970's, the nursing home was graced with one of its most famous residents when Robert Joseph Portner, a grandson to Robert Portner who also went by Robert Portner III, came to the facility. Quite popular, he continued to live there until his death from colon cancer in 1984.

In 1978, Sills decided to sell the Manassas Manor nursing home, but it was not until April of the following year that the facility was sold to the Prince William Hospital Corporation. When the new administration took over control, they decided to rename the facility. Honoring and commemorating the past, the hospital decided to change the name of the facility to Annaburg Manor, a name the facility still keeps today.

Portner Tower

While Sills' ownership and running of Manassas Manor had started off strong, his policies and actions soon became unsuitable for that of a nursing home and his employees had become increasingly unhappy with him. Depending on who you talk to, one could argue that his greatest downfall came when he made the decision to tear down the Portner Tower shortly before he sold the facility.

While he left the edifice standing throughout construction of the facility as well as the years since, he felt that it had become too much of a safety hazard in trying to keep local children from playing on the crumbling and decaying structure. On September 16, 1977, bulldozers made their way out to the site of the tower, ready to tear it down. The previous June, the tower had been heavily vandalized and the Manassas Manor officials had ordered it torn down. This request, however, never went before the City Manager, C. M. Moyer, Jr., or the City Council, yet someone within the City government had authorized the demolition request.

Fortunately, two members of the Manassas City Council, James Payne and Stuart Vetter, saw the bulldozers arrive and immediately asked that the work be stopped until after the council returned from a convention the following week. Over the course of the next seven months, local protesters and petitioners tried everything that they could to save the structure, including drafting plans to have it declared a local landmark. Unfortunately, the tower did not meet the standards by which it needed to be declared a landmark. Other attempts to save the tower included obtaining an easement on that particular piece of property so that it could be fenced off and restored. To the dismay of council members, mortgage holders on the property did not agree to an easement for the City.

In the end, every effort was to no avail. In the end the final decision rested in the hands of Sills himself. Out of options, Moyer advised Sills to take care of the structure as he saw fit. Sills was faced with the decision of fencing off the small piece of land where the tower stood and allow for future restoration, or to proceed with its destruction. Though he personally hoped Sills would fence it off, Moyer did not expect him to do that, and he was right.

By April 24, 1978, after standing proud for 86 years, the demolition of the Portner Tower began. By the end of the following week, all that remained of the structure was a pile of red sandstone and ivy. The pile of rubble continued to sit there over the next few weeks as people drove past the site, some in respect for the loss, others to take a block of sandstone as a memento of the past. Before long, all of the remaining stones were hauled off and disposed of with no apparent regard for what they had once been a part of. When the Portner Tower was torn down, the City of Manassas lost what has often been considered one of the most famous landmarks the city has ever had.

In an editorial written by Randi Deiotte, then a writer for Manassas' *Journal Messenger*, she said:

> If the criterion for historical value in this area is tied to the Civil War, with nothing built after that time being worthy of preservation, we may find ourselves in a bad way indeed. Given our penchant for destroying or replacing that which is not new and shiny, it may be difficult to preserve anything of value from the past until it accumulates at least 100 years. Under such a set of guidelines the stone tower is fortunate to have survived as long as it did.[90]

Though it was written when the Tower's existence was being threatened, those words serve as a perfect example of the recklessness by which the Portner Tower and countless other historical structures have been destroyed in the "name of progress."

As the Tower was being demolished, Robert Dutton, then-Editorial Page Editor for the *Journal Messenger*, wrote a final, poignant tribute to the structure.

> The days of the Portner Tower have come to an end. The 86-year-old monument that stood for so long as a city landmark is being torn down. [...] It is all very sad because the structure has for so long been part of Manassas. Since its construction in 1892, as an exact replica of the tower located on the Rhine River in Germany, the monument has been one of the primary historical sites in the city. [...] Unfortunately, it appears the Manor owners have little regard for such things. Unfortunately for all of us...[91]

Annaburg: The Present

After the Prince William Hospital took control of the facility, the only thing that essentially changed was the name. In 1986, however, the facility's services were expanded when

Photos taken in 1979 of the crumbling Portner Tower. The Tower was torn down shortly after these pictures were taken.
Courtesy of Al Steidel

the hospital board had a retirement home built directly behind Annaburg Manor, naming it the Caton Merchant House in honor of the local businessman and philanthropist who founded Merchant's Tire and Auto. This new building would offer residents apartment-style rooms, complete with their own stoves and refrigerators, and a dining hall. To build the Caton Merchant House, however, Annaburg had to once more undergo a structural change.

The back porch of the house had to be removed and the door bricked up. This allowed for an enclosed hall to be built leading from the ground floor of the Caton Merchant House down to the basement of Annaburg Manor. In addition to this, one of the last remaining outbuildings from Annaburg's past had to be destroyed. The former powerhouse, which had been converted into a gardener's shed or storage shed, was torn down to allow for construction. Building began in the summer of 1986 and was completed by the end of the following year.

During the summer of 1998, Annaburg Manor was thrust into the national media spotlight over a highly controversial court case involving one of its patients. Hugh Finn, a newscaster from Kentucky, had been in a serious car accident which left him in a comatose, vegetative state. In 1998, Finn's wife decided to have her husband's feeding tube removed that summer, but shortly before it could, Finn's family stepped in with court orders and other legal proceedings to try and prevent the tube's removal. Not only did this case thrust the facility into the media spotlight, but it also got many people to start thinking about what they would do in situations like that, living wills, and the entire right-to-die issue. Four months later, in October, a court decided that since Finn's wife was his legal guardian, she did have the right to have his feeding tube removed. Eight days after it was removed, High Finn passed away.

Today, the facility still retains the same name and is owned by the Prince William Health System, a corporation that oversees the hospital, nursing home, retirement home, and various other aspects regarding the facilities. In 1999, the Prince William Health System announced plans to build a new nursing home facility. Citing a poor layout of the current facility as well as being electronically and structurally outdated, not to mention the far distance of the facility from the hospital, plans called for a new facility to be built on land directly behind the hospital. These plans were put on hold, however, when the hospital realized that this would utilize the last of the land the hospital complex contained. In March of 2003, an article appeared in the *Manassas Journal Messenger* announcing that two contractors had been selected to design a new nursing home each. The hospital decided that rather than build one big facility, they would build two smaller facilities, each with a capacity half of what Annaburg Manor now houses. The article, however, did not state where the new facilities would be built or when construction might begin. The Prince William Health System has announced that once the new facilities are completed, the current nursing home wings will be removed from Annaburg and the house restored, though its future use remains uncertain at the time of this printing. Whatever the fate of Annaburg is, the hospital will still retain control over the Caton Merchant House and Annaburg (the new nursing home will still carry the name Annaburg Manor).

Annaburg in Retrospect

When the family signed over their ownership of Annaburg to Breeden, did any of them realize what might become of their vast, leisurely playground of memories and family history? When asked what he thought of the use of his grandfather's mansion, Robert Portner III once said, "It keeps it, it preserves it."[92] Once has to wonder, though what Robert and Anna might think of what has become of Annaburg.

To quote the letter mentioned at the beginning of chapter six, Robert wrote:

For this reason I've taken my beloved Annaburg and improved it and I will continue to do this to give you there a pleasant childhood and to have a real homeland which brings you all together and to refresh in your minds your childhood. This home I wish to reserve for you all. Those of you who feel tired or sick can return to this place and remember what a beautiful childhood to regain health and fresh spirit and those who have had a hard time in life should regain their strength for a new beginning.

The sale of Annaburg in 1947 marked a new era for Manassas, Annaburg, and the Portner family. For Manassas, the presence of the family would no longer be felt, nor would citizens have a place to go for strolls or swims, or local children have a big empty house to play in. For Annaburg, its fate rested in the hands of the man who bought it. More importantly, fate was left to whom ever the piece of land that contained the house would be sold to, and what their desires were. As for the Portner family, one of the main reasons they sold the estate was that they saw it as a farm, and a farm by "society" standards was a hassle. Once it was sold, each of the children could move on with their adult lives and their own families without having to worry about what was happening to the "big house" in Manassas.

After a period of 64 years, the Portner reign over Annaburg had ended. Even though the family and its ownership of Annaburg were gone, many lasting memories, legends, and markers of the Portner legacy would live on in the hearts and minds of the citizens of this small and quiet town.

When one looks back at pictures of Annaburg in her glory days, one must wonder how a place as stately as this could have become what it is today. While the overall character of the manor house is still there, it has lost a lot of the definable integrity it once possessed. In the words of one preservationist, "It has happened a lot. We threw our heritage out wholesale in the 1950's-60's." The residents of Manassas, however, are privileged to have such a building still standing. To Manassas, Annaburg represents the last direct tie to the Portner family and the estate that helped to define the shape of Manassas and Prince William County so many years ago. But more importantly, it represents the connection that this small town once had to a remarkable man and a taste of the benefits big business of that time had to offer; benefits the town might not have ever experienced had Robert not bought the farm so long ago.

In 1977, E. R. Conner III, then-Curator of the Manassas Museum, wrote a letter to Manassas Mayor Harry J. Parrish. Though he was writing about the fate of the Portner Tower, a part of the letter can be used to summarize Portner and Annaburg perfectly.

> If Robert Portner's accomplishments had been limited to Manassas, it would have been more than enough to insure him the respect of those who knew him here. Annaburg and its dependencies were ostentatious, perhaps garish by today's standards, but such architecture was what the style of the times demanded. From a practical standpoint, it may be argued that the Annaburg Tower in particular [was] the height of useless ornament. To be sure, it was built by a sentimental old man longing for the medieval fortresses of his native Germany. By all accounts it never served any purpose under the sun other than a cosmetic one, but that is what makes this building unique. [Annaburg] was the expression of a man and his age.

In 1837 a child was born, a child who would grow up to create many new things and leave a lasting mark on a country he adopted as his new homeland and an industry he cherished and helped define. Robert Portner's death in 1906 can be seen as a pivotal point when things began to go downhill. In ten short years, his brewing empire would be shut down by Prohibition, never to reopen due to the unfortunate, if not untimely, deaths of all of his six sons before Prohibition was lifted. The only thing left was his beloved Annaburg.

Unfortunately, a two-thousand-acre private estate cannot last long as a thriving community expands and grows around it. With Robert's children too busy with their own adult lives to worry about the farm, it became only a matter of time before the property was sold and was left to the mercy of a developer. The sale of Annaburg not only ended the Portner family's direct ties to Manassas, but with a few quick strokes of a pen, one of the shortest dynasties in America came to a quiet end.

Endnotes

[81] Cora Lee Cardwell, *Following the Dream.*
[82] Letter from G. Kenneth Lyons to the Manassas Museum, 1994.
[83] Prince William County Deed Book 125, p. 487.
[84] Prince William County Deed Book 56, p. 344.
[85] Prince William County Deed Book 43, p. 209.
[86] Prince William County Deed Book 37, p. 59.
[87] Prince William County Deed Book 46, p. 275.
[88] Prince William County Deed Book 50, p. 127.
[89] Prince William County Deed Book 50, p. 431.
[90] *Journal Messenger.* 28 September, 1977.
[91] *Journal Messenger.* 25 April, 1978.
[92] Dean Owen, *The Potomac News.* 9 November 1981.

Annaburg—1920's
Annaburg in the 1920's after the family had converted it back to use as a summer home.
Courtesy of Peggy E. M. Portner

Annaburg—1930's
Photo of the house in the 1930's probably during the time the estate was used for the Piedmont Dairy Festival
Courtesy of Nancy Ralls Southworth

Photo of Jane Roseberry sitting on the fountain at Annaburg, c.1929. Jane's father-in-law, Albert Roseberry, was caretaker of Annaburg at the time.
Courtesy of Jackie Roseberry Shepherd

Annaburg, April, 1956
Courtesy of Manasas Museum System

Abandoned Annaburg, March 1960
Photo taken by LeRoy C. Sloper
Courtesy of Manassas Museum System

In 1960, the seven and a half acres the house sat on was sold to J. Kennedy Sills, who converted it into a nursing home, opening in 1965 as the Manassas Manor nursing home. Sills operated the facility until he sold it in 1979 to the Prince William Hospital. Its new owners changed the name to Annaburg Manor and continue to use the facility today. This is how the nursing home looked in May of 2000.

2002 Portner Reunion at Annaburg
Courtesy of Anna Schoellkopf Lacher

Postscript

After nine years, countless hours of hard work and research, and two editions, I now believe that I have truly finished the book on Portner and Annaburg. Along the way, I met and became friends with people I never would have met otherwise. By far, I owe the greatest amount of thanks to the late-Kitty Arrington because without her suggestion, this book may never have been written, much less published! Also, I cannot begin to thank the descendants of Robert and Anna Portner enough for all of their help and constant encouragement. Many times I thought I would never get this project finished, but each letter I received was filled with emotion and excitement, knowing that their grandfather or great-grandfather was being written about. I have to admit that on a number of occasions that is what kept me going!

Now that I am at the end the only thing left to do is to thank everyone who has helped me along the way. As much as I would like to there is no way to list every descendant of the Portner family who has helped me over the years, but please know that I can not begin to thank you enough! I will try to list everyone who is not associated with the family who has helped, but if I do forget anyone, please know how much I appreciated your help!

Individuals:
Hilda M. Breeden*
George Combs
Sara Costello
Dr. Peter Dedek, formerly of Radford University
Tim Dennée
William H. & Pamela T. Gay
Claudia Kilmer
Kris Lloyd of the Lyceum
P. Leigh Pandolfi
Dr. John Reynolds of Longwood University
Susan K. Shaw
Jackie R. Shepherd
Ronald R. Turner
(Ret.) Gen. Bo Williams*

Staff:
Annaburg Manor Nursing Home:
    Ada Kohn
    Keith Meyers (formerly of the facility)
    Cathy Miller
    Synovia Porter
    Harley Tabak (formerly of the facility)
    David Tucker (formerly of the facility)
Bull Run Regional Library:
    Tish Como
    Bev Veness
    Don Wilson
Manassas Museum:
    Scott Brown (formerly of the Museum)
    Jason Hall (formerly of the Museum)
    Scott Harris (formerly of the Museum)
    Laura Peake Yakulis (formerly of the Museum)
    Melinda Herzog
    Roxanna Adams
    Dave Purschwitz (formerly of the Museum)

---

* Deceased

Bibliography

Books

Brick-Turin, Alan. "End Game: Anti-Prohibition in Alexandria." Dissertation, George Mason University. 1996.

Brockett, F. L., and George W. Rock. *A Concise History of the City of Alexandria, VA from 1669 to 1883, with a Directory of Reliable Business Houses in the City.* Alexandria: Gazette Book and Job Office, 1883: 66-67, 113

Byrd, Ethel M. *Town of Manassas and Old Prince William.* Manassas: 35-6, 55-6, 66-8, 71, 82-7, 90, 98

Caldwell, Cora Lee. *Following the Dream: the History of Manassas Baptist Church 1884-1984.* 1984: 19-21, 61-2.

Chandler, Margaret Terry, Sylvia M. Garnett. *Social Register Washington 1941.* New York: Social Register Association, 1940: 36, 46, 92, 110.

Cox, Ethelyn. *Historic Alexandria Virginia Street by Street.* McLean: EPM Publications, 1976: 166, 170.

Goode, James M. *Best Addresses.* Washington, D.C.: Smithsonian Institution Press: 34-36.

Goode, James M. *Capital Losses.* Washington, D.C.: Smithsonian Institution Press, 1979: 101-3

Glazier, Ira A. and Filby, P. Williams. Eds. *Germans to America*, vol. 5. Wilmington, De: Scholarly Resources: 171.

Griggs, Nora. *Virginia Old Births Index: 1876-1879.*

Lloyd House Staff. *Obituary notices from the Alexandria Gazette 1784-1915.* Bowie, Md.: Heritage Books, 1987: 256.

Loth, Calder. *The Virginia Landmarks Register.* Charlottesville, Va.: University of Virginia.

Manassas Museum. *75th Anniversary of the Manassas National Jubilee of Peace (July 1911).* Manassas: 1986: 4-6.

Mills, Charles A. *Echoes of Manassas*. Manassas: REF Typesetting & Publishing, 1988: 24-7.

Morrill, Penny. *Who Built Alexandria*. Alexandria, Va. 1979: 10.

Mulvaney, Kathleen. *Manassas: A Place of Passages*. Charleston: Arcadia, 1999: 16, 18, 39, 70, 98-9, 116

Parsons Engineering Science, Inc. *Maritime Archaeology at Keith's Warf and Battery Cove (44AZ119) Ford's Landing, Alexandria, Virginia*. Washington, D.C. 1993: 54-69, 357-374.

Rabatin, June, ed. *Count the Ties to Manassas*. Manassas: REF Typesetting & Publishing, 1984: 24-7

Scheel, Eugene M. *Crossroads and Corners*. Historic Prince William, 1996: 99-100.

Schuricht, Herrmann. *The German Element in Virginia*. Baltimore, Md.: Genealogical Publishing Company, 1977: 186-7.

Simmons, Catherine T. *Manassas, Virginia: 1886-1986.* Manassas: REF Typesetting, 1986: 35-6, 55-6, 66-8, 71, 85-6, 121-2.

Templeman, Eleanor Lee, and Netherton, Nan. *Northern Virginia Heritage*, 1966: 188.

Tortora, Phyllis and Eubank, Keith. *Survey of Historic Costume.* 3rd Ed. New York, NY, 1998: 348.

Turner, Ronald Ray. *Prince William County, Virginia 1805-1955 Businesses.* Manassas, 1999: 145, 182, 185.

Turner, Ronald Ray. *Prince William County, Virginia World War I Draft Registrations.* Manassas, 2000: 175.

Tyler, Lyon Gardiner. *Men of Mark in Virginia, Vol. 5.* Washington, D.C.: Men of Mark Publishing Company, 1909: 350-4.

Tyler, Lyon Gardiner. *Encyclopedia of Virginia Biography, vol. 3.* Washington, D.C.: Men of Mark Publishing Company, 1915: 235-6.

Wieder, Laurie C., Ed. *Prince William: A Past to Preserve.* Prince William: Prince William County Historical Commission, 1998: 154

Business Directory of the Principle Cities & Villages of Virginia for 1873-4: 263.

Catalogue of Hampden-Sydney College: 1776-1926: 163.

Journal of the Patent Office Society. January, 1950. Vol. XXXII, no. 1: 72-76.

Passenger and Immigration Lists Index: 1986-90 Cummulation. Vol. 3, O-Z: 1871.

1870 Alexandria, Virginia City Directory: 429.

1871 Alexandria City Directory.

1876-7 Alexandria General & Business Directory.

1877-8 Alexandria Directory: 364.

1895 Alexandria City Directory: 162.

1897-8 Alexandria County Business Directory: 171.

1899 Alexandria Directory.

1907 Alexandria Directory: 157.

1907 Richmond's Alexandria Directory: 265.

1915 Alexandria City Directory: 272.

1917 Alexandria Business Register: 213.

1919 Washington Directory: 226.

Newspapers

Alexandria Gazette

"Meeting of Citizens." *Alexandria Gazette*. 17 April, 1865: 2.

"Died." *Alexandria Gazette*. 28 July, 1873: 2.

"Launch to-morrow." *Alexandria Gazette*. 30 October 1876: 3.

"Launch of the "Robert Portner." *Alexandria Gazette*. 31 October 1876: 2.

"Another new vessel." *Alexandria Gazette*. 1 November 1876: 3.

"Robert Portner Brewing Company, Alexandria, VA." *Alexandria Gazette*.

"Letter from Manassas." *Alexandria Gazette*. 26 September 1887: 1.

"Prince William Notes." *Alexandria Gazette.* 9 July 1892.

"Manassas Notes." *Alexandria Gazette.* 25 July 1892.

"Manassas Notes." *Alexandria Gazette.* 8 October 1892.

"Engelhardt brewery destroyed by fire in the West End." *Alexandria Gazette.* 18 August 1893.

"Manassas." *Alexandria Gazette.* 31 May 1895.

"Clara L. Portner." *Alexandria Gazette.* 17 January, 1899.

"Death of Mr. Portner." *Alexandria Gazette.* 23 January, 1900: 3.

"Death of Robert Portner." *Alexandria Gazette.* 29 May, 1906: 3.

"Death of Mrs. Portner." *Alexandria Gazette.* 13 July 1912: 1.

"Death of H. H. Portner." *Alexandria Gazette.* 9 February 1916: 2.

"Death of former resident." *Alexandria Gazette.* 1 November 1919: 1.

"German influences in the settlement of Alexandria, Va." *Alexandria Gazette.* 5 March, 1954.

Fairfax County Herald

"Mrs. Robert Portner announces the engagement of her daughter, Etta Valer Portner." *Fairfax County Herald.* 6 November 1908: 3.

"Portner will case." *Fairfax County Herald.* 8 August 1920: 2.

"Believe beer is coming." *Fairfax County Herald.* 17 February 1933: 1.

Fredericksburg Daily Star

"Notice." *Fredericksburg Daily Star.* 2 April 1881: 2.

"W. P. Meredith and Miss Portner to wed." *Fredericksburg Daily Star.* 28 October 1908: 2.

"Miss Portner elopes." *Fredericksburg Daily Star.* 23 March 1911: 2.

"Late Mrs. Robt. Portner." *Fredericksburg Daily Star.* 22 July 1912: 2.

"Marriages." *Fredericksburg Daily Star.* 6 June 1913: 2.

"Portner-Moncure." *Fredericksburg Daily Star*. 10 June 1913: 2.

"Flood-Portner." *Fredericksburg Daily Star*. 20 April 1914: 2.

"Deaths" *Fredericksburg Daily Star*. 18 December 1917: 4.

"O. C. Portner dead." *Fredericksburg Daily Star*. 1 November 1924: 2.

(Fredericksburg) Free Lance Star

"Mr. Robert Portner, Jr." *Free Lance Star*. 25 January 1900: 2.

"The funeral of Anna Portner Flood." *Free Lance Star*. 30 March 1916: 2.

"Paul Portner dead." *Free Lance Star*. 4 November 1919.

"Congressman Flood dead." *Free Lance Star*. 10 December 1924: 1.

"Alvin O. Portner, Virginian, dead." *Free Lance Star*. 21 December 1931: 11.

"Mrs. Ralls to be interred at Aquia." *Free Lance Star*. 27 August 1941: 7.

(Manassas) Journal Messenger

"Manassas Manor nursing home gets first patient." *Journal Messenger*. 25 February 1965: A1-2.

"Mrs. Anna P. Flood." *Journal Messenger*. 4 August 1966: 7A.

"Annaburg was one of the nation's finest mansions." *Journal Messenger*. 8 May 1969: 5.

"Liberia: place of prominence." *Journal Messenger*. 8 May 1969.

"Local nursing home is one of country's finest." *Journal Messenger*. 8 May 1969: 6.

"Piedmont Dairy Festival was big evening in 1930's." *Journal Messenger*. 8 May 1969: 7.

"Council fighting to save historic tower." *Journal Messenger*. 26 September 1977: A1.

"City acting properly in saving old tower." *Journal Messenger.* 28 September 1977.

"Historical group to meet tonight." *Journal Messenger.* 1 November 1977: A3.

"The walls came crumbling down." *Journal Messenger.* 24 April 1978.

"Landmark demolition a discouraging site." *Journal Messenger.* 25 April 1978.

"Manassas Manor resident relives some experiences of his youth." *Journal Messenger.* 27 November 1978: A5.

"Manassas Manor becomes Annaburg." *Journal Messenger.* 19 February 1979: A1, A3.

Journal Messenger. 9 October 1979.

"Historic home saved; converted into apartments." *Journal Messenger.* 8 December 1984: A7.

Journal Messenger. 19 February 1989.

"Gatehouse gets spruced up." *Journal Messenger.* 19 May 1989: B1.

"Annaburg Manor provides hospital care in home-like setting." *Journal Messenger.* February 1994: 32.

"Nursing home to be rebuilt." *Journal Messenger.* 4 May 1999: A1.

Manassas Democrat

"Leases Prince William Hotel." *Manassas Democrat.* 28 July 1910: 1.

"Prince William Hotel will open Saturday." *Manassas Democrat.* 13 October 1910.

"Prince William Hotel burns to ground, rescue sleeping guests from death." *Manassas Democrat.* 15 December 1910: 1.

"Jubilee trumpet proclaims peace and brotherhood." *Manassas Democrat.* 13 July 1911: 1.

"Mrs. Robert Portner extremely ill." *Manassas Democrat.* 11 July 1912: 1.

"Mrs. Robt. Portner dies of paralysis." *Manassas Democrat.* 18 July 1912: 1.

"A tribute." *Manassas Democrat.* 18 July 1912: 1.

"Miss Anna V. Portner to be wedded April 18." *Manassas Democrat.* 26 March 1914: 1.

"The Flood-Portner wedding Saturday." *Manassas Democrat.* 16 April 1914: 1.

Manassas Journal

Advertisement, The Goodwin House. *Manassas Journal.* 14 August 1896.

"Vienna Cabinet lager beer." *Manassas Journal.* 14 August 1896.

"Annaburg, the home of Mr. Robert Portner." *Manassas Journal.* 7 September 1904: 1.

"Real estate column." *Manassas Journal.* 7 September 1904.

"Mr. Portner dead." *Manassas Journal.* 1 June 1906.

"Resolution of Respect." *Manassas Journal.* 1 June 1906.

"Robert Portner's will." *Manassas Journal.* 15 June 1906.

"Cornerstone laying." *Manassas Journal.* 3 August 1906: 1.

"Latest acquisition of Eastern College." *Manassas Journal*. 13 August 1909.

"Light plant installed." *Manassas Journal*. 8 April 1910: 1.

"Prince William Hotel destroyed." *Manassas Journal*. 16 December 1910: 1.

"Peace Jubilee." *Manassas Journal*. 28 July, 1911.

"Death of Mrs. Portner." *Manassas Journal*. July 1912.

Manassas Journal. 23 April 1915.

"Herman Portner is dead." *Manassas Journal*. 11 February 1916.

"Edward G. Portner died in Washington." *Manassas Journal*. 21 December 1917.

"Paul Portner dies after long illness." *Manassas Journal*. 31 October 1919: 1.

"New jury selected." *Manassas Journal*. 16 July 1920: 1.

"Portner will case continues." *Manassas Journal*. 23 July 1920: 1.

"Contest over will continues." *Manassas Journal*. 30 July 1920: 1.

"Court sustains Portner's will." *Manassas Journal.* 6 August 1920: 1.

"Portner will case decided." *Manassas Journal.* 16 June 1922: 1.

"Prominent man died suddenly." *Manassas Journal.* 6 November 1924: 1.

"Dairy festival at Manassas." *Manassas Journal.* 11 June 1931: 1.

"Who remembers when?" *Manassas Journal.* December 1935; 26 June 1958: 2A (reprint).

"Dairy festival postponed." *Manassas Journal.* 19 August 1937: 1.

Manassas Messenger

"Portner Estate sold to Jack Breeden." *Manassas Messenger.* 14 February 1947.

"William Payne Meredith." *Manassas Messenger.* 5 September 1947: 1.

New York Times

"A. L. Humes marries." *New York Times*. 2 April 1919: 11.

"Court bars service of divorce papers." *New York Times*. 18 November 1921: 10.

"Congressman Flood dies in Washington." *New York Times*. 9 December 1921.

"Graham divorce stands." *New York Times*. 16 May 1923: 3.

"Lawyer buys duplex in new 5th Av. House." *New York Times*. 24 February 1929: Sec. 12, P. 2.

"Augustine Humes, lawyer 53 years." *New York Times*. 26 September 1952: 21.

"Mrs. Augustine Humes." *New York Times*. 5 February 1954: 19.

Potomac News

"A Portner comes back to his 'heimat land'." *Potomac News*. 25 April 1975: C1.

Potomac News. 9 November 1981: A1, A5.

"Centuries preserve classic mansion." *Potomac News*. 24 January 1986: B1-2.

"Nursing home will replace Annaburg." *Potomac News*. 4 May 1999.

Prince William Journal

"New site planned for Annaburg." *Prince William Journal*. 4 May 1999: A7.

"Manassas Planning Commission approves land use permit." *Prince William Journal*. 21 January 2000: A3.

"Annaburg Manor receives permit OK." *Prince William Journal*. 14 March 2000: A3.

(Washington) Evening Star

"A big brewing establishment." *Evening Star*. 25 July 1891.

"Mr. and Mrs. Robert Portner announce the marriage of their daughter Alma Meta." *Evening Star*. 17 April 1903: 5.

"In the world of society." *Evening Star*. 1 November 1908: Sec. 7, P. 4.

"In the world of society." *Evening Star*. 1 December 1908: 7.

"In the world of society." *Evening Star*. 16 December 1908: 7.

"In the world of society." *Evening Star*. 18 April 1914: 7.

"Flood-Portner." *Evening Star*. 19 April 1914: Sec. 7, P. 1.

"Deaths." *Evening Star*. 9 February 1916: 7.

"Representative and Mrs. Henry Delaware W. Flood announce the engagement of Mrs. Flood's sister." *Evening Star*. 15 June 1919: Sec. 3, P. 1.

"Portner-Derby nuptuals." *Evening Star*. 19 June 1919: 8.

"Portner-Derby wedding plans." *Evening Star*. 21 June 1919: 7.

"The wedding of Miss Hildegarde Portner and Lieut. Palmer Derby." *Evening Star*. 22 June 1919: Sec. 3, P. 1.

"Deaths." *Evening Star*. 18 May 1923: 7.

"Oscar C. Portner dies suddenly." *Evening Star*. 31 October 1924: 4.

"Mrs. Oscar C. Portner is claimed by death." *Evening Star*. 8 July 1929: 9.

Washington Daily News

"More on air-conditioning." *Washington Daily News*. 27 July 1950: 46.

Washington Post

"Talks to the Farmers." *Washington Post*. 22 August 1895: 3.

"O. C. Portner, prominent capital realtor, dies." *Washington Post*. 1 November 1924: 2.

"Deaths." *Washington Post*. 5 March 1931.

"Deaths." *Washington Post*. 20 December 1931.

"Estate of $186,307 given to Capital man." *Washington Post*. 22 December 1931.

"Deaths." *Washington Post*. 27 August 1941: 24.

"Mrs. Hilda Derby." *Washington Post*. 24 May 1944: 8.

"Deaths." *Washington Post*. 2 September 1947: 2B.

"New license is denied to Dunbar Hotel." *Washington Post*. 28 April 1951: 1B.

"Frosty steins stepping stones in air conditioning progress."
Washington Post. 6 July 1952.

"Beer really responsible for comforts of air conditioning; Alexandria, Va., brewer took out patents on idea back in 1880." *Washington Post.* 14 August 1957.

"Deaths." *Washington Post.* 9 July 1965.

"Anna Flood, husband was in Congress." *Washington Post.* 2 August 1966.

"Two new apartment buildings planned for 15 Street NW." *Washington Post.* 15 April 1978: E5.

"Tribute to Dunbar at library opening stirs old memories." *Washington Post, D.C. Weekly.* 4 October 1979: 5.

"Fort Hunt, Manassas farmhouse named State historic landmarks." *Washington Post.* 17 January 1980: Va5.

"Toasting the Tivoli." *Washington Post.* 1 July 1993: T24.

"Health system to build better nursing home." *Washington Post, Prince William Extra.* 5 May 1999: 1.

Periodicals

Bragg, Patrick Timothy. "The Robert Portner Brewing Company of Alexandria, Virginia." *The Fireside Sentinel*. Vol. V, no. 9. September 1991. Pp. 113-122.

Cressey, Pamela T. "Shuter's Hill: The first lager brewery in Alexandria." *Alexandria Archaeology*. Vol. XI, no. 6. June 1993. Pp. 6-7.

DiGiovanni, Tom. "It's the big building across from Manassas Shopping Center." *The Grape Vine*. Vol. 1, no. 2. August 1985. Pp. 1-2.

Gallagher, Ray. "Dry law killed biggest business in 1916." *Alexandria Port Packet*. 1-7 February 1978.

Harris, Scott. "Gilded Age Entrepreneur: The Career of Robert Portner." *Word From The Junction*. Vol. 10, no. 1. January-February 1992.

Harris, Scott, Ed. "The Prince William Hotel fire of 1910." *Word From the Junction*. Vol. 11, no. 2. March-April 1993.

Harvey, Douglas K. "Victorian Patriarch: The Private Life of Robert Portner." *Word From The Junction*. Vol. 10, no. 2. March-April 1992.

_____. "A hundred bottles of beer on the ground…" *Alexandria Archaeology Volunteer News*. Vol. XVI, no. 1: 1, 9.

_____. *Journal of the Patent Office Society*. Vol. XXXII, no. 1. January 1950. Pp. 72-6.

Killmer, Paul. "Annaburg revisited." *Museum News*. Vol. II, no. 7. July 1984.

Leonard, Richard. "Maritime Alexandria: The shipbuilding revives – for a while." *Alexandria Archaeology Volunteer News*. Vol. X, no. 11. November 1992. P. 5.

Miller, T. Michael. "Alexandria's Crystal Palaces." *The Fireside Sentinel*. Vol. V, no. 11. November 1991. P. 138.

Ramsberger, Peter. "Notable neighbor: once the city's largest employer." *The Gazette Packet*. 11 June 1998.

Ramsberger, Peter. "A new life for Portner's brewery." *The Gazette Packet.* 11 June 1998: 33.

Shephard, Steve. "Even more than we had expected for: the Ford plant excavations." *Alexandria Archaeology Volunteer News.* Vol. VIII, no. 2. February 1990. Pp. 1-2.

Tilp, Frederick. "Tall ships 100 years ago." *The Alexandria Port Packet.* Vol. 1, no. 29. August 26-September 2, 1976. Pp. 1, 5.

Internet

All About Beer. <http://allaboutbeer.com>

American Brewery History Page. <http://www.beerhistory.com>

Antique Bottles. <http://antiquebottles.com/>

Beer Definitions. <http://www.tufts.edu/~dleister/beerdefs.htm>

Flood, Henry De La Warr (1865-1921) Bibliographical Information. <http://bioguides.congress.gov/>

Greenville Business and Living – Greenville: Spring 1888

<http://www.greenville-business/1998/February/Greenville Spring1888.htm>

Norfolk County Webpage. <http://hometown.aol.com/otterleigh/page2b.htm>

Our Lives at the Millennium – Air conditioning developments. <http://www.sun-herald.com/2000/ fron19.htm>

PEI History Department: Panic of 1893. <http://www.pei-intl.com/Research/PANICS/1893/ 1893.HTM>

Roanoke.Com Weekly Online Magazine. <http://www.roanoke.com/magazine/100years/1121drink.html>

The Charlotte Observer – Local Ads from December 1899. <http://www.meckhis.org/exhibit/century/189912/default.htm>

Tobacco Warehouse District – Craghead Street. <http://www.ci.danville.va.us/twd/ craghead.htm>

Tobacco Warehouse District – Success Stories. <http://www.ci.danville.va.us/twd/ success.htm>

Other Sources

International Association of Chiefs of Police. "History of 515 North Washington Street."

Manassas Historic Site Files: Annaburg. Bull Run Regional Library, RELIC Room.

Manassas Historic Site Files: Hynson House. Bull Run Regional Library, RELIC Room.

Manassas Historic Site Files: Liberia. Bull Run Regional Library, RELIC Room.

Manassas Historic Site Files: Masonic Temple. Bull Run Regional Library, RELIC Room.

Manassas Historic Site Files: Portner Gate House. Bull Run Regional Library, RELIC Room.

Portner family Bible

Portner, Robert. Personal Memoirs. Unpublished. 1890 – 1903.

Records from George Washington University

Records from Hampden-Sydney College

Records from IBM Corporate Archives

Records from Massachusetts Institute of Technology

Records from Rock Creek Cemetery

Records from Virginia Military Institute

The Lyceum exhibit information packet: "Robert Portner: Brewer of the Gilded Age."

Transcripts. "Supreme Court of Appeals of Virginia, Portner et al v. Portner Executors, et al." State Supreme Court of Virginia, Richmond, Virginia. 1922.

Valaer, Peter. Personal Memoirs. Unpublished. c.1970.

Virginia Historic Landmarks Commission Survey Form: Annaburg

Virginia Historic Landmarks Commission Survey Form: Hynson House Annex #1

Virginia Historic Landmarks Commission Survey Form: Liberia

Virginia Historic Landmarks Commission Survey Form:

    Masonic Lodge

Virginia Historic Landmarks Commission Survey Form:

    Portner Gate House

Virginia Historic Landmarks Commission Survey Form:
    R. S. Hynson House

Index

A

Abner, Edward, 13, 14, 22, 23, 24
Agnew, John P. C., 139, 141, 142, 154
Alexandria County Lighting Company, 195
Alexandria Marine Railroad and Shipbuilding Company, 139
Alexandria Marine Railway Company, 139
Alexandria Marine Railway, Shipbuilding and Coal Company, 142
Aller. See Ships
Amaranth. See Ships
American Brewers' Association, 130
American Film Corporation, 119
American Security and Trust Company, 92, 97, 144, 193
Anheuser-Busch. See Breweries
Annaburg, 54-6, 65, 68-9, 85, 92-3, 95-8, 101, 127-8, 130, 172, 183, 193, 200, 209, 211, 212-3, 220-1, 224-5; 1917 Inventory, 286; Abandoned, 293; Air-conditioning installed, 255; Bought by Portner, 51; Bought by Prince William Hospital, 312; Breedens move to Liberia, 303; Caton Merchant House built, 316; Converted to nursing home, 309; Cornerstone laid, 70, 256; Deer Park, 277; Description of Mathis house, 249; Description of new house, 262, 271; Effects of sale, 320; First house moved, 256; Gardens, 275; Gatehouse renovated, 306; Govt. lease, 210; Grave found, 258; Grounds, 274; Liberia, 278; Liberia converted to dairy farm, 280; Liberia donated to City, 304; Lots sold to Compton, 301; New facility planned, 318; New house designed, 68; New house finished, 260; Nursing home opens, 311; Original house moved, 69; Permanent Portner home, 281; Portner Tower, 273, 313, 295, 296, 322; Portner Tower demolished, 315; Public auction, 293; Purchased by Mathis, 247; Purchased by Portner, 248; Renamed Annaburg Manor, 312; Returned to summer home, 284; Sold to Breeden, 300, 320; Sold to Sills, 309; Source of name, 248; Steam heat added, 281; Subdivided, 302; Vandalized, 299; Windemere, 278, 282
Annapolis Roads Yacht Club, 195
Anti-Saloon League, 108, 110, 111
Armstrong, Louis B., 160, 311
Arrington, Catherine "Kitty", 294
Ashby, Turner, 187
Augusta Victoria. See Ships

B

Bailey, James A., 167
Baldwin, Percy McKnight, 80, 83, 102, 155
Baltimore Yacht Club, 195
Bartlett, John D., 163, 170
Barth, Samuel, 16
Barthold, Richard, 84

Bartholomay, Henry, 55, 62, 83, 244
Barzegar, Luke, 260
Baumgarten, Baroness Marie, 229
Bausch & Lamb Optical Company, 189
Beach, S. Furgeson, 28
Beauregard, Gen. P. G. T.. *See* Civil War Commanders
Belle Haven Apartment Building, 121
Bellevue Hotel, 194, 209, 211
Beuchert, George H., 102, 114
Biehl, George, 43
Biehle, Jacob, 32, 131
Birkett, James F., 284, 301
Black, George, 250
Blomquist & Henkel, 44
Blücher, General, 197
Blundon, Francis A., 153
Bouffet, Mr., 305
Boyle, David, 150
Boyle-Robertson Construction Company, 103
Bradford, Grace, 306
Breeden, I. J., 300, 305, 309, 319
Breweries: Abner-Drury, 24; Anheuser-Busch, 41, 125; Christian Heurich Brewing Company, 24, 171; Continental Brewery, 67; George Juenneman, 162; Jacob von Valaer, 33; Klein's, 53; Miller Brewing Company, 125; Philip Best Brewing Company, 148; Shuter's Hill, 28; Yuengling, 32
Brewery Workers' Union, 106
Briarcliff School. *See* Schools
Brinkley, William H., 167
Brunkhorst, Mr., 59
Bryan, William Jennings, 229
Bull Run Hunt Club, 196
Bullen, George, 244

Byrd, Ethel Maddox, 1, 252, 254, 296
Byrd, Harry Flood, 228
Byrd, Richard Evelyn, 229
Byrd, Thomas Bolling, 229

C

Calloway, Cab, 160
Cameron Run Hunt and Country Club, 196
Campbell-Heights, 162
Cannon, Ira E., 172, 193, 247
Cannon, John, 172, 247
Capital Construction Company, 154, 157, 159, 188, 193, 195, 208, 222
Capital Yacht Club, 195
Carnegie, Andrew, 2
Carry, Albert, 162, 171
Carry, Charles, 163, 170
Carter, Councilor Robert, 279
Carter, Robert, 279
Carter, Robert "King", 278
Castle Annaburg, 2, 3
Castle, Jacqueline Meredith. *See* Meredith, Jacqueline Cabell
Castle, William Donald, 206
Caton Merchant House. *See* Annaburg
Century Yacht Club, 195
City of New York. *See* Ships
Civil War Commanders: Beauregard, Gen. P. G. T., 279; Gwynne, 17-9; Jackson, Gen. Thomas "Stonewall", 280; Johnston, Gen. J. E., 279, 280; McDowell, Gen. Irvin, 279; Sickles, Gen. Daniel E., 280; Slough, John P., Brigadier General, 13, 17, 18, 20, 21; Slough, John P., Brigadier General, 12, 121; Taylor, H. L., Colonel, 12; Wyman, 17

357

Civil War Forts: Fort Beauregard, 250, 278, 303; Fort Ellsworth, 12; Fort Lyons, 12
Clark, Beauchamp "Champ", 229
Clark, Genevieve, 229
Clark, Valerie Graham. *See* Graham, Valerie
Clayton, William A., 153
Claytor, Dr. B. Lynn, 212
Cleveland, Grover, 67, 70, 78, 79, 128
Columbia. *See* Ships
Columbian University. *See* Schools
Commercial Yacht Club, 195
Compton, C. Lacey, 301
Congressional Country Club, 222
Conner, III, E. R. "Ren", 128, 322
Cook, Thomas, 145

D

Danville Military Academy. *See* Schools
Davis, Jefferson, 47-9, 279
Davis, Morgan, 44
de la Vergne, John C., 150
Dean & Foster. *See* Robert Portner Brewing Company: Bottlers
Deer Park Apartments, 304
Deiotte, Randi, 315
Denmead, Francis, 28, 29, 32
Dennee, Tim, 273
Derby, Claude Palmer, 237, 238
Derby, Hildegarde Portner. *See* Portner, Hildegarde Rose
Derby, Nancy Portner, 238
Derby, Palmer Portner, 238
Detwiler, William, 307
Deuster, Paul V., 244

Deutschland. *See* Ships
Dickerson, Ned, 212, 214, 215
Didden, Clement A., 151-4, 156
Donch's Brass Band, 141
Dougherty, George, 222, 223
Dougherty, Lida, 223
Dougherty, Mary Amanda, 219, 220, 221, 222, 223, 238, 293
Droops, E. H., 84
Dunbar Hotel, 159; Razed, 161; Sold, 161
Dunbar, Paul Lawrence, 159
Dunlop, Rev. E. Slater, 187
Dupre, H. Garland, 229
Dutton, Robert, 316

E

E. H. E.. *See* Robert Portner Brewing Company: Bottlers
Eastern College. *See* Schools
Ebstein, Professor, 60
Edens, John D., 297
Eichberg, Isaac, 136, 137
Eils, B. Edward J., 46, 53, 148, 150
Eils, Florence, 244
El Dorado House, 44
Ellington, Duke, 160
Emergency Hospital, 211, 212
Express Spark Plug Factory, 120

F

F. H. Finley & Son, 167
Faber, Louis, 45
Fielmayer, Edward, 38, 131
Finch School. *See* Schools
Finn, Hugh, 317
Fitzgerald, Ella, 160
Fitzgerald, N. W., 152
Flaake, Mr., 8, 10
Flood, III, Henry De La Warr, 231

Flood, Anna Florence Portner.
    See Portner, Anna Florence
Flood, Anna Portner, 231
Flood, Bolling Byrd, 229, 231
Flood, Eleanor Faulkner, 231
Flood, Sen. Henry De La Warr,
    108, 134, 209, 227, 228, 231,
    232, 237
Fort Beauregard. See Civil War
    Forts
Fort Ellsworth. See Civil War
    Forts
Fort Lyons. See Civil War Forts
Franics, E., 244
Frederick Wilhelm IV, 2
Frederick, Edward, 203
Friebus, Theodore, 152
Fürst Bismarck. See Ships

G

Gallagher, Ray, 116
Gardner, Dr., 85
Garfield, James A., 142
Garnett, Robert Sears, 205
Garnett, Sylvia Meredith. See
    Meredith, Sylvia Contee
Gawler & Sons, 96, 194, 201,
    205, 223, 239
George Washington University.
    See Schools, See Schools
George Washington University
    Hospital, 101
Georgetown University. See
    Schools
Gerde, Willi, 47
German Banking Company, 135,
    143
German Co-operative Building
    Association, 136, 143
German Orphan Asylum, 101,
    143
German Patriotic Aid
    Association, 142
Goodwin, Eppa, 253

Götzon, Count, 84
Graham, Elsa Portner. See
    Portner, Elsa Eugenia
Graham, Elzina K., 246
Graham, Hildegarde Portner,
    241
Graham, Lorimer C., 100, 241,
    246
Graham, Valerie, 241
Grant, Ulysses S., 128, 129, 141
Guenther, Mrs., 244
Guenther, Richard, 244
Gwynne. See Civil War
    Commanders

H

Hall, Adra Lion, 251
Hampden-Sydney College. See
    Schools
Herbner, Henry, 34
Herbort, Charles G., 53
Herman, Baron, 84
Hertzog, Hildegarde, 58, 59, 244
Heth, Robert M., 282
Higgins & Kell, 44
High Bridge Mansion, 33
Highland Apartments, 229
Hixson, George W., 250
Hoffman, Nicolas, 6
Hooff, Philip H., 14
Holton-Arms. See Schools
Hopkins, C. A. S., 172
Howard Theater, 160
Humes, Andrew Russell, 243
Humes, Augustine, 194, 214,
    238, 242
Humes, Augustine Leftwich, 242
Humes, Elsa Portner. See
    Portner, Elsa Eugenia
Humes, John Portner, 242
Humes, R. Alice Leftwich, 243
Hynson, Richard S., 176, 259

I

International Association of Chiefs of Police, 121
Inventions, 145: Brewing equipment, 123; Hutchinson stopper, 41; Lightning stopper, 41; pasteurization, 41

J

J. F. Hermann & Son, 167
James B. Ogden. See Ships
Johnson, John M., 155
Johnson, John T., 155
Johnston, Gen. J. E.. *See* Civil War Commanders
Jones, Jacob, 152
Jones, Minnie, 233
Jungenfeld, E., 150

K

Kaercher, Mr., 13, 14, 24, 25, 27, 131; Possible Identity, 27
Karl Hutter. *See* Robert Portner Brewing Company: Bottlers
King, Jr., Martin Luther, 160
Koehler, Alma Portner. *See* Portner, Alma Meta
Koehler, Julius H., 94, 96, 199, 200
Koehler, Robert Portner, 200, 201, 248, 300
Krausch, Theodore, 150
Kunding, Pastor J., 70

L

Lacher, Anna Portner Schoellkopf, 235
Leicht, Eugenia, 244
Leicht, John M., 67, 80, 82, 83, 131
Lewis, Marion Lewis, 253
Liberia. *See* Annaburg

Lincoln Theater, 160
Lincoln, Abraham, 7, 18, 20, 24, 279
Lion, Thomas C., 172
Lipscomb, Phillip, 254
Lucas, Bell, 57, 59
Lucas, W. R., 174
Lynch, Jr., M., 174
Lynch, William, 174
Lyons, Kenneth, 298

M

Mabley, "Moms", 160
MacCurdy, Joseph F., 195
Mackin, Reverend, 222
Madigan, Frank P., 163, 170
Madison Homes, Inc., 120
Magnetic Pigment Company, 188, 246
Manassas Improvement Corporation, 173
Manassas Peace Jubilee, 193
Mann, William Hodges, 108, 109, 110, 134
Marquis de Lafayette, 23
Marshall, Thomas R., 229
Martin, E. I., 200
Martin, Lucy, 229
Martin, Sen. Thomas S., 108, 109, 229
Massachusetts Institute of Technology. *See* Schools
Mastercraft Interiors, 118
Mathis, Anna C. H., 248, 249, 262
Mathis, Christian, 33, 34, 51, 247, 248, 262
McDonald, Dr., 85
McDowell, Gen. Irvin. *See* Civil War Commanders
McKellar, Kenneth D., 229
McKinley, William, 83, 91
McLean, Virginia B., 250
McPherson, John D., 248, 250

McPherson, Robert W., 70
Merchant, Anna, 97
Merchant, Rena, 254
Merchant, Robert W., 254
Merchant, William F., 193
Meredith, Elisha E., 97, 278
Meredith, Etta Portner. *See* Portner, Henriette Marie
Meredith, Jacqueline Cabell, 204, 205, 215
Meredith, Rose, 83, 204
Meredith, Sylvia Contee, 204, 205, 214, 215, 216, 296
Meredith, William Payne, 97, 100, 193, 194, 203, 205, 215
Miller Brewing Company. *See* Breweries
Mills, Charles A., 252
Mitchell, Harriet Bladen, 279
Moffitt, W. W., 172
Moncure, Nannie, 187, 189, 190
Moncure, Rev. George, 187
Montclair Military Academy. *See* Schools
Morgan, J. Pierpont, 2
Morrow, Robert C., 311
Mount Saint Mary's College. *See* Schools
Mount Vernon Cotton Company, 94, 120, 121
Moyer, Jr., C. M., 313, 314
Muhlhauser, Louise, 244
Muhlhauser, Paul, 38, 39, 53, 66, 126, 131, 244
Müller, Louis, 10
München. *See* Ships
Murphy, Rev. P. H., 187
Mutual Ice Company, 94
Mutual Life Insurance Company, 205

N

National Bank of Manassas, 93
National Cordage Company, 78
National Bank of Washington, 144
National Capital Brewing Company, 79: Brands, 170; Description, 164; Established, 163
National War Labor Board, 205
Necker. *See* Ships
Nelson, Effie, 297
Neurological Institute, 213
New York Trust Company, 200
Newman, W. A., 193
Newman, Oliver, 262
Nicol, C. E., 172
North Carolina State University. *See* Schools

O

Ogilby, Charles F. R., 194, 212, 215
Old, Ethel Mae, 194, 195

P

Pabst, Frederick, 148
Page, Capt. Nelson, 238
Panic of 1893, 78
Pantop's Academy. *See* Schools
Parker, M. M., 144
Parkway Motor Company, 119
Parrish, Harry J., 322
Pasteur, Louis, 145
Payne, James, 314
Peace Jubilee of 1911, 281, 295
Peele, Stanton C., 194
Peoda, Mr., 84
Peters, Reetzie, 186
Philadelphia and Reading Railway Corporation, 78
Piedmont Dairy Festival, 294
Pierce, Rev. U. G. B., 98, 199, 203, 238
Pitts, David M., 282
Poncho Villa, 229

Portner & Company, 18;, 27
Established, 14
Portner & Tillett, 171
Portner Apartments, 155, 158, 177, 187, 194, 209, 211, 221, 239; Built, 154; Sold, 159
Portner Brownstone Company, 171, 193
Portner House. *See* Portner's Landing
Portner Realty Company, 195, 208, 222, 282-4, 300, 301
Portner Tower. *See* Annaburg
Portner, III, Robert Joseph, 220, 221, 224, 255, 260, 300, 312, 319
Portner, IV, Robert Valar, 224
Portner, Alma Meta, 46, 55, 58, 66, 70, 84, 90, 91, 92, 93, 94, 213, 244; Biography, 199
Portner, Alvin Otto, 46, 55, 56, 58, 61, 65, 68, 94, 95, 96, 100, 101, 114, 126, 158, 203, 208, 209, 210, 212, 214, 226, 228, 244, 282; Biography, 191
Portner, Anna Florence, 56, 68, 95, 158, 203, 237, 244, 254, 300; Biography, 227
Portner, Anna von Valaer. *See* Anna von Valaer
Portner, Augusta, 2, 15, 92
Portner, Carl, 2, 3, 6, 12, 21, 22, 27, 126
Portner, Clara Louise, 56, 85, 89, 91, 244, 254
Portner, Edward George, 40, 48, 55, 56, 58, 60, 61, 65, 68, 70, 81, 82, 83, 84, 90, 91, 96, 97, 98, 100, 101, 102, 126, 186, 188, 203, 208, 219, 229, 244; Biography, 185
Portner, Edward Moncure, 189, 190
Portner, Edwin, 40, 85, 91

Portner, Elsa Eugenia, 68, 70, 95, 96, 211, 228, 238, 244, 300; Biography, 241
Portner, Felixine, 2, 15, 16, 23, 49, 50, 55, 57, 92, 126, 152, 244
Portner, Heinrich, 2, 197
Portner, Helen Barbara, 194, 195, 197
Portner, Henriette Marie, 46, 55, 58, 66, 70, 84, 86, 90, 91, 92, 93, 94, 95, 97, 158, 210, 212, 213, 214, 215, 216, 244, 296, 300; Biography, 203
Portner, Herman Henry, 55, 96, 100, 187, 203, 209, 214, 244, 282; Biography, 225
Portner, Hermann, 2, 3
Portner, Hildegarde Rose, 61, 62, 95, 96, 158, 211, 228, 244; Biography, 237
Portner, John Alexander Dougherty, 221, 224, 300
Portner, Louis, 2, 3, 4, 5, 10, 12, 16
Portner, Oscar Charles, 55, 57, 66, 93, 96, 100, 115, 158, 201, 203, 208, 238, 244, 254, 282, 284; Biography, 219
Portner, Otto, 2, 10, 12, 16, 27, 34, 45, Otto, 92, 126, 244
Portner, Paul Valer, 50, 55, 56, 59, 90, 91, 93, 95, 96, 100, 101, 114, 115, 116, 126, 193, 203, 226, 229, 238, 244, 282; Biography, 207
Portner, Robert: Arrested, 19; Banking, 135; Birth, 2; Bribe Offer, 18; Brings bicycle to Alexandria, 35; Brings bowling to Alexandria, 36; Buys Annaburg, 51; Buys family plot, 91; Buys land around Annaburg, 249; Buys Liberia, 278; Buys

Windemere, 70; Character description, 125; Citizenship, 7; Creates the Capital Const. Co., 154; Death, 96, 281; Designs Annaburg, 255; Early jobs, 3; Education, 2; Ends partnership with Recker, 25; Established early connections, 19; Family trips, 46, 55, 59, 60, 62, 65, 81, 82, 84, 90, 91, 92, 93, 95; Final will, 92; First business, 5; First family home, 39; Grocery in Alexandria, 10; Immigrates to America, 3; Inventions, 146; Leaves Philadelphia brewery, 45; Letter to children, 181; Manassas real estate, 171; McKinley's inauguration, 83; Meeting Anna, 33; Meeting the Prince of Liechtenstein, 62; Moves family back to America, 65; Moves family to Germany, 57; Moves family to Washington, 50; New Washington home, 53; New will, 69; Partnership with Recker, 8; Patents stolen, 66; Philadelphia brewery, 33; Philanthropy, 54, 93; Proposes marriage, 39; Retirement, 95; Second brewery, 162; Sells Mathis house, 259; Ship building, 137; Shooting, 16; Temporary retirement, 57; US Brewers Association, 143; Washington real estate, 151

Portner, Robert Francis, 47, 55, 56, 58, 60, 61, 65, 68, 70, 71, 84, 89, 90, 91, 126, 155, 158, 185, 186, 208, 219, 244

Portner's Arena, 119

Portner's Garden. *See* Robert Portner Brewery

Potomac Gardens. *See* Robert Portner Brewery

Portner's Landing, 120

Prince Johannes II, 62

Prince William Horseman's Association, 193

Prince William Hotel, 172-4

Princess Victoria Louise. See Ships

R

Rabey, Henry, 162

Ralls, John Milton, 189

Ralls, Nancy Moncure, 189

Recker, Frederick, 8, 9, 10, 11, 13, 14, 16, 17, 18, 21, 22, 23, 24, 25;

Red Cross, 119, 235

Reid, Ira, 99

Reid, James H., 136

Riggs Fire Insurance Company, 144

Robert Portner. See Ships

Robert Portner Brewery, 27; First Beer, 31; First Icehouse, 37; New advertising, 42; New building, 33; Portner's Garden, 34, 35, 36; Potomac Gardens, 34; Saloon, 43

Robert Portner Brewing Company, 77, 85, 93, 98, 113, 114, 121, 127, 170, 187, 188, 193, 208; 1894 description, 72; 1907 description, 102; Becomes the Robert Portner Corporation, 114; Brands, 80, 132; Brew masters, 131; Closed by Prohibition, 112, 114; Commentary, 122; Depot closings, 104; Depots, 78; Dissolved, 117; Electric power installed, 71; Incorporated, 53; Last bottling house, 103; New bottling

house, 94; New brew house, 72; New coal plant, 76; Produces malt extract, 84; Rail cars, 77; Rents vacant buildings, 115; Second strike, 107; Sells mineral water, 67; Telephones installed, 71Third icehouse built, 91; Washington depot, 151; Worker strike, 105
Robert Portner Corporation, 195, 222. *See* Robert Portner Brewing Company
Robinson, Arthur, 301
Rohr, Walser Conner, 252
Rose, Louise, 58, 62, 83, 244
Roseberry, Albert, 284, 306
Roseberry, John: Family, 306
Rosenthal, Albert, 137
Round, George Carr, 281

S

Saint Michael's Yacht Club, 195
Saunders, William H., 155
Schandein, Emil, 148
Schandein, Mrs., 244
Schneider, Joseph, 66, 131
Schneider, Justus, 137
Schneider, Louis, 57
Schools: Briarcliff School, 241; Columbian University, 89, 185, 186, 246; Danville Military Academy, 68, 69, 191; Eastern College, 173; Finch School, 241; Franklin School, 66, 219; George Washington University, 188, 246, *See* Schools; Georgetown University, 224; Hampden-Sydney College, 208; Holton-Arms, 237, 241; Massachusetts Institute of Technology, 89, 185, 188, 191, 192; Montclair Military Academy, 219; Mount Saint Joseph's College, 194; North Carolina State University, 188; Pantop's Academy, 207; Sidwell Friends, 223; University of Virginia, 192, 195, 208, 225; Virginia Military Institute, 68, 85, 90, 208, 225; Washington High School, 191
Schultz, Alfred J., 35
Schwartz, Mr., 38
Schwartzbach, Dr., 61
Seipp, Clara, 244
Seipp, Elsa, 244
Seward, William, 280
Shinn, Steven, 139
Ships: *Aller*, 57; *Amaranth*, 3; *Augusta Victoria*, 85; *City of New York*, 14; *Columbia*, 90; *Deutschland*, 92; *Fürst Bismarck*, 81, 84; *James B. Ogden*, 141; *München*, 65; *Necker*, 47; *Princess Victoria Louise*, 91, 92; *Robert Portner*, 141
Shoreham Apartments, 234
Sickles, Gen. Daniel E.. *See* Civil War Commanders
Sidwell Friends. *See* Schools
Siebel Institute, 186
Sills, John Kennedy, 309, 314
Simken, Henry, 144
Simonds, Bettie, 254
Simonds, John T., 254
Slough, John P., Brigadier General. *See* Civil War Commanders
Social Clubs, 23
Spieden, Albert, 297
Stanton, Edwin, 18, 20, 279
Steinkäuler, Lisbeth, 57, 59
Stoneleigh Court, 158
Stonewall Jackson Hotel, 176
Strange, Captain, 141

Strangmann, Augusta Portner.
  See Portner, Augusta
Strangmann, Carl, 46, 53, 68, 80,
  126, 163, 170, 244
Strangmann, Paula, 16
Strangmann, Louise, 126
Summers, Mrs., 66
Syme, Dr. William, 211, 212

T

Taft, William Howard, 281
Taylor, H. L., Colonel, 13, 17,
  See Civil War Commanders
Terney, C. F., 75
Thompson, J. S. B., 172
Thornton, J. B. T., 213
Tillett, John R., 99, 171, 193
Tivoli Brewery. *See* Robert
  Portner Brewing Company
Tivoli Way. *See* Portner's
  Landing
Torti Gallas CHK, 120
Tucker, Henry St. George, 108,
  109
Turberville, Ellen, 295
Twain, Mark, 128

U

United States Brewers
  Association, 143, 147, 150,
  180
United States Bureau of
  Engraving, 188
Union Memorial Hospital, 201
University of Virginia. *See*
  Schools
University Yacht Club, 195

V

Valaer Creamery, 280
Valaer, Christian, 126
Valaer, Hans, 92
Valaer, Peter, 100, 127, 188, 273

Van Roijen, Hildegarde Graham.
  See Graham, Hildegarde
  Portner
Vernier, Marie, 244
Vetter, Stuart, 314
Virginia Feed & Milling
  Corporation, 115, 116, 208,
  222
Virginia Flats, 153, 157
Virginia Glass Company. *See*
  Robert Portner Brewing
  Company: Bottlers
Vogt, John, 163, 170
Vogt, Oscar, 68, 172, 256
von der Westlaken, Peter, 83,
  131
von Gornberg, Baron, 59
von Holleben, Dr., 84
von Valaer, Anna, 33, 34, 38,
  39, 40, 46, 47, 49, 50, 53, 55,
  56, 59, 60, 61, 65, 68, 69, 70,
  82, 83, 89, 92, 93, 94, 95, 96,
  97, 98, 100, 101, 173, 204,
  247, 281, 282, 301, 310
von Valaer, Jacob, 33
von Valaer, Peter, 33, 97, 244

W

W. J. Sloane Company, 118
Waddell, J. Richard, 309
Warren Green Hotel, 174
Washington Gold Country Club,
  222
Washington High School. *See*
  Schools
Washington Home for
  Foundlings, 101
Weir, E. Wood, 301
Weir, Rebecca M., 301
Weir, Robert Carter, 247
Weir, William J., 250, 279
Weller, E. R., 103
Wilconxin, John W., 302
Wilkening, Anna, 244

Wilkening, Henry, 57, 68
Wilkening, Felixine Portner. *See*
  Portner, Felixine
Wilson, Woodrow, 229
Windemere, 70, 220, 303
Wolf, Fred W., 150
Wolters, Carl, 30, 32, 131
Wolters, Peter, 37, 131
Wood, Rev. Dr. Charles, 232
Woodmont Flats, 152, 157
Woodward and Lothrop, 118
Wright, Mrs., 83
Wylie, Andrew, Judge, 19, 20
Wyman. *See* Civil War
  Commanders

X

Xander, H., 84

Michael Gaines was born in Manassas, Virginia in 1977. A 1995 graduate of Osbourn High School in Manassas, he entered Longwood College to study History, concentrating on Historic Preservation. At Longwood, Gaines helped establish the Historic Preservation and History Clubs and was a member of Phi Kappa Tau fraternity.

From 1998 to 2000, Gaines worked and attended community college in northern Virginia. He entered Radford University in June 2000 and is currently pursuing a degree in English with double minors in History and Interior Design. Upon graduation in 2004, he plans to pursue a career in historic preservation.

In addition to this book, Gaines has written editorials for his hometown newspaper, the Manassas Journal Messenger, as well as stories for the Longwood College newspaper and has begun work on two new books.

In 2002, Gaines became the youngest author to be published by Heritage Books.

When not at university, he resides with his family in Manassas.